Evidence of Purpose

BY JOHN MARKS TEMPLETON

Discovering the Laws of Life

Is God the Only Reality?
(with Robert L. Herrmann)

Looking Forward (editor)

Riches for the Mind and Spirit (editor)

The Templeton Plan (with James Ellison)

Global Investing the Templeton Way
(with Norman Berryessa and Eric Kirzner)

The God Who Would Be Known
(with Robert L. Herrmann)

The Humble Approach

Evidence of Purpose

Scientists Discover the Creator

Edited by
John Marks Templeton

CONTINUUM • New York

1996
The Continuum Publishing Company
370 Lexington Avenue, New York, NY 10017

Printed in the United States of America

Library of Congress Cataloging-in-Publication Data

Evidence of purpose : scientists discover the creator / edited by John Marks Templeton.
        p.   cm.
    Includes bibliographic references.
    ISBN 0-8264-0649-1 (alk. paper)
    1. Teleology. 2. Causation. 3. Religion and science. I. Templeton, John, 1912–

BD541.E95 1994   94-13472
124—dc20   CIP

Contents

Introduction

The Purpose of This Book

This book was written to bring a new scientific perspective to the age-old question of purpose. It had been assumed since perhaps the middle of the last century that science had put to rest any idea that there was a Creator whose design had brought the universe its form and process. Yet there have been powerful dissenting voices even among the great scientists. Physicists like Albert Einstein openly and movingly spoke of the religious attitude as essential to good science and Sir James Jeans said that the universe was beginning to look not like a great machine but rather like a great thought. Astronomer Allen Sandage spoke of God in terms of the marvelous laws of nature, and Sir Arthur Eddington once wrote of a spiritual world that lies behind the universe we study.

But in the last twenty or thirty years the number of scientists raising philosophical and religious questions as a result of recent scientific discoveries has multiplied. This volume contains some of those questions—searching, exploratory, tentative but often profound—about ultimate reality and purpose and meaning. The scientists who have contributed to this book covered a broad spectrum of theological and philosophical persuasion. Yet they all express something of the wonder of the universe we begin to know through science, and all see evidence for a deep meaning written into the laws and processes of nature.

It is to be hoped that the reader will come to this collection of essays with the same spirit of humility that characterizes all good science. As we begin to understand our own limitations as finite creatures in a vast universe of infinite complexity and intricacy, perhaps we can be released from our prejudices—whether scientific, philosophical, or religious—and open our minds to the great plan of which we are a part.

Science as a Humbling Experience

Science in the past few decades has revolutionized our view of the universe and our place in it. Just a century ago science appeared to be tidying up our world, dispelling the illusions of gods and inexplicable miracles and finally providing us with an "objective" view. Yet today the credo of objectivity, together with its tight little mechanisms and clockwork images, is gone. Matter has lost its tangibility, space and time are no longer separable entities, and quantum physics has shown our world to be more like a symphony of wave forms in dynamic flux than some sort of mechanical contrivance.

Anthropologist Loren Eiseley talks about the illusions of science in his book, *The Firmament of Time*:

> A scientist writing around the turn of the century remarked that all of the past generations of men have lived and died in a world of illusions. The unconscious irony in his observation consists in the fact that this man assumed the progress of science to have been so great that a clear vision of the world without illusion was, by his own time, possible. It is needless to add that he wrote before Einstein, . . . at a time when Mendel was just about to be rediscovered, and before the advances in the study of radioactivity had made their impact—of both illumination and confusion—upon this century.

> Certainly science has moved forward. But when science progresses, it often opens vaster mysteries to our gaze. Moreover, science frequently discovers that it must abandon or modify what it once believed. Sometimes it ends by accepting what it has previously scorned. The simplistic idea that science marches undeviatingly down an ever broadening highway can scarcely be sustained by the historian of ideas.[1]

Scientific progress is always attended by the corrections of error, by sharp shifts in direction and emphasis. And the nature of the correction is again only tentative, only partially truth. And the illusions could hardly be said to have been dispelled. In fact, in a very real sense, what we have started with as the tangible—matter, energy, space, and time—now seems to bear some of the mystery of an illusion. Things are not what they seemed. In the words of science writer K.C. Cole:

> So much of science consists of things we can never see: light "waves" and charged "particles"; magnetic "fields" and gravitational "forces"; quantum "jumps" and electron "orbits." In fact, none of these phenomena is literally what we say it is. Light waves do not undulate through empty space in the same way that water waves ripple over a still pond; a field is only a mathematical description of the strength and direction of a force; an atom does not literally jump from one quantum state to another, and electrons do not really travel around the atomic nucleus in orbits. The words we use are merely metaphors. "When it comes to atoms," wrote Neils Bohr, "lan-

guage can be used only as in poetry. The poet, too, is not nearly so concerned with describing facts as with creating images.[2]

Many scientists would be quick to respond with the argument that some things in science are far more secure—the periodic table, the laws of thermodynamics, relativity, the genetic code, biological evolution—and that we are gradually building a foundation of fact toward a clear picture of reality. But not everyone agrees, especially among scientists interested in the philosophy of science, and they are joined by a large number of sociologists and historians of science. A forerunner in this critique of science is Thomas Kuhn, whose *Structure of Scientific Revolutions*, published in 1970, proposed a new interpretation of the history of science.[3] Kuhn argues that science goes through periods of normality during which an accepted paradigm—a broad conceptual framework—is employed and applied, and periods of revolution in which a given paradigm is shattered and replaced by a new one. Following Kuhn, a new emphasis was placed on the sociological factors influencing the development of science. As Arthur Peacocke, one of the contributors to this volume, once described it:

> Science came to be seen as a continuous social enterprise, and the rise and fall of theories and the use and replacement of concepts as involving a complex of personal, social, intellectual, and cultural interactions that often determined whether a theory was accepted or rejected. Theories are constructed, it was argued, in terms of the prevailing world view of the scientists involved: so to understand them one must understand the relevant world view. A new emphasis was therefore placed on the history of science, especially the sociological factors influencing its development. Thus a new area was opened up for the application of the expanding enterprise of the sociology of knowledge in general and of scientific knowledge in particular. However, it turns out that the "world view" of the scientist is an exceedingly complex and elusive entity—even more so when a *community* of scientists is involved.[4]

Out of this debate between extremists arguing for scientific truth as purely social construction and those arguing for science as final truth has come what is referred to as the critical realist position. Philosopher Ernan McMullin has suggested that the basic claim for scientific realism is that "the long-term success of a scientific theory gives reason to believe that something like the entities and structure postulated in the theory actually exists."[5] He proposes four qualifications for his definition: "(1) The theory must be a successful one over a significant period; (2) The explanatory success of the theory gives some reason, though not a conclusive warrant, to believe it; (3) What is believed is that the theoretical structures are *something like* the structures of the real; (4) No claim is made for a special, more basic, privileged, form of existence for the postulated entities." [6]

Even here we see the extent of provisionality assigned to theories. Terms like *significant period, some reason,* and *something like* are the essential elements of a valid approach to scientific truth in the new scientific era. This cautious approach, now accepted by a majority of working scientists, ought to instill in all of us a greater openness to the more philosophical and theological questions of meaning and purpose in our universe. There simply are no exclusive pathways to truth! Add to this the baffling questions of interpretation of quantum uncertainty at the subatomic level and the staggering size of the universe at the cosmic level and we marvel, as Paul Davies does in his chapter, on the unreasonable effectiveness of scientific study to comprehend nature and nature's laws.

Indeed, it is only in the past few decades that we have come to appreciate the enormity of the cosmos and the paucity of our knowledge of it. Timothy Ferris has given us some idea of the extent of our ignorance in his book, *Coming of Age in the Milky Way:*

> We might eventually obtain some sort of bedrock understanding of cosmic structure, but we will never understand the universe in detail; it is just too big and varied for that. If we possessed an atlas of our galaxy that devoted but a single page to each star system in the Milky Way (so that the sun and all its planets were crammed in one page), that atlas would run to more than ten million volumes of ten thousand pages each. It would take a library the size of Harvard's to house the atlas, and merely to flip through it, at the rate of a page per second, would require over ten thousand years. Add the details of planetary cartography, potential extraterrestrial biology, the subtleties of the scientific principles involved, and the historical dimensions of change, and it becomes clear that we are never going to learn more than a tiny fraction of the story of our galaxy alone—and there are a hundred billion more galaxies. As the physician Lewis Thomas writes, "The greatest of all the accomplishments of twentieth-century science has been the discovery of human ignorance." [7]

Yet, as Ferris goes on to point out, this realization carries with it a new awareness of the open-endedness of learning, of the vast storehouse of discovery and opportunity that is ours.

The New Data of Evolution

THE CREATIVITY OF THE COSMOS

This new horizon includes not only the universe without but also that within. The scientific study of our spiritual nature may well open up an infinity of discovery beyond our wildest expectations. In light of this, we might ask what has become of the century-old scientific ideas about humankind and our evolution. What has become of us? Are we just a blind mistake in the long and tortuous path of evolution, the gradual climb from stardust to sentient humankind? The incredible events of evolution are punctuated, we now know, with quite miraculous emergences and extinctions. The extraordinarily complex origin of life, the sudden early appearance of multicellular animals in great profusion in the Cambrian,[8] and the proliferation of mammals following the sudden extinction of the dinosaurs 65 million years ago argue for a marvelous creativity and connectedness. The process seems to seethe with new innovations and a superb timing that dispels any notion of blind chance. And the end result? Matter has become mind, and now contemplates its origin and its reason for being!

There is here no knockdown argument for design and purpose, but certainly there are strong hints of ultimate realities beyond the cosmos, just as Owen Gingerich says in his chapter. One of the strongest hints, in our opinion, relates to the new understanding of the creativity of the cosmos, its capacity for so-called self-organization. For, following the Big Bang, a most astounding story of creativity unfolds throughout time, from the void of space to galaxies, planets, crystals, life, and people. Science has heretofore been ruled by the Newtonian and thermodynamic paradigms, viewing the universe as either an unchanging and static machine, or as a process moving inexorably toward degeneration and decay. But current science leads us to look for a new paradigm, a universe fraught with creativity in the direction of cooperative and organizational processes. The gradual growth of complexity has been noted throughout the history of science, but it was given powerful support through the theory of biological evolution proposed by Charles Darwin and Alfred Russel Wallace. Subsequent developments in cosmological science have demonstrated that the increased complexity and diversity inherent in biological evolution have also been characteristic of the entire universe from its origin. Indeed, there appears to be a continuity of organization into novel and increasingly complex structures and relationships throughout the spectrum of transitions from stardust to thinking man. How did these changes come about? What processes are involved? The most likely candidate for this thrust toward diversity is a poorly studied category of earth's processes that the chemist usually defines as nonlinear, far-from-equilibrium, and irreversible. They are less well understood because they are complex and irregular processes that are usually studied by approximation. The general approach is to model the processes under study to some regular system that is linear. The problem with this approach is that the basic characteristic of the system, spontaneous order, is overlooked. Furthermore, it turns out that the majority of the processes of nature are of the nonlinear type.

A COMING REVOLUTION IN PHYSICS

Paul Davies, in his book, *The Cosmic Blueprint*, says that the discovery of the self-ordering character of nonlinear processes and the new awareness of their very frequent occurrence in nature has brought physicists to feel that their subject is poised for a major revolution. On one side will be the unifiers, those who seek to reduce all phenomena to a single explanation, to seek the ultimate principles that operate at the lowest and simplest level of physics. For the unifiers, the ultimate goal is a "theory of everything."[9] The other side is represented by the diversifiers, who see the universe as a holistic phenomenon, with the emphasis on organization and function as integrated wholes. The key ideas are complexity and connectedness rather than simplicity. The big question is whether the propensity of matter to "self-organize" is explainable by the known laws of physics or whether a completely new set of principles is involved. We agree with Davies that some scientific explanation is forthcoming, but would give even more emphasis to his plea that the concept of organizing principles in nature not be simply dismissed as "mystical" or "vitalistic."

From a theological perspective it is indeed tempting to see this remarkable self-organizing tendency as an expression of the intimate nature of the Creator's activity and identification with our universe. It certainly hints at purpose, and together with the many other "signals of transcendence" with which this book deals, makes a rather strong case for a higher purpose for our world. Certainly the cosmological evidence for a very special set of circumstances for the origin of living systems, and eventually mankind, the so-called anthropic principle, as presented by John Polkinghorne in his contribution to this volume, fits in this category.

ORIGIN OF LIVING SYSTEMS

When we face the issue of what is known about the biochemical mechanisms for the origin of living systems, we have to confess along with Dean Kenyon, author with Gary Steinman of *Biochemical Predestination*,[10] that there are serious reasons for doubting that any straightforward naturalistic explanation will be forthcoming. Kenyon, writing in the preface to a book entitled *The Mystery of Life's Origin: Reassessing Current Theories*, by Charles Thaxton, Walter Bradley, and Roger Olsen,[11] argues that most recent studies of biogenesis are so artificially simplified as to be useless; potentially interfering cross-reactions and the presence of optical isomers in prebiotic systems have been ignored. Kenyon also expresses concern for the enormous gap between the most complex "protocell" model systems of the laboratory and the simplest living cells such as Mycoplasma. He then concludes:

> Finally, in this brief summary of the reasons for my growing doubts that life on earth could have begun spontaneously by purely chemical and physical means, there is the problem of the origin of genetic, i.e., *biologically relevant*, information in biopolymers. No experimental system yet devised has provided the slightest clue as to how biologically meaningful sequences of subunits might have originated in prebiotic polynucleotides or polypeptides. Evidence for some degree of spontaneous sequence ordering has been published, but there is no indication whatsoever that the non-randomness is biologically significant. Until such evidence is forthcoming one certainly cannot claim that the possibility of a naturalistic origin of life has been demonstrated."[12]

Here again we are faced with a question of forces moving in the process of self-organization that seem to transcend the explanations of science. Perhaps a scientific explanation for this most unique event will eventually be provided, but we suspect it too will, by its surprising intricacy and elegance, suggest the purpose and the pleasure of the Creator.

THE ORIGIN OF THE DIVERSITY OF LIFE

Beyond life's origin we are confronted by a spectacular display of innovative and adaptive organisms interacting with an often incredibly supportive environment. Indeed, the actors in this drama exhibit such creativity that one biology writer, Louise Young, has described the process as "form set free to dance through time and space."[13] Just thirty years ago biological evolution was assumed to follow the Darwinian view of gradual increase in complexity of organisms with time. A simple mechanism of natural selection among a series of chance mutations seemed reasonable. But recent studies of the time course of appearance of new organisms reveal a startling set of discontinuities. Life appears almost before the earth has had sufficient time to cool, and variety and complexity of form appear without the expected simpler precursors. Primitive bacteria and unicellular photosynthetic organisms similar to the present blue-green algae appear as fossils dating to 3.5 billion years ago. The early production of oxygen by photosynthesis and the subsequent formation of an ozone layer to protect life from ultraviolet radiation were also crucial developments. It is a picture of a remarkable interplay between earth and its first living inhabitants, as Young says in *The Unfinished Universe*. It is one facet in the fascinating story of the creative forces still being revealed in the natural world. She writes:

Life altered the atmosphere and gentled the sunlight. It turned the naked rocks of the continents into friable soil and clothed them with a richly variegated mantle of green which captured the energy of our own star for the use of living things on earth, and it softened the force of the winds. In the seas life built great reefs that broke the impact of storm-driven waves. It sifted and piled up shining beaches along the shores. Working with amazing strength and endurance life transformed an ugly and barren landscape into a benign and beautiful place where wildflowers carpet the hillsides and birds embroider the air with song. The story of how all this came to pass is a shining example of the creative forces working within nature.[14]

The first appearance of microorganisms is followed by a long period of quiescence until about 1.5 billion years ago, when the first appearance of fossils of eukaryotic cells—those bearing specialized apparatus for inheritance (nucleus) and energy production (mitochondria) and sometimes motion (cilia). It was these more complex cells that provided the raw material for innovation and experimentation, for new relationships like colonial living and sexual reproduction. Some of the colony formers built the coral reefs, and some of the more modern examples are our termites and bees. Following the appearance of the first eukaryotic cells, another 800 million years passed before fossils of unicellular plants such as algae and fungi appear. This is followed, some 200 million years later, by the appearance of the first multicellular organisms; green algae, then primitive seaweeds and fungi. The union of separate cells carried the important possibility for specialization, division of labor into more efficient units that could still be mobilized for general needs in emergencies. Here is one of the first examples of the wholeness and interconnectedness of living systems. One additional fossil type is found dating to this period, the first multicellular animals, looking somewhat like the later jellyfish, segmented worms, and corals.

Then at about 570 million years ago, soft-shelled aquatic animals suddenly appear, and these are followed at 500 million years ago by aquatic animals with hard skeletons and a bone-protected central nerve cord, the first fish. Because of the hard body parts, these organisms readily fossilize, and their remains are broadly distributed and demonstrate spectacular variety and numbers.

The first land organisms appear at about 400 million years ago, at which time the biosphere had been altered to provide oxygen at present levels and a protective ozone layer. The transition to land involved plants in the intertidal zone, organisms with strong body parts, anchoring structures, and heavy cell walls to avoid desiccation. Louise Young tells us that there is a certain mystery about this transition to the land. The doctrine of slow alteration by chance mutation and selection would argue for retention of easy environments for maximum survival. Yet the adaptation to land proved enormously successful despite the more stringent requirements of structure and nutrition. Although only 30 percent of the earth's surface is land, over 80 percent of all species are terrestrial, and these are the most complex organisms known. Life seems not to follow the path of least resistance. As Young puts it: "There is something within life, within nonliving matter, too, that is not passive—a nisus, a striving that is stimulated by challenge. Steadily throughout geologic time life has moved out from easy to difficult environments and now has populated almost every nook and cranny of the globe, from the frozen wastes of Antarctica to the boiling sulfur-laden vents at the bottom of the sea." [15]

The first land plants left their fossil imprint 400 million years ago. They photosynthesized through green porous stems and had root hairs that gripped the soil and brought water to the branches. It is probable that the very important symbiotic relationship between plants and nitrogen-fixing bacteria occurred at this very early stage. Nitrogen in the metabolic form of ammonia is crucial to life, but it is probable that the denitrifying bacteria of the early biosphere could not supply the larger demands of terrestrial plants. Here a creative association of two very different organisms occurred; a primitive anaerobic bacterium with a powerful enzyme system called nitrogenase, capable of reducing relatively plentiful atmospheric nitrogen to ammonia, and a photosynthetic plant with a root system to provide nourishment and a protected location for the bacterium. Symbiosis is seen throughout the present biosphere, and remains one of the most crucial relationships on earth.

Young tells us that the first land animals are found in fossils dating to about 390 million years ago.[16] They were spiderlike and air-breathing and they eventually gave rise to some thirty-two distinct body plans, including sponges, corals, annelids (earthworms, etc.), arthropods (insects, spiders, etc.), mollusks, echinoderms (starfishes, sea urchins, sand dollars), and chordates (vertebrates, etc.). All these organisms have come to us by this stupendous evolutionary path—tortuous, devious, full of pitfalls and dead ends, festooned with the successful and littered with the debris of the failures. Some failures were of immense proportions, and were often out of the hands of the participants. The comet that apparently struck the earth 65 million years ago left the dinosaurs with no choice—they all perished.

Yet the removal of the dinosaurs provided an open door for the warm-blooded mammals including ourselves. And their removal also coincided with an explosive appearance of the angiosperms—the flowering plants. Within a few million years, a tick of the clock by evolutionary standards, the entire face of the planet changed. It is said that the appearance of these plants, bringing with them crucial high-energy food sources for the proliferating mammalian species, occurred so suddenly that Darwin referred to them as an "abominable mystery." Eiseley says of this sudden coincidence of the high-energy-requiring mammals and the flowering plants that it represents one of the supreme achievements in the evolution of life.[17] One cannot view such marvelously coincident phenomena as flowers and warm-blooded creatures without realizing that all of nature exhibits a connectedness, an exquisite inter-linkage. Flowers did indeed change the face of the planet. The English poet Francis Thompson once wrote that one could not pluck a flower without troubling a star. And Eiseley comments: "Without the gift of flowers and the infinite diversity of their fruits, man and bird, if they had continued to exist at all, would be today unrecognizable. Archaeopteryx, the lizard-bird, might still be snapping at beetles on a sequoia limb; man might still be a nocturnal insectivore gnawing a roach in the dark. The weight of a petal has changed the face of the world and made it ours."[18]

One can call such a coincidence only happenstance, but it would seem to be repeated throughout the evolutionary process, and to suggest that something much deeper and more profound is going on. Someone has said that coincidence is God's way of remaining anonymous!

THE ORIGIN OF HUMANKIND

The final chapter in the evolution of life is the most profound of all—the origin of humankind. It contains the strongest evidence for purpose, since it brings with it that most wondrous phenomenon, of which Sir John Eccles writes at length in his chapter, that of human self-consciousness. Arthur Peacocke also addresses this highly significant development, pointing out that there is no mechanistic explanation, no knowledge of the biological and physical worlds, which would explain why we have the "experience of subjectivity."

Very recent anthropological data and new genetic data suggest the possibility of a single recent geographical origin for *Homo sapiens* in Africa.[19,20,21] Populations of this species migrated out of Africa perhaps one hundred thousand years ago into the rest of the world, replacing existing primitive human populations, like the Neanderthals, which they encountered.

The new genetic evidence comes from studies of mitochondrial DNA (mt DNA). Mt DNA is found only in mitochondria, the cell organelles that provide the bulk of cellular energy in most organisms. It has two distinguishing characteristics. One is that it is distinct from the DNA of the nucleus and the second is that its mode of inheritance is maternal. Whereas nuclear genes are inherited from both parents and shuffled in sexual reproduction, mitochondrial genes are contributed only by the female sex cells, and so are handed down from generation to generation by the mother only. Additionally, mitochondrial genes are much more frequently mutated, a factor that makes mt DNA much more useful as a molecular clock, a device for assigning a date to every branching point on the genealogical tree.[22]

The initial work with human mt DNA has been carried out by Allan Wilson and coworkers at Berkeley. What they have done is to compare mt DNA from about 150 women from 5 geographical populations throughout the world—Asia, Africa, Europe, Australia, and New Guinea. When the DNA sequences were compared, the most striking thing was that there was little difference between the various groups, which implies that they separated from each other only recently. Another thing that was observed was that DNAs fell into two main groups—one that represented only sub-Saharan Africans, and the other that represented individuals from all groups. And it was also evident that the sub-Saharan African group was the longest established of all. That is, the greatest sequence divergence—the largest number of mutational differences—was found when comparing the African group's mt DNA with a reference DNA. Thus, the mt DNAs from the sub-Saharan Africans were derived from a common ancestor of all modern humans. This so-called mitochondrial Eve was from South or East Africa and was probably derived from an ancestor of the present-day Khoisan people of South Africa, perhaps one hundred thousand years ago. It is possible that these Bushmen are descended from a series of wandering bands that had separated from an original small population elsewhere, and that *all of us* are derived from the same small population!

This astounding conclusion, which would make human evolution a rather colossal emergence, is based upon several important assumptions about the mt DNA methodology. First of all, genetic similarities must be directly proportional to the recency of their divergence from a common ancestor. Secondly, the mt DNA mutation rate must be constant. Thirdly, there must be no selection processes either to retain or cull out certain genes. It is also assumed that there was relatively little mixing of the ancestral population with other hominids as it migrated out of Africa, a process that would give an erroneously early date for our maternal ancestor.

Some support for these assumptions, together with the most recent fossil evidence and population genetics analyses, suggests the recent origin of modern humans in Africa.

THE REMARKABLE PACE OF HUMAN EVOLUTION

Once modern humans became established there was a veritable explosion of innovation. Painting, engraving, and tool manufacture changed so quickly that archaeologists divide the periods from thirty-five thousand years ago to ten thousand years ago into six separate cultural periods, each with its own style of technology and innovations. David Wilcox, one of the contributors to this volume, has pointed out in another context that by contrast the Neanderthal populations displayed cultural stasis like *Homo erectus*. The Mousterian tool culture that they developed appeared around one hundred thousand years ago and remained basically uniform across Europe for sixty-five thousand years. The modern humans that apparently replaced the Neanderthals were, in less than half their tenure, walking on the moon![23]

What were these early modern humans like? Most emphatically, they were artistic. Perhaps this is a reflection of their forced confinement in caves during periods of bitter cold, but the contemporary Neanderthals did not draw in their cave dwellings. And what art these moderns produced! The seventeen-thousand-year-old Lascaux Cave, the most spectacular of the caves of Ice Age Europe, is filled with vivid images of animal activity. And such caves dot the map of Europe and the Mideast. Along with cave paintings we also find pieces of engraved bone, often with curious sets of markings that appear to have some mathematical significance, and a rapidly accelerating innovation in tool manufacture.

What were these people of the caves and the grasslands really like? Clearly, they were radically different from anyone who had gone before in terms of artistry and ingenuity, symbolism, and ritual. They were from Africa, perhaps with their roots in that Khoisan tribe of perhaps one hundred thousand years ago. They must have come to Europe and Asia shortly after their origin, for we find them in the Israeli caves seventy thousand years ago and in France, Britain, and southern Russia more than thirty thousand years ago. Their skin probably was black, and the archaic human populations—Neanderthals and others—they encountered in Europe were probably white. Over time, *sapiens* would have become paler, an evolutionary adaptation to the decrease in the sun's intensity that would then enhance their capacity to synthesize vitamin D. Also over time, they would replace Neanderthals and other archaic humans, perhaps in something of the way that 17th-and 18th-century Europeans replaced the American Indians, though there is relatively little evidence of interbreeding of the modern humans of seventy thousand years ago with their archaic counterparts.

THE DEEPER MEANING OF HUMAN EVOLUTION

Many intriguing questions remain to be answered scientifically, but from a theological perspective the recent emergence of *Homo sapiens* with all their new capabilities does encourage a serious look at the biblical picture of creation. Scripture begins the story with the words: "Let us make man in our own image, in our likeness, and let them rule over the fish of the sea and the birds of the air, over the livestock, over all the earth, and over all the creatures that move along the ground. So God created man in his own image, in the image of God he created him; male and female he created them."[24]

We are not surprised by the recent origin and rapid evolution of modern humans. It does indeed seem a quantum leap from the animal world to a creature with such great potentialities for creativity, ethical reasoning, and altruism—a "kingdom-level speciation." It might be argued that the other primates are not only anatomically and genetically like us but that they too have characteristics that we ordinarily associate with humanness. Certainly the chimpanzee is capable of tool use, can perform sign language, show empathy and build long-term relationships. However, there is no evidence that they make their simple tools according to a pattern, as though they had a conceptual image of what they were making, nor that their use of sign language has any sense of grammatical arrangement—any syntax—which is the essence of language.[25] Behaviorally, chimps show no ethical sense or any particular evidence for feelings of guilt if, for example, they have killed a fellow chimp. World authority Jane Goodall refers to them as the "innocent killers."[26]

The exclusively human characteristics that appear crucial are reason, language, and responsibility, and it seems highly unlikely that these are the "elaborations or epiphenomena resulting from unguided material events" as paleontologist Stephen Gould has suggested. However, it is interesting that he is impressed with the uniqueness of our origin, for he says: "We are an improbable and fragile entity, fortunately successful after precarious beginnings as a small population in Africa, not the predictable end result of a global tendency. We are a thing, an item of history, not an embodiment of general principles."[27]

Yet the general principle—self-organization—has been there in all its fruitfulness since the stars first began to shine. And it has moved with marvelous creativity within a structure of opportunity and cooperativeness toward ever higher levels of complexity and sophistication to arrive at us!

We may not be the end of the story, with our attributes of self-awareness and self-conscious purpose, as Sir John Eccles describes them in his chapter. But we are surely a remarkable beginning of a new era of evolution in which matter becomes mind and the spirit soars!

The nature of what we are biologically still eludes us, and we shout for an even deeper meaning that may never come by way of our very best and most sophisticated genetics and anthropology. As with the countless stars, we too are a universe of complexity, a deeper reality, to be known fully, not in material but in spiritual terms, as an image of the Creator who purposed it so to be.

1

Owen Gingerich

Dare a Scientist Believe in Design?

Conus cedonulli is, literally, the "I yield to none" cone. In the eighteenth century this handsomely patterned shell became the most celebrated and sought-after molluscan rarity. Two specimens were known in Europe in the early 1700s, one of which became the prize of the king of Portugal's collection. In 1796 the other was auctioned for 243 guilders at a sale in which Vermeer's masterpiece, "Woman in Blue Reading a Letter," fetched a mere 43 guilders!

Cone shells, *cedonulli* among them, are considered among the most "advanced" mollusks because their anatomy includes a toxic harpoon that can spring out of the apex end of the shell. In some species the sting can be deadly even to humans.

Our first reaction upon hearing about the cone shells may well be: what wonderful design! And we may be even more impressed and probably puzzled to learn that the exquisite pattern on the shell is, during the animal's lifetime, covered by an opaque periostracum, rendering the pattern virtually invisible and therefore perplexingly useless either for survival or sexual attraction. To think in terms of deliberate design is an almost intuitive response, yet such thoughts have become strangely taboo in contemporary scientific circles. *Conus cedonulli* thus becomes a jumping-off place for consideration of the question, "Dare a scientist believe in design?"

Consider what happened when a report on studies of the mollusk toxins recently appeared in *Science* magazine (along with an illustration of both *Conus cedonulli* and the Vermeer painting).[1] A supplementary news article, entitled "Science Digests the Secrets of Voracious Killer Snails" remarked that "the great diversity and specificity of toxins in the venoms of the cone snails are due to the intense evolutionary pressure on the snails to stop their prey quickly, since they can't chase it down."[2]

Very promptly a letter to the editor objected that this language implied that some real pressure was driving the snails to develop the toxins. "The reality is that those snails that produced toxins that immobilized their prey quickly tended to obtain food more often than those possessing slower-acting or no toxins, and thus over time the population of cone shells became dominated by those possessing the fast-acting agents. There was no pressure! In the vernacular, 'If it works, it works; if it don't, it don't.'"[3]

The response shows clearly the current philosophical orthodoxy about the nondirected nature of evolution. It also typifies the enormous change of view that has occurred over the past century with respect to the wonders of the biological world.

What is now seen as the zigzag, largely accidental path to amazing organisms with astonishing adaptations was in earlier times routinely interpreted as the design of an intelligent Creator. The long neck of the giraffe, which so well adapts the creature to an environment where food is available high off the ground, would have been seen, in William Paley's words, as a "mark of contrivance, in proof of design, and of a designing Creator."[4] "Who gave white bears and white wolves to the snowy regions of the North, and as food for the bears the whale, and for the wolves, birds' eggs?" asked Johannes Kepler two centuries earlier.[5] "Great is our Lord and great his virtue and of his wisdom there is no number!" he exclaims in answer. "Use every sense for perceiving your Creator."

Even Jean-Jacques Rousseau, not best known as a theist, declared, "It is impossible for me to conceive that a system of beings can be so wisely regulated without the existence of some intelligent cause which affects such regulation. . . . I believe, therefore, that the world is governed by a wise and powerful Will."[6]

The notion of design suggests, of course, the existence of a goal-directed or end-directed process, what can aptly be termed teleology. Ernst Mayr, a leading evolutionist who has written very clearly on the modern philosophy of evolution, wisely remarks that it is futile to attempt to clarify the concept of teleology without discriminating between different types of end-directed processes. There are some kinds of inanimate natural processes that do have an end point, for example, and there are also goal-directed processes in genetically controlled organisms. "The third category, organic adaptness, is not directed toward an end but rather an adaptation to the environment in the widest sense of the word, acquired during evolution, largely guided by natural selection. The fourth teleology, the cosmic one, is not supported by scientific evidence."[7] So much then, for a role for the Creator in modern biology.

"Man was not the goal of evolution, which evidently had no goal," wrote G. G. Simpson in a more visceral fashion. "He was not planned, in an operation wholly planless."[8]

Yet, despite the articulate denials of cosmic teleology by the leading evolutionists of our age, there still remain enough astonishing details of the natural order to evoke a feeling of awe—so much so that cosmologists have even given it a name: the anthropic principle. The discussion arose originally when some physicists noticed that even small variations in some of the constants of nature would have led to a universe in which life could not exist. For example, had the original energy of the Big Bang explosion been less, the universe would have fallen back onto itself long before there had been time to build the elements required for life and to produce from them intelligent, sentient beings. Had the energy been more, it is quite possible that the density would have dropped too swiftly for stars and galaxies to form. These and many other details were so extraordinarily right that it seemed the universe had been expressly designed for humankind. Such was the original context that led to the anthropic principle.

One of the first scientists to consider how the environment itself made life possible was the Harvard chemist L. J. Henderson. Early in this century, after Darwin's emphasis on the fitness of organisms for their various environments, Henderson wrote a fascinating book entitled *The Fitness of the Environment*, which pointed out that the organisms themselves would not exist except for certain properties of matter. He argued for the uniqueness of carbon as the chemical basis of life, and everything we have learned since then, from the nature of the hydrogen bond to the structure of DNA, reinforces his argument. But today it is possible to go still further and to probe the origin of carbon itself, through its synthesis deep inside evolving stars.

Carbon is the fourth most common atom in our galaxy, after hydrogen, helium, and oxygen. A carbon nucleus can be made by merging three helium nuclei, but a triple collision is tolerably rare. It would be easier if two helium nuclei would stick together to form beryllium, but beryllium is not very stable. Nevertheless, sometimes before the two helium nuclei can come unstuck, a third helium nucleus strikes home, and a carbon nucleus results. And here the details of the internal energy levels of the carbon nucleus become interesting: it turns out that there is precisely the right resonance within the carbon that helps this process along.

Let me digress a bit to remind you about resonance. You've no doubt heard that opera singers such as Enrico Caruso could shatter a wine glass by singing just the right note with enough volume. I don't doubt the story, because in the lectures at our Science Center at Harvard, about half a dozen wine glasses are shattered each year using sound waves. It's necessary to tune the audio generator through the frequency spectrum to just the right note where the glass begins to vibrate—the specific resonance for that particular goblet—and then to turn up the volume so that the glass vibrates more and more violently until it flies apart.

The specific resonances within atomic nuclei are something like that, except in this case the particular energy enables the parts to stick together rather than to fly apart. In the carbon atom, the resonance just happens to match the combined energy of the beryllium atom and a colliding helium nucleus. Without it, there would be relatively few carbon atoms. Similarly, the internal details of the oxygen nucleus play a critical role. Oxygen can be formed by combining helium and carbon nuclei, but the corresponding resonance level in the oxygen nucleus is half a percent too low for the combination to stay together easily. Had the resonance level in the carbon been 4 percent lower, there would be essentially no carbon. Had that level in the oxygen been only half a percent higher, virtually all of the carbon would have been converted to oxygen. Without that carbon abundance, neither you nor I would be here now.

I am told that Fred Hoyle, who together with Willy Fowler found this remarkable nuclear arrangement, has said that nothing has shaken his atheism as much as this discovery. Occasionally Fred Hoyle and I have sat down to discuss one or another astronomical or historical point, but I never had enough nerve to ask him if his atheism had really been shaken by finding the nuclear resonance structure of carbon and oxygen. However, the answer came rather clearly in the November 1981 issue of the Cal Tech alumni magazine, where he wrote:

> Would you not say to yourself, "Some supercalculating intellect must have designed the properties of the carbon atom, otherwise the chance of my finding such an atom through the blind forces of nature would be utterly minuscule." Of course you would. . . . A common sense interpretation of the facts suggests that a superintellect has monkeyed with physics, as well

as with chemistry and biology, and that there are no blind forces worth speaking about in nature. The numbers one calculates from the facts seem to me so overwhelming as to put this conclusion almost beyond question.[9]

Not so long ago I used the carbon and oxygen resonance in a lecture at a university in the Midwest, and in the question period I was interrogated by a philosopher who wanted to know if I could quantify the argument by Bayesian probabilities. Now I'll confess that, at the time, I hadn't a clue that Bayesian statistics meant evaluating a proposition on the basis of an original probability and new relevant evidence. But even knowing how to handle that would hardly have enabled me to perform a convincing calculation, that is, a probability so overwhelming as to be tantamount to a proof that super-intelligent design was involved in the placement of the resonance levels.

Clearly my petitioner was daring me to convince him, despite the fact that I had already proclaimed that arguments from design are in the eyes of the beholder, and simply cannot be construed as proofs to convince skeptics. Furthermore, in posing his question he had already pointed out the quicksands of using numerology to prove the existence of divine order in the cosmos. So now I hasten to dampen any notion that I intended the resonance levels in carbon and oxygen nuclei to demonstrate the efficacy of design or to prove the existence of God.

Even William Paley, with his famous watch and his conclusion that it pointed to the existence of a watchmaker, said that "My opinion of Astronomy has always been, that it is *not* the best medium through which to prove the agency of an intelligent creator; but that, this being proved, it shows, beyond all other sciences, the magnificence of his operations."[10]

For me, it is not a matter of proofs and demonstrations, but of making sense of the astonishing cosmic order that the sciences repeatedly reveal. Fred Hoyle and I differ on lots of questions, but on this we agree: a common sense and satisfying interpretation of our world suggests the designing hand of a superintelligence. Impressive as the evidences of design in the astrophysical world may be, however, I personally find even more remarkable those from the biological realm. As Walt Whitman proclaimed, "A leaf of grass is no less than the journey work of the stars."[11] I would go still further and assert that stellar evolution is child's play compared to the complexity of DNA in grass or mice. Whitman goes on, musing that,

The tree toad is a chef-d'oeuvre for the highest,
And the running blackberry would adorn the parlors of heaven,
And the narrowest hinge in my hand puts to scorn all machinery,
And the cow crunching with depress'd head surpasses any statue,
And a mouse is miracle enough to stagger sextillions of infidels.

Even Hoyle, by his allusion to the biology, seems to agree that the formation of, say, DNA, is so improbable as to require a superintelligence. Such biochemical arguments were popularized about forty years ago by Lecomte du Noüy in his book *Human Destiny*. Du Noüy estimated the probability of forming a two-thousand atom protein as something like one part in 10^{321}. He wrote, "Events which, even when we admit very numerous experiments, reactions, or shakings per second, *need an infinitely longer time than the estimated duration of the earth in order to have one chance, on the average, to manifest themselves can, it would seem, be considered as impossible in the human sense.*"[12]

Du Noüy went on to say, "To study the most interesting phenomena, namely Life and eventually Man, we are therefore, forced to call on antichance, as Eddington called it; a cheater who systematically violates the laws of large numbers, the statistical laws which deny any individuality to the particles considered."[13]

The game plan for evolutionary theory, however, is to find the accidental, contingent ways in which these unlikely and seemingly impossible events could have taken place. The evolutionists do not seek an automatic scheme—mechanistic in the sense that Newtonian mechanics is determined —but some random pathways whose existence could be at least partially retraced by induction from the fragmentary historical record. But when the working procedure becomes raised to a philosophy of nature, the practitioners begin to place their faith in the roulette of chance and they find du Noüy and Hoyle an aggravation to their assumptions about the meaninglessness of the universe.

Despite the reluctance of many evolutionary theorists, such as Ernst Mayr who states, "Cosmic teleology must be rejected by science. . . . I do not think there is a modern scientist left who still believes in it,"[14] there does seem to be enough evidence of design in the universe to give some pause. Even G. G. Simpson wrote, "Man *did* originate after a tremendously long sequence of events in which both chance and orientation played a part. . . . The result *is* the most highly endowed organization of matter that has yet appeared on earth—and we certainly have no good reason to believe there is any higher in the universe. To think that this result is insignificant would be unworthy of that high endowment."[15] In fact, scientists who wish to deny the role of design seem to have taken over the anthropic principle. Briefly stated, they have turned the original argument on its head. Rather than accepting that we are here because of a deliberate supernatural design, they claim that the universe simply must be this way *because* we are here; had the universe been otherwise, we would not be here to observe ourselves, and that is that. Such is almost precisely the view enunciated by Stephen Hawking in his inaugural lecture as Lucasian Professor at Cambridge University—an illustrious chair once held by Isaac Newton—and a view of nature repeated by Hawking in his best-selling *A Brief History of Time*.[16] As I said, I am doubtful that you can convert a skeptic by the argument of design, and the discussions of the anthropic principle seem to prove the point.

But once again I return to my central question, "Dare a scientist believe in design?" and I pause to remark on the somewhat curious status of "belief" within science. A year ago I conducted a workshop for a rather diverse group of Christians, and I asked, "Can a theist believe in evolution?" I got a variety of responses, but it didn't occur to any of them to challenge what it might mean to "*believe*" in evolution. Does that mean to have faith in evolution in a religious sense? I have heard one leading paleontologist announce himself as a "devout evolutionist" when asked his faith, and I guess that is a possibility. But when pressed, most scientists would, I think, claim only that they accept evolution as a working hypothesis. In everyday, non-philosophical usage, most people, scientists included, would say that they believe in the results of science and that they believe the results of science to be true. Yet, and this is the anomalous part, most scientists would be mildly offended at the thought that their beliefs constituted an act of faith in a largely unproved but intricate system of coherencies.

Actually, surprisingly little in science itself is accepted by "proof." Let's take Newtonian mechanics as an example. Newton had no proof that the earth moved, or that the sun was the center of the planetary system. Yet, without that assumption, his system did not make much sense. What he had was an elaborate and highly successful scheme of both explanation and prediction, and most people had no trouble believing it, but what they were accepting as truth was a grand scheme whose validity rested on its coherency, not on any proof. Thus, when a convincing stellar parallax was measured in 1838, or when Foucault swung his famous pendulum at 2 A.M. on Wednesday morning, January 8, 1851, these supposed proofs of the revolution and of the rotation of the earth did not produce a sudden, newfound acceptance of the heliocentric cosmology. The battle had long since been won by a persuasiveness that rested not on proof but on coherency.

Now if we understand that science's great success has been in the production of a remarkably coherent view of nature rather than in an intricately dovetailed set of proofs, then I would argue that a belief in design can also have a legitimate place in human understanding even if it falls short of proof. What is needed is a consistent and coherent worldview, and at least for some of us, the universe is easier to comprehend if we assume that it has both purpose and design, even if this cannot be proven with a tight logical deduction.

Nevertheless, there has been a persistent criticism that arguments from design will cause scientific investigators to give up too easily. If the resonance levels of carbon and oxygen are seen as a miracle of creation, would a Christian physicist try to understand more deeply why, from the mechanistic view of physics, the levels are that particular way and not in some other configuration? Might it not be potentially detrimental to the faith to explain a miracle? And so we come face-to-face with our original query, "Dare a scientist believe in supernatural design?"

There is, I shall argue, no contradiction between holding a staunch belief in supernatural design and being a creative scientist, and perhaps no one illustrates this point better than the seventeenth-century astronomer Johannes Kepler. He was one of the most creative astronomers of all time, a man who played a major role in bringing about the acceptance of the Copernican system through the efficacy of his tables of planetary motion.

Now one of the principal reasons Kepler was a Copernican arose from his deeply held belief that the sun-centered arrangement reflected the divine design of the cosmos: the sun at the center was the image of God, the outer surface of the star-studded heavenly sphere was the image of Christ, and the intermediate planetary space represented the Holy Spirit. These were not ephemeral notions of his student years, but a constant obsession that inspired and drove him through his entire life.

Today Kepler is best remembered for his discovery of the elliptical form of the planets' orbits. This discovery and another, the so-called law of areas, are chronicled in his *Astronomia nova*, truly the New Astronomy. In its introduction he defended his Copernicanism from the point of view that the heavens declare the glory of God:

> I implore my reader not to forget the divine goodness conferred on mankind, and which the psalmist urges him especially to consider. When he has returned from church and entered on the study of astronomy, may he praise and glorify the wisdom and greatness of the creator.... Let him not only extol the bounty of God in the preservation of living creatures of all kinds by the strength and stability of the earth, but also let him acknowledge the wisdom of the Creator in its motion, so abstruse, so admirable.
>
> If someone is so dumb that he cannot grasp the science of astronomy, or so weak that he cannot believe Copernicus without offending his piety, I advise him to mind his own business, to quit this worldly pursuit, to stay at home and cultivate his own garden, and when he turns his eyes toward the visible heavens (the only way he sees them), let him with his whole heart pour forth praise and gratitude to God the Creator. Let him assure himself that he is serving God no less than the astronomer to whom God has granted the privilege of seeing more clearly with the eyes of the mind.[17]

A detailed study of Kepler's life reveals an evolution of ideas on a number of topics, such as whether planets have "souls" that guide them. He had grown up in an age when philosophers still attributed heavenly motions in part to the individual intelligences of the planets, and in his first, youthful treatise, he endorsed the idea of animate souls as moving intelligences of the planets. But by the time of his mature work he could flatly state that, "I deny that celestial movements are the work of Mind." However, on his views of God as a geometer and of a universe filled with God's geometrical designs Kepler was unwavering.

Kepler's life and works provide central evidence that an individual can be both a creative scientist and a believer in divine design in the universe, and that indeed the very motivation for the scientific research can stem from a desire to trace God's handiwork.

In the centuries that followed, many scientists took inspiration from the idea that the heavens declared the glory of God, but God's hand appeared less and less in their physical explanations. In a sense, one of the fundamental consequences of the scientific revolution, in which the ancient geocentric universe gave way to a vast heliocentric plan governed by gravitation, was the secularization of the natural world.

Darwin's theory was of a quite different sort from Newton's. He sought some fundamental explanation for patterns of similarities as well as differences within the biological kingdoms, and a way to understand the remarkable adaptation of the organisms beyond a simple attribution to God's designing hand. Darwin's explanation eventually relied on historical contingency rather than mechanical necessity. As such, his theory lacked the compelling predictive power that arises from the necessity of gravitation, or of conservation of angular momentum, or of any number of physical laws. But what it lacked in sheer predictive power it achieved in its immense explanatory power, a spectacular new coherency of understanding.

With the secularization of the physical world that followed in the wake of the scientific revolution of the sixteenth and seventeenth centuries, the community became divided between the deists, who put God outside the universe as the Spirit who set it all into motion according to physical laws, and the theists, who still maintained an active role for God within the world. This was, of course, a theological or philosophical option, not a decision required by any scientific observations of the world itself. After Darwin's evolutionary theory was raised to a philosophy, with its inherent denial of design, the apparent choice swung more sharply from deism/theism to atheism/theism. Science remained a neutral way of explaining things, neither anti-God nor atheistic. Many people were (and are) extremely uncomfortable with a way of looking at the universe that did not explicitly require the hand of God. But it did not mean the universe was actually like that, just that science generally has no other way of working.

Nevertheless, random opportunism (as opposed to design) has been raised to such a level of scientific orthodoxy that some of our contemporaries forget that this is just a tactic of science, an assumption, and not a guaranteed principle of reality. Few, however, have enunciated the mechanistic credo so stridently as the evolutionary biologist and historian of science William B. Provine, who has recently written,

> When Darwin deduced the theory of natural selection to explain the adaptations in which he had previously seen the handiwork of God, he knew that he was committing cultural murder. He understood immediately that if natural selection explained adaptations, and evolution by descent were true, then the argument from design was dead and all that went with it, namely the existence of a personal god, free will, life after death, immutable moral laws, and ultimate meaning in life. The immediate reactions to Darwin's *On the Origin of Species* exhibit, in addition to favorable and admiring responses from a relatively few scientists, an understandable fear and disgust that has never disappeared from Western culture.[18]

Provine, in defending the gospel of meaninglessness, goes on to say that if modern evolutionary biology is true, then lofty desires such as divinely inspired moral laws and some kind of ultimate meaning in life are hopeless. I am not sure why Professor Provine has such fear and loathing of design, but apparently, despite the example of Kepler (and of Newton and many others), he is still afraid that the arguments from design may block the march of science. Such a view is perhaps not totally unfounded. Let me explain.

Several years ago I participated in a remarkable conference of theists and atheists in Dallas. One session considered the origin of life, and a group of Christian biochemists argued that the historical record was nonscientific since it was impossible to perform scientific experiments on history. Furthermore, they amassed considerable evidence that the current scenarios of the chemical evolution of life were untenable. One of the atheists aligned against them, Professor Clifford Matthews from the University of Chicago, conceded that their criticisms had considerable validity. Calling their book on *The Mystery of Life's Origin*[19] brilliant, he summarized their arguments with respect to the standard picture of chemical evolution as saying, "(1) the evidence is weak, (2) the premises are wrong, and (3) the whole thing is impossible."

I soon found myself in the somewhat anomalous position that to me, the atheists' approach was much more interesting than the theists'. That particular group of Christian biochemists had concluded that ordinary science did not work in such a historical situation, that is, with respect to the origin of life, and they attempted to delineate an alternative "origin science" in which the explicit guiding hand of God could make possible what was otherwise beyond any probability. The reason I admired the atheist biochemists so much was that they had not given up. They were still proposing ingenious avenues whereby catalytic effects in the chemistry made the events far more likely. "Let us not flee to a supernaturalistic explanation," they said, "let us not retreat from the laboratory."

Now it might be that the chemistry of life's origins *is* forever beyond human comprehension, but I see no way to establish that scientifically. Therefore it seems to me to be part of science to keep trying, even if ultimately there is no accessible answer.

Am I contradicting myself to say, on the one hand, that the resonance levels in carbon and oxygen point to a superintelligent design, and on the other hand, that science must continue to search for underlying reasons why the resonance levels are that way and not some other way? I think not, for even if it is shown that those levels had to be the way they are because of some fundamental, invariable reason, there is still the miracle of design that led it so, choice or not. Therefore, I see no reason that an appreciation of the astonishing details of design should prevent us from trying to search further into their underlying causes. Hence I am not prepared to concede that arguments from design are necessarily contrascientific in their nature.

Perhaps part of Provine's outrage came because he was responding to Phillip Johnson, professor of law at Berkeley, who is an articulate legal champion of the right to believe in God as Creator and Designer, and a critic of an evolutionary process running entirely by chance.[20] Earlier I mentioned the incredible odds calculated by Lecomte du Noüy against the chance formation of a protein molecule. Since we do have proteins, and since a mechanistic science has been highly successful, the overwhelming reaction has just been to ignore du Noüy, since he is so obviously wrong. But is he? For science to overcome the odds, it is necessary for us to postulate catalysts and unknown pathways to make the formation of life from inert matter enormously easier, and it is of course precisely such pathways that are the challenge of science to find. But is not the existence of such pathways also evidence of design? And are they not inevitable? That is what materialists such as Provine do not want to hear, but as Hoyle says, the numbers one calculates put the matter beyond question.

So, while I differ from those Christian biochemists who postulate some new kind of "origin science," I do think a science totally devoid of the idea of design may be in danger of running into a blank wall. And this brings me to ask again, is the idea of design a threat to science? and I answer no, perhaps design might even be a necessary ingredient in science.

In reflecting on these questions I have attempted, in a somewhat guarded way, to delineate a place for design both in the world of science and in the world of theology. As Kepler once said of astrology, the stars impel, but they do not compel.[21] There is persuasion here, but no proof. However, even in the hands of secular philosophers the modern mythologies of the heavens, the beginnings and endings implied in the Big Bang, give hints of ultimate realities beyond the universe itself. Milton Munitz, in his closely argued book, *Cosmic Understanding*,[22] declares that our cosmology leads logically to the idea of a transcendence beyond time and space, giving lie to the notion that the cosmos is all there is, or was, or ever will be.

Munitz, in coming to the concept of transcendence, describes it as unknowable, which is somewhat paradoxical, since if the transcendence is unknowable then we cannot know that it is unknowable. Could the unknowable have revealed itself? Logic is defied by the idea that the unknowable might have communicated to us, but coherence is not. For me, it makes sense to suppose that the superintelligence, the transcendence, the ground of being in Paul Tillich's formulation, has revealed itself through prophets in all ages, and supremely in the life of Jesus Christ.

To believe this requires accepting teleology and purpose. But I think that the philosophers might rightfully point out that purpose transcends design, that is, there can be purpose without design; God could work God's purposes even in a universe without apparent design, or with designs beyond our finite comprehension. It would be possible to be a theist and a Christian even in the absence of observed design.

Nevertheless, just as I believe that the Book of Scripture illumines the pathway to God, so I believe that the Book of Nature, with its astonishing details—the blade of grass, the *Conus cedonulli*, or the resonance levels of the carbon atom—also suggests a God of purpose and a God of design. And I think my belief makes me no less a scientist.

To conclude, I turn once again to Kepler, who wrote, "If I have been allured into brashness by the wonderful beauty of thy works, or if I have loved my own glory among men, while advancing in work destined for thy glory, gently and mercifully pardon me: and finally, deign graciously to cause that these demonstrations may lead to thy glory and to the salvation of souls, and nowhere be an obstacle to that. Amen."[23]

2

Russell Stannard

God's Purpose in and Beyond Time

Modern physics and cosmology impact in a number of ways upon our understanding of a God who purposefully creates and sustains the world. First, let us look at the way God relates to time:

Purpose implies looking to the future. As far as we conscious human beings are concerned, the future is uncertain, so the attainment of our goals must be a matter of conjecture. But for God it is different. The traditional belief in his omniscience has as a corollary an acceptance that God knows everything that is to happen. Whereas we can do no more than *hope* that things will work out satisfactorily, he *knows* his purpose will be accomplished. Herein lies a fundamental difference between the concept of purpose as applied to God and to ourselves.

But *can* God know the future before it has happened? If even I do not know how I shall decide to act on a future occasion, how can God know my decision and the consequences that will stem from it? If the future is in some sense already decided, does that not close the options and inhibit the exercise of free will—an equally vital feature of Christian belief? Indeed, to do full justice to traditional beliefs one must include the idea of predestination—God not only knows the future, but according to his divine purpose, *determines* that future (including our own individual salvation or otherwise).

It has never been easy to reconcile the notion of human free will with the idea of divine foreknowledge and predestination. Because the firsthand experience of our own free will is so persuasive and seemingly incontestable, there is a natural tendency to resolve the tension by downplaying the importance, or indeed the correctness, of the belief in God's omniscience. This leads to arguments in which nothing is allowed that in any way diminishes, or appears to diminish, the concept of free will as conventionally understood. But herein lies a danger: that we create a conception of God shorn of his distinctive characteristics—a God conforming to our own image, clothed in human limitations.

It is my belief that an appreciation of modern physics, in the form of Einstein's theory of relativity, can go a long way toward redressing the balance of this argument. To my mind, today's physics faces us with the need to accept, like it or not, that the future does in some special sense already exist. Not that this in any way affects the manner in which we human beings live our lives—for us the future will always remain uncertain and dependent on our current decisions and actions. But the fact that the future is in some sense already out there, does lend plausibility to the idea that an Intelligence operating in some altogether different way to ourselves could have access to it. That being the case, God's purpose does have that added quality of assurance about it that is lacking in human purpose. God's omniscience then reflects back on us in that we, through faith, can accept with confidence that God's kingdom will undoubtedly prevail in the end.

I begin by giving a simple account of the relevant ideas to be drawn from the theory of relativity for the benefit of readers not already acquainted with them:

I want you to imagine an astronaut in a high-speed spacecraft, and a mission controller at Houston. The astronaut leaves Earth at a speed of nine-tenths the speed of light. (The speed of light is 186,000 miles per second, so this is clearly a practical impossibility. However, it is more striking to illustrate the principles with somewhat exaggerated examples!) Relativity theory is able to show that, with the astronaut and the controller in relative motion, they do not agree on the distance the craft has to travel to reach a distant planet. At the particular speed we have chosen, the astronaut considers the distance to be about half that estimated by the controller. Nor is this the only effect of their relative speed. The two not only differ in their estimates of distance, but also of time. According to the controller, time for the astronaut passes at about half the rate it does for himself. Thus, everything happening in the craft—the clocks, the astronaut's breathing, his heartbeats, his aging processes—everything has slowed down by a factor of a half.

Not that the astronaut will be aware of this; a slow clock looked at with a brain in which the thinking processes have been slowed down by the same factor, appears perfectly normal. Which of the two observers is right in his assessment of distance and time? It is impossible to distinguish. Will the astronaut not realize that something must be wrong when, because of his slowed-down clock, he arrives at his destination in half the time it should have taken? No. Remember, he thinks the journey distance is only half that which the controller claims it to be. Both the astronaut and the mission controller have sets of measurements that are entirely self-consistent; there are no grounds for claiming one to have precedence over the other.

Confusing? It certainly seems that way when one first becomes acquainted with relativity. We are accustomed to thinking that we all inhabit a common three-dimensional space, so should agree on distance measurements in that space. We are also used to thinking that we live out our lives in a common time, so should agree on the separation in time between any two events. How is it feasible to have such disagreements?

Let me give you an analogy: suppose in the middle of a lecture I were to hold up an object—a pencil, say. What would the members of the audience see? They would each see something different. Some would see a long pencil, others a short one, others something in between. Confusing? No. We think nothing of such differing observations. We realize that what each person sees is merely a two-dimensional projection of what in reality extends into three dimensions. The two-dimensional projection is at right angles to the line of sight, and this line of sight will vary depending on where the observer is seated relative to the pencil. We are unperturbed by the different observations because we know that when each observer makes due allowance for how the pencil extends *along* his or her line of sight, Pythagoras's theorem applied to three dimensions comes up with identical results for the true length of the pencil.

Analogous considerations apply to the case of the astronaut and the mission controller. Here the two observers differ over the distance of the journey and the time of the journey. How are we to understand this? Einstein's solution to the problem is that we are *not* dealing with a three-dimensional space and a one-dimensional time, each being independent of the other. We are dealing with a *four*-dimensional reality: the three dimensions of space plus a fourth dimension closely related to time. What are the "objects" to be found in this space-time? They must be characterized by four coordinates (x, y, z, t), one for each of the dimensions. In other words, they must be events. One event might be the launch from Earth of the spacecraft at a specific time; another would be its arrival at the distant planet at some later time. Besides locating these pointlike events in space-time, we might be interested in the four-dimensional separation between two events. What would be the separation between the events marking the launch and the arrival of the spacecraft? We have seen that the two observers do not agree about either the spatial or the temporal separation of the events. But this must not worry us unduly; these are but projections of the four-dimensional reality (a three-dimensional and a one-dimensional projection respectively). From our analogy of the pencil we know that these can be different depending upon the vantage point from which one views the object. In the case of four-dimensional space-time, one observer will have a different vantage point from another observer if they are in relative motion. So what result do the astronaut and controller get when each takes his three-and-one-dimensional projections and combines them (via Pythagoras's theorem applied to four dimensions) to obtain the separation in four dimensions of the two events? They arrive at identically the same answer. It is the four-dimensional separation of two events that *all* observers agree on. This is the reason why physicists regard reality as four-dimensional.

It is an extraordinary conception. There is no point in trying to visualize it; our minds do not have that capability. One simply has to rely on the mathematics to lead us to this conclusion, and on the experiments to check its correctness.

Just how radical the theory is can be appreciated by reflecting on Einstein's remark that it is now more natural to think of physical reality as "a four-dimensional existence instead of, hitherto, the evolution of a three-dimensional existence." [1] Space and time form a seamless union. Time does not exist alongside space, but equally important, it does not exist alongside space-time either—it is integrally *part of space-time itself.* It makes no sense to think of space-time evolving *in* time because there is no other physical time in which such evolution could take place. Space-time, and the events that are etched into the fabric of space-time do not evolve—they do not change—they simply are.

Note how all the points in space-time exist on an equal footing. Just as each point in space exists at each point in time (as we are accustomed to accepting) so each point in time exists at each point in space—which is something new. Note further that, although for each point in time there exist earlier times and later times, there is no special point called "now"—one that distinguishes past events that no longer exist from future events that are yet to exist. I repeat, *all* events exist on an equal footing—*they all* exist.

Now, this conclusion is completely counterintuitive. We are accustomed to think that the only events that exist are those that exist at this particular instant—the one designated "now." Existence is confined purely to the present. This conviction is so strong that even certain physicists are reluctant to accept that it could be otherwise. But the reasoning is compelling, particularly when one takes into account a further consequence of relativity about which there can be no argument—its revision of the concept of simultaneity:

A fast baseball breaks the batter's bat. The bat breaks at the same time as the ball hits it; the events are simultaneous. That is true in conventional Newtonian mechanics; it is true also in Einstein's relativity. Our understanding of the simultaneity of events occurring at the same point in space is unchanged. What is interesting in relativity theory is what it has to say about events occurring in *different* locations:

At Houston it is 12:00 noon exactly. The controller wonders what the astronaut is doing at this precise moment in time far out in space. He cannot know immediately; it takes time for the information to travel at the speed of light from the craft to the base. But eventually he receives the requisite signals. Knowing the distance of the craft from Houston at any time, and making allowance for the time taken for each of the signals to travel from the craft, he is able to work out which event must have occurred in the craft at noon, Houston time. These calculations reveal that the astronaut had just started to do a series of exercises on his bicycle machine. Thus, according to the controller, he now knows that the astronaut started his exercises at the instant the Houston clock had indicated noon. So much for the controller. The astronaut has likewise been thinking, longingly, of what might have been happening back at Houston. He receives signals from home, and carries out analogous calculations to those that were done by the controller. He concludes that at the instant he had begun his exercises, the clock at Houston had been reading 12:10. There is a disagreement. Whereas the controller concluded that the event marking the start of the astronaut's exercises was simultaneous with the Houston clock showing 12:00, the astronaut concludes that his starting the exercises was simultaneous with the Houston clock showing 12:10. The fact that they disagree is not altogether surprising. Their conclusions can be arrived at only after calculation, and as we have already seen they do not agree about the distances and times to be included in the calculations.

The loss of agreement over the simultaneity of spatially separated events has serious repercussions for those anxious to retain the idea that only events that occur "now" can truly be thought to exist (prior events no longer existing, and future ones not yet existing). In speaking of such contemporary events, one presumably needs to include events occurring "now" in locations other than where one happens to be oneself. But in the above example, there is no agreement as to which event in the control room at Houston existed at the same time as the astronaut commenced his exercises on the craft—the clock reading 12:00, or the clock reading 12:10. Indeed, there is no need to confine the possibilities to these two. Depending on one's speed relative to Houston, there can be any number of possibilities. There is no way to decide between them. Each observer is taking a different slice through four-dimensional space-time. Each alternative is equally valid. The way out of the problem is to concede that *all* events in Houston exist along with the event happening in the craft. The disagreement is not about which event *exists*, but about which of these events should carry the same coordinate as the one in the craft.

In this way, physicists have to come to terms with a future that is seemingly not as tenuous and uncertain as our practical experience of life would have us believe. If, in some mysterious sense of the word *exist*, it is valid to say that the future "exists" on a par with the present, this must surely go some way toward adding plausibility to the idea that God might have knowledge of it. His having knowledge of it then lends a distinctive quality to the notion of "purpose" as applied to God.

But, I hear you say, if the future already exists, what does that do for my free will? Under such circumstances can *I* be said to have a meaningful purpose in life? Do I have a choice as to whether I cooperate with God's purpose for me? Am I not reduced to the level of an automation? Also, if physics does not pick out any special instant of time to be called *now*, where does the concept of "now" come from? Where do we get the notion of an uncertain future? And if nothing is changing, what about the flow of time—where does that come in?

Here we touch on one of the truly great mysteries: the fact that we have two entirely different approaches to the concept of *time*. So far I have spoken about "time" exclusively in the way that concept is addressed in physics. Let us now see how this same word *time* is used in a different context—the description of what it is to be a conscious human being:

On examining the contents of the conscious mind we find mental experiences—feelings, decisions, sensory experiences, etc. These occur in sequence. What separates one experience from the next? We call it "time." We are able to estimate and compare these separations or intervals of time. This might be done through noting the extent to which the memory of a past experience has faded—the greater the separation in time, the greater the degree of fading. Or possibly the estimate is based on the number of other experiences we have had subsequent to the one in question. The precise mechanism by which we subjectively assess the passage of time is not at all well understood. All we know is that, somehow, we are able to do it—semi-quantitatively at least.

Although we call this separation between mental experiences "time," it does not follow that this is the same "time" as is used in the description of the physical world. For one thing, mental states occur in time but not in space, and we know now how indissoluble is the link between space and time in the physical domain.

For each experience there are other experiences on either side of it in the sequence, with one exception—the experience that marks the end of the sequence. This end point of the sequence occurs at the point in time we designate "now." It is only in consciousness that the "now" instant acquires its special status.

Only through the recognition that we use the word *time* in two distinct ways can it make sense to say that all of time, including the future, exists now. What this means is that all of *physical* time exists at the instant of *mental* time called "now" (and indeed, at every other instant of mental time).

It is perhaps unfortunate that the same word *time* is used in two such dissimilar contexts. The reason it is, of course, has to do with the fact that, despite the distinctiveness of physical time and mental time, there is a close correspondence between them. A sensory experience that is part of the mental sequence (e.g., the hearing of a shot now) is correlated to a feature of space-time (the firing of a gun at a particular point in space-time). The "now" of mental time is correlated to a particular instant of physical time. Although, as I have said, *all* of physical time exists now, consciousness (not physics) singles out one particular instant as having special significance for the "now" of mental time.

A short while later (according to mental time, that is) the "now" correlates to a different physical time. The differences between the two physical times, judged on a clock, when compared with the perceived lapse of mental time, gives rise to a "flow" of time. Note that without there being two distinct types of time, there could be no flow. A flow is a change of something in a given time. The flow from a hosepipe, for example, is the volume of water emitted in a given time. The change in time in a given time means nothing—unless we are talking of two different times.

Perhaps an analogy might help: You are watching a news broadcast on television. There has been a railway crash. Rescuers are at work, survivors are being taken out from the wreckage, politicians declare to a reporter that there will be a full inquiry. You are caught up in the drama as it unfolds. But then the scene switches to the studio. The reporter you have just seen, now in the role of newscaster, points out that what you have been watching was something he had recorded earlier in the evening; the broadcast had not been a live one, as you had previously assumed. While you had been caught up in a story that was evolving in time, the whole story, unknown to yourself, already existed on videotape in the studio. While you could experience the story only a little at a time, the newscaster had access to all of it. For you it was uncertain how the story would develop. For the newscaster there was no uncertainty; he had access to the full contents of the videotape; he knew infallibly what followed after each incident shown. However, the fact that there was such a videotape, and the newscaster was in a privileged position regarding that tape, does not mean that the participants in the story were thereby reduced to the level of automatons. The video is a record of normal human beings saying and doing what they normally do—making decisions and exercising their free will—and you were involved in the broadcast in exactly the same way as you would have been had it been live.

Thus what I am saying is this: As conscious human beings we live out our lives as a sequence of conscious mental experiences. These are set in mental time with its dynamic "now" separating a past that cannot be changed from a future that is uncertain and dependent upon current decisions. We possess free will and are to be held responsible for our decisions. We are free to pursue our purposes and to decide whether or not to conform our will to that of God. In this context, God (in a role analogous to that of the reporter) is properly thought of as an active participant with us in life's evolving drama. This freedom is not in any way to be thought of as diminished by the knowledge that etched into the fabric of relativistic space-time there exists a "videotape" of the whole of our physical lives—including those parts that occur at physical times correlated with instants of mental time that lie in the future. Those parts may be accessible to God (in his other capacity as the transcendental divine newscaster); they are not accessible to us.

That then is the first lesson I want us to draw from modern physics. In my view, relativity theory contains within it a warning to those who pay inadequate attention to those aspects of traditional Christian belief to do with God's foreknowledge and his complete assurance that his purposes will be fulfilled.

A second way in which relativity theory enriches our appreciation of God's relation to the world comes from what it has to say about the early history of the universe. As is now well-known, the universe began with a Big Bang. It is to be noted that when one speaks of the expansion of the universe in this connection one is not referring to a movement of matter away from one particular point in space out into the rest of that space. The expansion is the expansion of space itself. It is rather as though we have a rubber sheet on which there are painted various dots to represent the matter—the galaxies. As the edges of the sheet are pulled, the dots separate, simulating the way the galaxies are receding from each other. Thus the Big Bang sees not only the creation of matter, but also the creation of space itself. And because we now know through relativity theory that space is locked into space-time, the Big Bang also marks the beginning of time; there is no time before the Big Bang.

This is not an altogether new idea. St. Augustine was of the view that the moment of creation might also mark the creation of time itself. Big Bang theory supports this conjecture. But this being the case, we must abandon the widespread belief that initially God was on his own and then at some point in time decided to create the universe. The moment of the Big Bang must not be thought of as being especially invested with God's creative power, everything else subsequently being a consequence of this unique act. The instant of the Big Bang happens to mark one particular end of the time axis—that and nothing more. God's creative power is *uniformly* distributed throughout the whole of the space-time framework. His traditional roles as Creator and Sustainer merge. His purpose is at work throughout time and space and is not to be thought of as confined to a once-off initial act.

The above is predicated on the idea that the Big Bang marks the beginning of time. I should perhaps mention that this might not be the case; there is another possibility. This emerges when one considers the future development of the universe, and what that might imply about its past. How the universe will continue to develop is as yet uncertain. Either it will continue to expand forever or, if there is sufficient matter in the universe, the gravitational attraction will be strong enough to bring the expansion to an eventual halt, and thereafter pull all the matter together again into a Big Crunch. What would happen then is open to speculation. It could be followed by a further expansion. If this were the case, the universe would be of an oscillating type. Under these circumstances, the Big Bang would *not* mark the moment of creation, rather it would be merely the most recent of the big bounces. That being so, time would exist prior to the Big Bang, contrary to what we earlier supposed. But then there is raised the question of when the series of oscillations began. Possibly there was no beginning to them, there being an infinite number of them. This would be a second way in which the idea of God getting the universe going at one point in time would be inappropriate, and again one would have to go over to a view of God such that his creative purpose is invested equally everywhere and at all times.

Thus we see that relativity and the cosmology based upon it open up new possibilities for us to explore as to how God relates to Creation. But all this is predicated on the idea that the world does indeed owe its existence to a Creator God. There are, however, aspects of modern physics, and speculations arising from it, that appear to cast doubt on the need for a Creator God at all. The universe might have spontaneously created itself.

Rumors are currently circulating that physicists are on the verge of a theory capable of explaining everything about the universe, including how it came into existence. There are two components to the argument. The first concerns the problem of how the universe could create itself out of nothing, using no preexisting ingredients. This is not as difficult as it might seem. True, when we look around we see lots of matter, and matter is something rather than nothing. But according to relativity theory, matter is a locked-up form of energy, and energy can be either positive or negative. Two objects bound together by a gravitational force need to be supplied with energy to pull them apart; we say that in the bound state they have negative gravitational energy. How much negative energy is there in the universe? A plausible case can be made for saying that there is as much negative energy in the universe as positive energy locked up in the matter. In other words, the total energy/matter in the universe is zero.

What is true of energy is true also of some other physical properties. Take electric charge. There is clearly a lot of electrical charge in the universe. The nucleus of every atom has positive charge; the electrons outside the nucleus have negative charge. But note again: positive and negative. What is the net amount of electric charge in the universe? Again the answer is zero. In this way we begin to see how it is perfectly possible to have a universe that is made of nothing—albeit an ingenious rearrangement of nothing!

The second hurdle to be negotiated if the universe is to make itself is how to bring about this arrangement. The universe began with the Big Bang. But why? How did it come about? One suggestion invokes the quantum theory. According to this theory, events do not have to have deterministic causes. From any given state of affairs one can predict only the relative probabilities of various possible outcomes. The Big Bang might have been a quantum fluctuation of some kind. As such it requires no explanation. One simply says that there was a finite chance of this happening—and it did so happen.

It is a fascinating speculation. No wonder many physicists are excited by it. But does this mean that one can now dispense with the God hypothesis, as some are moved to claim? Does one now replace the idea of God creating the world—presumably for a purpose—and put it all down to a mindless, random, quantum fluctuation? No. It is one thing to say that everything derives from a quantum event, but that still leaves unanswered the question of why the process was governed by the laws of quantum mechanics rather than some other conceivable set of physical laws. How did the laws themselves arise? Is this where one needs a God to make a decision?

A possible counter to this argument for God is expressed in the hope that one day physicists will have a theory of everything. As science continues its relentless progress, the point will be reached where they will be able fully to account for everything that happens or could happen in the world. Moreover, so it is claimed, when that goal is achieved, one will recognize that the laws so uncovered will have a quality about them that will make plain that they constitute the only conceivable, self-consistent set of laws. The universe is the way it is because it could not have been otherwise. In other words, not only do we not require a God to bring about the Big Bang (quantum mechanics does it for you), but quantum mechanics governs the process because there could be no other kind of mechanics. The theory, therefore, makes a purposeful God entirely redundant.

This goal I believe to be illusory. The reason is that the language of physics is mathematics; we are engaged in developing a mathematical model of the world. We can, therefore, learn something of the general nature of the laws of physics, together with the conditions they must satisfy, by studying the general properties of mathematics:

Each mathematical structure is built on a set of axioms. The rest of the structure consists of theorems that can be derived from those axioms. From within the structure one can verify how the theorems logically and inevitably follow from the axioms. However, one *cannot* justify the original choice of axioms. Such a justification would have to be supplied from outside the system. Not only that, but in 1931, the mathematician Kurt Gödel demonstrated that it was impossible to prove from within the methods open to many important areas of mathematics (including elementary arithmetic) that the axioms are consistent—meaning that conclusions drawn from them could never lead to contradictions. Even if it were possible to prove consistency for a particular mathematical system, that same system would not be complete. In other words, from within the system it was impossible to prove the truth of all the true statements contained in that system.

This inherent, unavoidable lack of completeness must reflect itself in whatever mathematical system models the working of our universe. As creatures belonging to that physical world, we shall be included as part of that model. It follows that we shall never be able to justify the choice of axioms in the model—and consequently the physical laws to which those axioms correspond. Nor shall we be able to account for all the true statements that can be made about the universe. For these reasons the goal of a complete theory of everything is unattainable, and the claim to have disproved the need of a purposeful creating and sustaining God is false.

3

Paul Davies

The Unreasonable Effectiveness of Science

Science and the Demystification of Nature

Human beings have always been struck by the complex harmony and intricate organization of the physical world. The movement of the heavenly bodies across the sky, the rhythms of the seasons, the pattern of a snowflake, the myriads of living creatures so well adapted to their environment—all these things seem too well arranged to be a mindless accident. It was only natural that our ancestors attributed the elaborate order of the universe to the purposeful workings of a deity.

The rise of science served to extend the range of nature's marvels, so that today we have discovered order in the deepest recesses of the atom and among the grandest collection of galaxies. But science has also provided its own reasons for this order. No longer do we need explicit theological explanations for snowflakes, or even for living organisms. The laws of nature are such that matter and energy can organize *themselves* into complex forms and systems. It now seems plausible that, given the laws of physics, the existence and nature of all physical systems can be accounted for in terms of ordinary physical processes.

Some people have concluded from this that science has robbed the universe of mystery and purpose, that the elaborate arrangement of the physical world is merely the meaningless outworking of mechanistic laws and random juxtapositions of clodlike particles. It is a sentiment well captured by the words of two eminent Nobel laureates. The biologist Jacques Monod writes: "The ancient covenant is in pieces: man at last knows that he is alone in the unfeeling immensity of the universe, out of which he has emerged only by chance. Neither his destiny nor his duty have been written down."[1] The physicist Steven Weinberg echoes this dismal sentiment: "The more the universe seems comprehensible, the more it also seems pointless."[2]

However, not all scientists find it so easy to accept the "miracle of nature" as a brute fact. It is all very well proclaiming that the laws of physics plus the cosmic initial conditions explain the universe, but this begs the question of where those laws and conditions came from in the first place. Science may be powerfully successful in explaining the universe, but how do we explain science? Why does science—based on the notion of eternal laws of physics—work, and work so well? As our understanding of the basic processes of nature advances, so it becomes increasingly clear that what we call scientific laws are not just any old laws, but are remarkably special in a number of intriguing ways.[3]

Cosmic Unity

Consider first the general orderliness of the universe. There are limitless ways in which the cosmos might have been totally chaotic. It might have had no laws at all, or laws that caused matter to behave in disorderly or unstable ways. One could also imagine a universe in which conditions changed from moment to moment in a complicated or random fashion, or even in which everything abruptly ceased to exist. There seems to be no logical obstacle to the idea of such unruly universes. But the real universe is not like this. It is highly ordered, and this order persists in a dependable manner. There exist well-defined physical laws and definite cause-effect relationships that we can rely upon.

The physical world is not arbitrarily regulated; it is ordered in a very particular way, poised between the twin extremes of simple regimented orderliness and random complexity: it is neither a crystal nor a random gas. The universe is undeniably complex, but its complexity is of an *organized* variety. Moreover, this organization was not built into the universe at its origin. It has emerged from primeval chaos in a sequence of self-organizing processes that have progressively enriched and complexified the evolving universe in a more or less unidirectional matter.[4] It is easy to imagine a world that, while ordered, nevertheless does not possess the right sort of forces or conditions for the emergence of complex organization. Some scientists have been so struck by the uncanny efficiency of self-organizing processes in nature that they have suggested the existence of a type of optimization principle,[5] whereby the universe evolves to create maximum richness and diversity. The fact that this rich and complex variety emerges from the featureless inferno of the Big Bang, and does so as a consequence of laws of stunning simplicity and generality, indicates some sort of matching of means to ends that has a distinct teleological flavor to it.

The very fact that we can even talk meaningful about "the universe" as an all-embracing concept already indicates an underlying unity and coherence in nature. The physical world consists of a multiplicity of objects and systems, but they are structured in such a way that, taken together, they form a unified and consistent whole. For example, the various forces of nature are not just a haphazard conjuction of disparate influences. They dovetail together in a mutually supportive way that bestows upon nature a stability and harmony. Although this subtle coherence is hard to capture in a precise way, it is obvious to most practicing scientists. I like to compare doing science with completing a crossword puzzle. In conducting experiments, scientists enter into a dialogue with nature, from which they obtain clues to the underlying regularities. When these clues are "solved"—usually in the form of mathematical laws—it is like filling in a missing word. What we find is that the "words" gleaned from different branches of science form a coherent, interlocking matrix, and not just a "laundry list" of separate principles juxtaposed.

To elaborate this point, it is particularly striking, for example, how processes that occur on a microscopic scale—say in nuclear physics—seem to be fine-tuned to produce interesting and varied effects on a much larger scale, for example in astrophysics. Consider the death of stars in supernova explosions. Part of the explosive force is due to the action of the elusive subatomic particle called the neutrino. Neutrinos are almost entirely devoid of physical properties: the average cosmic neutrino could penetrate many light years of solid lead. Yet these ghostly entities can still, under the extreme conditions near the center of a dying massive star, pack enough punch to blast much of the stellar material into space. The resulting detritus is richly laced with heavy elements of the sort from which planet Earth is made. We can thus attribute the existence of terrestrial-like planets, with their special propensity to spawn complex material forms and systems, to the qualities of a subatomic particle so feeble in its effects that it might well have gone forever undetected.

In addition to this coherent interweaving of the various aspects of nature, there is the question of nature's curious uniformity. Laws of physics discovered in the laboratory apply equally well to the atoms of a distant galaxy. The electrons that make the image on your television screen have exactly the same mass, charge, and magnetic moment as those on the moon, or at the edge of the observable universe. Furthermore, these properties do not change detectably from one moment to the next.

Nature's Ingenuity

The subtle harmony of nature is perhaps manifested most forcefully in the field of subatomic particle physics. Here mathematical physics achieves its greatest successes. But a full understanding of the microworld of subnuclear processes requires the deployment of several branches of advanced mathematics in a delicate way. Progress is often hard. One finds that a straightforward application of mathematics gets you so far, and then you get stuck. Some internal inconsistency appears, or else the theory yields wildly unacceptable results. Then someone discovers a clever mathematical trick, perhaps an obscure loophole in a theorem or an elegant reformulation of the original problem in new mathematical guise, and, hey presto, everything falls into place! It is impossible to resist the urge to proclaim nature at least as clever as the scientist for "spotting" the trick and exploiting it. One often hears theoretical physicists, speaking in the highly informal and colloquial way that they do, promoting their particular theory with the quip that it is so clever/subtle/elegant it is hard to imagine nature not taking advantage of it!

Sometimes it is the other way about, and the scientists are puzzled by what seems to be some arbitrariness or profligacy on nature's behalf. Physicists are often to be heard asking, "Why would nature bother with this?" or "What is the point of that?" Though uttered in a lighthearted spirit, there is a serious content too. Experience has shown that nature does share our sense of economy, efficiency, beauty, and mathematical subtlety, and this approach to research can often pay dividends. Most physicists believe that beneath the complexities of their subject lies an elegant and powerful unity, and that progress can be made by spotting the mathematical "tricks" that nature has exploited to generate an interestingly diverse and complex universe from this underlying simplicity.

There is a feeling among physicists that everything that exists in nature must have a "place" or a role as a part of some wider scheme; that each facet of physical reality should link in with the others in a "natural" and logical way. "Who ordered that?" exclaimed an astonished Isadore Rabi when the muon was discovered. The muon is a particle more or less identical to the electron in all respects except mass, which is 206.8 times greater. This big brother to the electron is unstable, and rapidly decays, so it is not a permanent feature of matter. Nevertheless it seems to be an elementary particle in its own right and not a composite of other particles. Rabi's reaction is typical. What is the muon for? Why does nature need another sort of electron, especially one that disappears so promptly. How would the world be different if the muon did not exist?

The hope and expectation is that the existence of the muon, and other "gratuitous" particles, can be explained as part of some all-embracing unification of particle physics, probably involving a branch of mathematics known as group theory, which can be used to connect together apparently distinct particles into unified families according to certain abstract mathematical symmetries. The groups have definite rules about how they can be represented and combined together, and how many of each type of particle they describe. Hopefully a group theoretical description will emerge that commends itself on other grounds, but which will also automatically incorporate the correct number of particles. Nature's apparent profligacy will then be seen as a necessary consequence of some deeper unifying symmetry. If so, nature will once again be shown to share our sense of economy, with "a place for everything and everything in its place." Current research trends strongly indicate this will be so.

The Anthropic Principle

The strange harmony of nature becomes even more intriguing when we take into account the existence of living organisms. The fact that biological systems have very special requirements, and that these requirements are met by nature, has attracted much comment by scientists. In 1913 the Harvard biochemist Lawrence Henderson, impressed by the way that life on Earth seemed to depend crucially on some rather peculiar properties of water and other chemicals, wrote: "The properties of matter and the course of cosmic evolution are now seen to be intimately related to the structure of the living being and to its activities; . . . the biologist may now rightly regard the Universe in its very essence as biocentric." [6]

In the 1960s the astronomer Fred Hoyle was struck by the fact that the element carbon, so crucial to terrestrial life, exists in abundance in the universe only by courtesy of a lucky fluke. Carbon nuclei are made by a rather delicate process involving the simultaneous encounter of three helium nuclei inside the cores of large stars. Because of the rarity of triple nuclear encounters, the reaction can proceed at a significant rate only at certain well-defined energies (called resonances), where the reaction rate is greatly amplified by quantum effects. By good fortune one of these resonances is positioned just about right to correspond to the sort of energies that helium nuclei have inside large stars. Hoyle was so impressed by this "monstrous accident," he was prompted to comment that it was as if "the laws of nuclear physics have been deliberately designed with regard to the consequences they produce inside the stars." [7] Later he was to expound the view that the universe looks like a "put-up job" as though somebody had been "monkeying" with the laws of physics. [8]

These cases are just samples. Quite a list of "lucky accidents" and "coincidences" has been compiled since, most notably by the astrophysicists Brandon Carter, Bernard Carr, and Martin Ress. [9] Taken together they provide impressive evidence that life as we know it depends very sensitively on the form of the laws of physics, and on some seemingly fortuitous accidents in the actual values that nature has chosen for various particle masses, force strengths, and so on. If we could play God, and select values for these natural quantities at whim by twiddling a set of knobs, we would find that almost all knob settings would render the universe uninhabitable. Some knobs would have to be fine-tuned to enormous precision if life is to flourish in the universe.

It is of course a truism that we can only observe a universe that is consistent with our own existence. This linkage between human observership and the laws and conditions of the universe is known as the anthropic principle. In the trivial form just stated, the anthropic principle does not assert that our existence *compels* the laws of physics to have the form they do, nor need one conclude that the laws have been deliberately designed with *Homo sapiens* in mind. On the other hand, the fact that even slight changes to the way things are might render the universe unobservable is surely a fact of deep significance.

Accident or Intelligent Design?

The early Greek philosophers recognized that the order and harmony of the cosmos demanded explanation, but the idea that these felicitous properties derive from a creator working to a preconceived plan was well formulated only in the Christian era. In the twelfth century, Aquinas offered the view that natural bodies act as if guided toward a definite goal or end "so as to obtain the best result." This fitting of means to ends implies, argued Aquinas, an intention. But seeing as natural bodies lack consciousness, they cannot supply that intention themselves. "Therefore some intelligent being exists by whom all natural things are directed to their end; and this being we call God." [10]

Aquinas's argument collapsed in the seventeenth century with the development of Newton's mechanics. Newton's laws explain the motion of material bodies quite satisfactorily in terms of inertia and proximate forces without the need for an overall plan, divine supervision, or any form of teleology. Nevertheless, this shift of worldview did not entirely eliminate the idea that the world must have been designed for a purpose. One could still puzzle, as did Newton himself, over the way in which material bodies have been arranged in the universe. For many scientists it was too much to suppose that the subtle and harmonious organization of nature is the result of mere chance. Thus Robert Boyle wrote:

> The excellent contrivance of that great system of the world, and especially the curious fabric of the bodies of the animals and the uses of their sensories and other parts, have been made the great motives that in all ages and nations induced philosophers to acknowledge a Deity as the author of these admirable structures.[11]

It was Boyle who drew the famous comparison between the universe and a clockwork mechanism, which was most eloquently elaborated by William Paley in the eighteenth century. Suppose, argued Paley, that you were "crossing a heath" and came upon a watch lying on the ground. On inspecting the watch you observe the intricate organization of its parts and how they are arranged together in a cooperative way to achieve a collective end. Even if you had never seen a watch and had no idea of its function, you would still be led to conclude from this inspection that this was a contrivance designed for a purpose. Paley then went on to argue that, when we consider the much more elaborate contrivances of nature, we should reach the same conclusion even more forcefully.

The weakness of this argument is that it proceeds by analogy. The mechanistic universe is analogous to the watch; the watch had a designer, so therefore the universe must have had a designer. One might as well say that the universe is like an organism, so therefore it must have grown from a fetus in a cosmic womb! Clearly no analogical argument can amount to a proof. The best it can do is to offer support for a hypothesis. The degree of support will depend on how persuasive you find the analogy to be. There is clearly a point at which nature would look so contrived that even the most ardent skeptic would believe it had been designed for a purpose. Our present understanding of nature does not provide compulsive proof of design. It is conceivable, however, that more compelling evidence exists in nature, but is hidden in some way from us. Perhaps we will only become aware of the "architect's trademark" when we achieve a certain level of scientific attainment. This possibility forms the theme of the novel *Contact* by the astronomer Carl Sagan,[12] in which a message is subtly embedded in the digits of pi—

a number that is incorporated into the very structure of the universe—and accessible only by the use of sophisticated computer analysis.

Although analogical arguments are merely suggestive, they are frequently accepted. Consider, for example, the existence of a physical world. One's immediate experiences always refer to a mental world of sensory impressions, which has the status of a map or model of the really-existing world "out there." Yet a map or a model is also just an analogy. An even greater leap of faith is required when we conclude that there exist other minds besides our own. Our experience of other human beings derives entirely from interactions with their bodies: we cannot perceive their minds directly. Certainly other people behave *as if* they share our own mental experiences, but we can never know that. The conclusion that other minds exist is based on analogy with our own behavior and experiences.

It is in the biological realm that one encounters the most arresting examples of "the contrivances of nature," where the adaptation of means to ends is legendary. It is hard to imagine, for example, that the eye is not meant to provide the faculty of sight, or that the wings of a bird are not intended for flight. To Paley and many others such intricate and successful adaptation indicated providential arrangement by an intelligent designer. Alas, Darwin's theory of evolution eliminated this argument by demonstrating that complex organization efficiently adapted to the environment could arise as a result of random mutations and natural selection. No designer is needed to produce an eye or a wing. Such organs appear as a result of perfectly ordinary natural processes.[13]

Given the blow that Darwin dealt to the design argument, it is curious that it has made a reappearance. In its new form the argument is directed not to the material objects of the universe as such, but to the underlying laws, where it is immune from Darwinian attack. The essence of Darwinian evolution is variation and selection. This depends on nature's being able to select from a collection of similar, competing, individuals. When it comes to the laws of physics and the initial cosmological conditions, however, there is no obvious ensemble of competitors. The laws and initial conditions are apparently unique to our universe. If it is the case that the existence of life requires the laws of physics and the initial conditions to be fine-tuned to high precision, and that fine-tuning does in fact obtain, then the suggestion of design seems compelling.

But just how fine does the tuning have to be to convince a skeptic? One can always shrug aside any number of "coincidences" with the comment that they are a lucky but meaningless quirk of fate. Again, it is a question of personal judgment. The problem is that there is no natural way to quantify the intrinsic improbability of the known "coincidences." What is needed is a sort of metatheory—a theory of theories—that supplies a well-defined probability for each range of values of any parameter that is allegedly fine-tuned. No such metatheory is available, or has to my knowledge even been proposed. Until it is, the impression of "something fishy going on" must remain entirely subjective.

Other Worlds

Undoubtedly the most serious challenge to the design argument comes from the hypothesis of many universes, or multiple realities. The basic idea is that the universe we see is but one among a vast ensemble. When deployed as an attack on the design argument, the theory proposes that all possible physical conditions are represented somewhere among the ensemble, and that the reason why our own particular universe looks designed is because only in those universes that have that seemingly contrived form will life (and hence consciousness) be able to arise. Hence it is no surprise that we find ourselves in a universe so propitiously suited to biological requirements. It has been "anthropically selected."

The various universes must be considered to be in some sense "parallel" or coexisting realities. Though such a hypothesis may seem bizarre, it is supported, in one version or another, by many physicists as a natural interpretation of quantum mechanics. An alternative, and less outrageous proposal, is that what we have been calling "the universe" might be just a small patch of an infinite system extended in space. If we could look beyond the ten billion or so light-years accessible to our instruments, we might find regions of the universe that are very different from ours.

So can evidence for design equally well be taken as evidence for many universes? In some respects the answer is undoubtedly yes. For example, the spatial organization of the cosmos on a large scale is important for life. If the universe were highly irregular, it might produce black holes, or turbulent gas rather than well-ordered galaxies containing life-encouraging stars and planets. If matter was distributed at random, chaos would generally prevail. But here and there, purely by chance, an oasis of order would arise, permitting life to form. Although such oases would be almost unthinkably rare, it is no surprise that we find ourselves inhabiting one, for we could not live elsewhere. So the cosmic order need not be attributed to the providential arrangement of things, but rather to the inevitable selection effect connected with our own existence.

In spite of the apparent ease with which the many-universes theory can account for what would otherwise be considered remarkable features of the universe, the theory faces a number of serious objections. Not least of these is Ockham's razor: one must introduce a vast (indeed infinite) complexity to explain the regularities of just one universe. This "blunderbuss" approach to explaining the specialness of our universe is scientifically questionable. Another problem is that the theory can explain only those aspects of nature that are relevant to the existence of conscious life, otherwise there is no selection mechanism. Many of the best examples of design, such as the ingenuity and unity of particle physics, have little obvious connection with biology.

Another point that is often glossed over is the fact that in all of the many-universe theories that derive from real physics (as opposed to simply fantasizing about the existence of other worlds) the laws of physics are the same in all the worlds. The selection of universes on offer is restricted to those that are *physically* possible, as opposed to those that can be imagined. There will be many more universes that are logically possible, but contradict the laws of physics. So we cannot account for nature's *lawfulness* this way, unless one extends the many-universes idea to encompass all possible modes of behavior. Imagine a vast stack of alternative realities for which any notion of law, order, or regularity of any kind is absent. Physical processes are entirely random. However, just as a monkey tinkering with a typewriter will eventually type Shakespeare, so somewhere among that vast stack of realities will be worlds that are partially ordered, just by chance. Can anthropic reasoning be used to conclude that any given observer will perceive an ordered world, mind-boggling rare though such a world may be relative to its chaotic competitors? I think the answer is clearly no, because anthropic arguments work only for aspects of nature that are crucial to life. If there is utter lawlessness, then the overwhelming number of randomly selected inhabited worlds will be ordered only in ways that are essential to the preservation of life. There is no reason, for example, why the charge of the electron need remain absolutely fixed, or why different electrons should have exactly the same charge. Minor variations would not be life-threatening. But what else keeps the value fixed—and fixed to such astonishing precision—if it is not a law of physics? One could, perhaps, imagine an ensemble of universes with a selection of laws, so that each universe comes with a complete and fixed set of laws. We could then perhaps use anthropic reasoning to explain why at least some of the laws we observe are what they are. But this theory must still presuppose the concept of law, and begs the question of where those laws come from, and how they "attach" themselves to universes in an "eternal way."

The Cosmic Code

Another of Einstein's famous remarks is that the only incomprehensible thing about the universe is that it is comprehensible. The success of the scientific enterprise can often blind us to the astonishing fact that science works. Though it is usually taken for granted, it is both incredibly fortunate and deeply mysterious that we are able to fathom the workings of nature by use of the scientific method. The purpose of science is to uncover patterns and regularities in nature, but the raw data of observation rarely exhibit explicit regularities. Nature's order is hidden from us: the book of nature is written in a sort of code. To make progress in science we need to crack the cosmic code, to dig beneath the raw data, and uncover the hidden order. To return to the crossword analogy, the clues are highly cryptic, and require some considerable ingenuity to solve.

What is so remarkable is that human beings can actually perform this code-breaking operation. Why has the human mind the capacity to "unlock the secrets of nature" and make a reasonable success at completing nature's "cryptic crossword"? It is easy to imagine worlds in which the regularities of nature are transparent at a glance or impenetrably complicated or subtle, requiring far more brainpower than humans possess to decode them. In fact, the cosmic code seems almost attuned to human capabilities. This is all the more mysterious on account of the fact that human intellectual powers are presumably determined by biological evolution, and have absolutely no connection with doing science. Our brains have evolved to cope with survival "in the jungle," a far cry from describing the laws of electromagnetism or the structure of the atom. "Why should our cognitive processes have turned themselves to such an extravagant quest as the understanding of the entire Universe?" asks John Barrow. "Why should it be *us*? None of the sophisticated ideas involved appear to offer any selective advantage to be exploited during the pre-conscious period of our evolution. . . . How fortuitous that our minds (or at least the minds of some) should be poised to fathom the depths of Nature's secrets." [14]

The effectiveness of science seems especially odd given the limitations of human educational development. It usually requires at least fifteen years before a student achieves a sufficient grasp of science to make a contribution to fundamental research. Yet major advances in fundamental science are usually made by men and women in their twenties. The combination of educational progress and waning creativity hem in the scientist, providing a brief, but crucial "window of opportunity" to contribute. Yet these intellectual restrictions presumably have their roots in mundane aspects of evolutionary biology, connected with the human life span, the structure of the brain, and the social organization of our species. It is odd that the durations involved are such as to permit creative scientific endeavor. Again, one can imagine a world in which we all had plenty of time to learn the necessary facts and concepts to do fundamental science, or another world in which it would take so many years to learn all the necessary things that death would intervene, or one's creative years would pass, long before the educational phase was finished.

No feature of this uncanny "tuning" of the human mind to the workings of nature is more striking than mathematics. Mathematics is the product of the higher human intellect, yet it finds ready application to the most basic processes of nature, such as subatomic particle physics. The fact that "mathematics works" when applied to the physical world—and works so stunningly well—demands explanation, for it is not clear we have any absolute right to expect that the world should be well described by our mathematics.

Much has been written about the "unreasonable effectiveness" of mathematics in science (to use Eugene Wigner's famous phrase).[15] If mathematical ability has evolved by accident rather than in response to environmental pressures, then it is a truly astonishing coincidence that mathematics finds such ready application to the physical universe. If, on the other hand, mathematical ability does have some obscure survival value and has evolved by natural selection, we are still faced with the mystery of why the laws of nature are mathematical. After all, surviving "in the jungle" does not require knowledge of the *laws* of nature, only of their manifestations. We have seen how the laws themselves are in code, and not connected in a simple way at all to the actual physical phenomena subject to those laws. Survival depends on an appreciation of how the world is, not of any hidden underlying order. Certainly it cannot depend on the hidden order within atomic nuclei, or in blank holes, or in subatomic particles that are produced on Earth only inside particle accelerator machines.

It is sometimes argued that as the brain is a product of physical processes it should reflect the nature of those processes, including their mathematical character. But there is, in fact, no direct connection between the laws of physics and the structure of the brain. The thing that distinguishes the brain from a kilogram of ordinary matter is its complex organized form, in particular the elaborate interconnections between neurones. This wiring pattern cannot be explained by the laws of physics alone. It depends on many other factors, including a host of chance events that must have occurred during evolutionary history. Whatever laws may have helped shape the structure of the human brain (such as Mendel's laws of genetics) they bear no simple relationship to the laws of physics.

Conclusion

A careful study of the laws of physics suggests that they are not just "any old" set of laws, but special in a number of intriguing ways: in their coherence and harmony, their economy, their universality and dependability, their encouragement of diversity and complexity without total chaos, and so forth. Perhaps the oddest feature of all is the way that the laws are "decodable" by human beings, i.e., that science works so unreasonably well, especially in regard to its mathematical content. Also mysterious is the fact that these particular laws, which receive such succinct and elegant expression when cast in terms of human mathematics, nevertheless encourage the emergence from primeval featurelessness of a sufficiently rich and sufficiently organized complexity to permit the evolution of intelligent organisms in the universe, organisms that produce the very same mathematics as pertain to these laws. This self-reflective, self-consistent loop is all the more remarkable when account is taken of the fine-tuning of parameters needed for it to occur. Attempts to explain this "too good to be true" arrangement by invoking an infinity of random universes require metaphysical assumptions at least as questionable as those of design.

The success of human science and mathematics and the anthropic fine-tuning that is apparently a prerequisite for the very existence of humanlike beings, strongly suggests that our existence is linked into the laws of the universe at the most basic level. Far from being a trivial and incidental by-product of random and meaningless physical processes, it seems that conscious organisms are a fundamental feature of the cosmos. That is not to say that the species *Homo sapiens* as such is preordained, but the emergence somewhere, sometime in the universe of intelligent organisms capable of reflecting on the significance of the cosmos is, I believe, written into the laws of nature. Clearly, the universe could have been otherwise. The fact that it is as it is, and that its form is linked so intimately with our own existence, is powerful evidence that the universe exists for a purpose, and that in our small yet significant way, we are part of that purpose.

4

Walter R. Hearn

Evidence of Purpose in the Universe

"I am writing this chapter on purpose."

Is the writer referring to *intent* or *content*? Though not immediately clear from that sentence, the context suggests content, since this book asks about "evidence of purpose in the universe." Further, to modify the verb *writing* with the phrase *on purpose* would sound redundant. Everyone knows from experience that writing is done intentionally, generally for the purpose of communicating. I wrote that opening sentence as a reminder that human beings are well acquainted with purpose.

Can one write aimlessly? Sometimes people "doodle" in notebooks or on paper napkins, not to communicate but to pass the time or trigger the imagination. Even if we cannot say why we are doing it, scribbling "for no reason" represents one course of action among alternative possibilities. At a dismal lecture, for example, one could choose to do something else, like yawning noisily or leaving the room—which probably *would* communicate.

Human beings are not always making choices, or always conscious of making choices, or always conscious. A dull speech (or a dull chapter) can put us to sleep *despite* our intentions. Part of our humanity consists in a capacity to sense the difference between acting purposefully and being in a semiconscious or unconscious state. The idea to which I am trying to awaken you now is that as human persons we experience the phenomenon of personal *agency*, of "consciousness of conscious action." My direct knowledge of that phenomenon is a vivid fact to me, the single piece of data most "real" in my encounter with the rest of the universe.

I find myself living as a purposeful actor in a universe I did not create. To me that constitutes "evidence of purpose in the universe." Planet earth, at least, is full of people, and hence (if other people are like me) is full of purpose. Billions of people living today, or known from the past through their writings, have extrapolated from that evidence to the concept that purpose lied "behind" our existence as purposeful creatures.

If the experience and the extrapolation are so widespread, why does that not settle the issue?

Science As Challenger of Religious Concepts

The problem with that purposive concept of the world—one might say the only problem with it—is that in essence it is a religious view. Some people today are convinced that a religious view of the world is inherently false, untrustworthy, or at least inferior to a scientific view. Others believe that for a religious view to have credence, it must sound like or be attuned to the most up-to-date scientific description of the world.

Science, as a recognized way of knowing, dates back only about three hundred years. Many early scientists believed that purpose lay behind the world because they were devout believers in the God of the Bible. Astronomer Johannes Kepler (1571-1630), for example, thought the universe had been created and was upheld by a divine Creator; in exploring the physical world he was unfolding "the admirable wisdom of God."

Modern scientists are often assumed to ignore or look down on a theistic view of the world. Yet in this volume scientists appreciative of a religious view discuss such topics as cosmology, the anthropic principle, quantum mechanics, chaos theory, and the ordered complexity of genetic information. Clearly, from many areas of science, evidence can be cited to indicate that, in its intricacy and intelligibility, the universe resembles a chapter or a whole book rather than an aimless doodle.

Actually, the world as we know it through science is more like a complete encyclopedia (with yearbooks coming out annually) or a vast library. Today it is hardly bizarre to conclude that what scientists explore seems "written" in a way that can be understood.

Scientific analysis of a physical "text" or "data base" can of course be carried on without assuming that the data contain a message. A scientist's conviction that the universe is more than a meaningless scribble is likely to be held on essentially religious grounds. Scientists are seldom strangers to belief. They believe that an experiment will work, say, or at least that something to be learned from today's experiment will help make sense of tomorrow's. Scientists hope, often believe, sometimes pray, that their grants will be renewed. Scientists tend to trust their colleagues. In practice, doing science is not so different from exercising personal religious faith. Part of the process is working from data at hand to draw inferences leading beyond those data.

No single "scientific method" is followed to the letter by all scientists. The actual practice of science is almost as denominational or "sectarian" as religion, but certain generalities apply. Some familiar generalities, however, are misstatements, such as the idea that science deals only with *objective knowledge*, religion only with *subjective belief.*

Scientist-philosopher Michael Polanyi (1891-1976) showed rather convincingly that all knowledge, including scientific knowledge, is *personal.* Thus even science has a tacit subjective component. A scientist makes subjective choices, first in choosing some branch of science as a career, then every day of that career in choosing problems to work on, the methods to solve them, how to interpret the results, and so on. Before any of us takes up science (or religion), we are first human persons, decision-making *agents* whose acts are inherently purposeful.

It is necessary to add quickly that in studying physical things as objects, scientists seek to be as objective as possible. Philosopher-theologian Martin Buber (1878-1965) called the relationship of scientists to whatever they study an "I-it" relationship. The personal relationship more characteristic of religious experience he called an "I-Thou" relationship. In science the "I" lays down logical rules by which the game is played, but the basis of religious experience can be characterized as primarily "fiducial" rather than logical.

As transcendent Creator, a divine "Thou" is in a position to lay down the rules. For a theist, however, the personal attributes of the *Thou* in a religious encounter make the relationship more reciprocal. At least that is the way I see it, without presuming to speak for all theists (who believe in a "living God" as "author" of the universe) or even for all Christians. I picture religious experience as a relationship between persons based on mutual trust.

Put simply, scientific knowledge is obtained by keeping ourselves out of the picture as much as possible, religious knowledge from putting ourselves into the picture as much as possible. Note that I said *knowledge* in both instances. Scientific knowledge is gained at a sacrifice of a big part of our human repertoire: while treating things external to ourselves as objects to be known, we must ourselves remain unknown.

We acquire religious knowledge at a different price, becoming vulnerable to being known as we really are. *Knowing* in this religious sense is much like loving. Knowing a loved one depends on giving up the rule-making prerogative for a mutual "giving in" to each other. Both ways of knowing require the exercise of a certain amount of trust (i.e., *faith*). In pursuit of scientific knowledge, we trust that out logic will apply to new situations and that we can eliminate or compensate for our personal biases. In seeking religious knowledge, we trust that the "rules of engagement" will be consistent and that the One to whom we give ourselves will prove trustworthy.

The power of scientific methodology lies chiefly in its relatively objective (i.e., publicly intersubjective) verification process. When scientists succeed in controlling extraneous variables, making careful measurements, and providing accurate descriptions of their experiments, the same results can be obtained by other experimenters who follow the same rules—if the rules continue to apply. Scientists generally have so much faith in the consistency of the natural world that when an experiment goes haywire they do not even consider the possibility that the rules might have changed. Even nontheists and atheists are confident that the universe operates in a logically consistent way.

Nothing in religious knowledge corresponds to the (relative) objectivity of scientific verification. That is why a religious position is so easily caricatured as being "mere belief" rather than "real knowledge." The philosophical basis of science is generally considered to be empiricism, which emphasizes experience (from observation and experiment) as the only legitimate source of knowledge. A religious approach to knowledge can be empirical even though it differs from a scientific approach in certain respects.

Although its dominant personal element keeps it from being tested by others in the same way that scientific hypotheses are tested, religious conviction is testable for internal consistency and for coherence with what one can know from other avenues of experience, including science. A mature religious faith is one that has been tested in many circumstances.

Scientists' willingness to remain personally aloof in formulating and testing their hypotheses has yielded statements of great generality—but only about certain matters and with some definite limitations. Most scientific statements, for example, are framed as statistical probabilities, sacrificing certainty for generality. Even scientific "laws" stated in the precise language of mathematics have boundary conditions outside of which they do not apply. The scientific approach is poorly adapted to the study of truly unprecedented events or genuinely unique objects. Given a "one-of-a-kind" object, scientists may analyze it (i.e., take it apart) for recognizable components, observe it over time to see if it does anything familiar, or simply shelve it until something similar comes along to make a comparative study possible. Scientific generalities are derived by induction from specific examples, but one needs more than a single point to plot a curve.

The difficulty of making statements applicable to the universe as a whole is suggested in the parody of a typical examination question in science courses: "Define universe and give three examples." The universe is full of things to study scientifically, their great diversity accounting for the fragmentation of science into many disciplines and subdisciplines. But to say something about "all there is" stretches science to its limit and beyond. (Is this the *only* universe? The only *possible* universe? Has it *always* existed, in some form or another? etc.)

Equally challenging at another extreme is the problem of making scientific statements about an individual human being. There are plenty of human beings to study comparatively, but each of us is like a unique "universe." Confronted with a one-of-a-kind phenomenon, as vast and remote as the whole universe or as proximate and intimate to the scientist as a human person, the scientific approach begins to show its limitations. Some limitations are methodological; others represent a clash with social values. In a humane democratic society, scientists cannot experiment on fellow beings, even those who are near death, without their informed consent. Society values scientific knowledge, but not at any price. Scientists who arrogantly push against such restrictions are caricatured in the "mad scientists" of science fiction and horror movies.

The above comparison of science and religion as two valid ways of knowing will seem quite elementary to anyone familiar with both. I regard these two ways of knowing as very similar in some respects but quite different in others. We are, I believe, much richer for having available to us more than one way of knowing.

Purposelessness: Evidence or Inference

My own experience of leading a purposeful life, amplified by my religious experience as a Christian, forms a basis for my understanding of what lies behind my existence. In my view, I exist because the Creator of the universe wants me to—and the whole universe exists for a similar reason. What evidence could compel me to deny that divine purpose lies behind the universe?

"You should withhold belief until you have objective proof."

Religious faith is sometimes caricatured as "believing in something despite the evidence," but as I have described it, exercising religious faith is more like exploring an inference that goes beyond the evidence at hand. A scientist with confidence in a hypothesis (a proposed solution to a problem) will commit laboratory resources to testing it by trying to disprove it and alternative hypotheses. Most scientists constantly do "thought experiments," costing nothing but their time, to eliminate faulty ideas without having to go to the greater time and expense of physical experimentation.

Apprentice scientists are taught to exercise skepticism toward untested hypotheses. The public nature of scientific validation makes open skepticism an appropriate stance. If a scientist is not sufficiently skeptical about a favored idea, other scientists who hold rival opinions certainly will be. Scientists learn to examine their own ideas critically before publishing them, because significant ideas will almost certainly be examined critically after publication. The scientific publication process has skepticism built into it; a journal editor will send a paper to several referees for critical evaluation before accepting it. "The literature" (i.e., the content of refereed journals) is considered trustworthy because scientists trust the refereeing process to weed out what is trivial, false, or incompletely disclosed. What gets published has already been challenged, but the act of publication invites further challenge.

The personal element that renders religious convictions inaccessible to public verification also imbues them with a kind of intensity. Religious convictions are what people bet their lives on, not just another experiment or a professional career.

The competition of ideas in science is like a game in which the best ideas eventually win. Scientists, who expect some of their own ideas to be proved wrong as part of the game, generally delight in discovering flaws in someone else's ideas. That is how one "advances" toward the goal. Discovery of deliberate fraud will bring a scientific career to a tragic end, but most careers can survive a few mistaken ideas if the scientist has some good ideas as well. One benefit of "scientific objectivity" is freedom to complete vigorously in the arena of ideas without feeling that one is struggling against other human beings. Science can be fun partly because it need not be a deadly game to play.

Individuals with religious convictions also expect to encounter skepticism in the open marketplace of competitive ideas. "Believers" learn by experience to examine their convictions critically because, as in science, to make them public is to invite skeptical response. Mature believers tend to treat the religious ideas of others with respect, not because all ideas are equally valid but because such ideas are at the core of people's lives.

A faith that a person lives by is less likely to be changed by logical arguments than by an alternative faith lived out in another person's life. That is the way the game of religious commitment is played. Though living out one's faith may be joyful, it is ultimately a more serious game than commitment to a scientific career. Skeptics of religious ideas, therefore, should be willing to demonstrate the cohesiveness and comprehensiveness of their alternative conviction.

A challenge to my belief in the existence of a personal, purposeful Author of the universe is subject to such a challenge by anyone who believes otherwise. But what kind of challenge by anyone who believes otherwise. But what kind of challenge could be offered in the name of *science?*

"Scientific progress has rendered such questions irrelevant."

The undeniable success of a scientific approach undeniably lies in its narrowness, the keenness of its cutting edge. Historically, empirical investigation became a new way of looking at the world when scientists freed themselves from preoccupation with final causes (teleology), leaving the scholarly debate of ultimate questions to philosophers and theologians. Scientists focus on proximate questions, such as *how* things work, instead of *why* things exist. Plenty of effort is required to work out a chain of cause-and-effect in the physical world without exploring what either end of that chain is anchored to. The self-limitation of science to examining only secondary or mechanical causes should signal immediately that science has no capacity to deal with the existence—or nonexistence—of a purpose "behind the universe."

In its practice as well as its philosophy, science works by a process of elimination. Science is not so much a way of getting at truth as it is of getting rid of error. Scientific work is frequently compared to detective work, as one suspect after another is found to have an alibi or is eliminated on the basis of physical evidence or for other reasons. The inductive method homes in on the best available solution to a problem by eliminating less-satisfying solutions, though it never reaches absolute certainty because all of the potentially significant evidence is not available. An important clue might turn up years later.

Nevertheless, hypotheses (proposed solutions) that continue to stand up through experiments designed to test their validity are considered "true enough" until proven otherwise. Scientists, generally uncomfortable with words like *true* and *proven*, are more likely to say that certain hypotheses "are strongly supported by the evidence."

Philosophical positions unwarranted by science, but claiming scientific warrant, are properly called "scientisms." In my opinion, to say anything at all about ultimate purpose requires stepping outside the normal boundaries of science, even though individuals who deny divine purpose may claim that their argument rests on "what science tells us." The irrelevance of certain questions *within* science does tell us something, however, about the limited relevance *of* science to some of the deepest human concerns.

"You can't extrapolate from human purpose to overall purpose."

Let us assume, for argument, that scientific methodology *did* provide the only "real knowledge." How much is actually known about the universe *as a whole?* Obviously, a lot is known about the workings of various components and systems within the universe.

Suppose that a relatively exhaustive description of the workings of some isolated system as a continuous cause-and-effect sequence *could* be taken as evidence of "absence of purpose" from that system. To extrapolate from "purposeless" systems to an absence of purpose behind the whole universe would require a leap of faith of the same dimensions as my extrapolation from the purposefulness I detect in "my own system." In other words, disbelievers in overall purpose are in a philosophical position equivalent to that of believers in overall purpose: they must reach beyond the data at hand.

From scientific considerations alone, we do not know, and cannot know, if ours is the only universe—or the only possible universe. ("Define universe and give three examples.") Nor can a scientist know *me* as a purposeful being—unless I choose to let him or her know me "in person."

"Your sense of individual human purpose is only an illusion."

Mention of personhood brings up another kind of challenge to the position I have taken. Perhaps I am deceiving myself about being a purposeful agent. If I am self-deluded about having "free will" to make choices, any extrapolation to a will behind the world is based on a false premise. Perhaps I am not really an "I" at all, just a complex "it." Perhaps my personhood is an illusion, an epiphenomenon of a highly complex nervous system.

Direct research on neural systems and indirect research on artificial intelligence in brain-simulating computers have not yet taken the "mind/brain" problem away from philosophers. In the classical position taken by materialistic monists, mind and brain are identical; interactionist dualists regard mind and brain as separate but interacting entities. An intermediate "comprehensive realism" that makes sense to me was set forth by Donald M. MacKay (1922-1987) in his 1975 Henry Drummond lectures (published as *Brains, Machines, and Persons*, Eerdmans, 1980).

Mackay, then chair of the Department of Communication and Neuroscience at the University of Keele in England, argued for a "logical indeterminacy" principle (not to be confused with Heisenberg's principle of physical indeterminacy), according to which an external observer's account of human agency can neither correspond to nor contravene the "inside" or "I" story known to that individual. That is, no matter how complete a description of my brain function a scientist may be able to give in the future, it cannot invalidate the reality of my free will as a human person.

"You are a product of millennia of mindless evolutionary steps."

But what of the challenge to my human significance from an evolutionary explanation of human origins? In many people's minds, the most direct attack on the concept of divine purpose has come from Charles Darwin (1809-82) and his followers. Darwin saw the living world of nature as unfolding (evolving as a result of the action of natural forces, with no direction or purpose from outside nature. Up to the mid-nineteenth century, all of nature was believed to have come into existence by divine fiat only a few thousand years before, with essentially nothing having changed since. Although an overly literal reading of Genesis had been questioned by various theological scholars, for centuries a static view of nature made scientific as well as religious sense.

By Darwin's time, canals dug across Britain through Cambria (Wales), Devon, and other regions had revealed fossil remains of ancient animals characteristic of sedimentary strata that now bear the names of those regions. Soon a whole geologic column could be constructed showing a progression of forms that had once lived on the earth. It became obvious that the earth had a much longer history than previously thought, and that many changes had occurred on its surface.

Darwin's own observations of "natural history," including those he made in little-known parts of the New World on a voyage of HMS *Beagle*, convinced him of the dynamic character of the living world. He proposed a natural mechanism for "the preservation of favored races in the struggle for life" (subtitle of his most famous book, *The Origin of Species*, 1859), which, operating in a changed environment, could be expected eventually to produce new species. Noting the many varieties of pigeons that had been produced by pigeon breeders who selected for desired traits, Darwin saw nature itself as a "breeder of pigeons" and of all other living things. "Natural" selection of naturally occurring variations could have produced all forms of life, Darwin reasoned, starting from an undifferentiated but potentially variable stock.

Subsequent development of population genetics and eventually of molecular genetics put Darwin's proposal of a mechanism for adaptation and speciation on a broader scientific basis. Failure to complete the fossil record with intermediate forms connecting major taxa has left the overall *macro-*

evolutionary ("microbe-to-man") proposal in the realm of inference despite a recent flood of structural data on DNA, RNA, and proteins on which to base "molecular clocks." Proponents of punctuated equilibria have argued that the fossil evidence is complete enough to challenge evolutionary gradualism, and that mass extinctions may have kept Darwinian principles from dominating the history of life.

Development of all life from a single life-form remains a plausible inference, and *micro*evolution at the species level seems to be well supported by scientific evidence. The challenge to the idea of purpose in the name of evolution comes not from scientific evidence but from a philosophical scientism properly termed *evolutionism*. A typical assertion is that of paleontologist George Gaylord Simpson (1902-84) in *The Meaning of Evolution*, (1949, p. 344): "Man is the result of a purposeless and materialistic process that did not have him in mind. He was not planned."

When freed from association with a static, unchanging world, however, the concept of divine creation is not negated by discovery of evolutionary mechanisms. Indeed, Darwin showed that evolutionary processes could be *creative*. His model for natural selection was "artificial" selection, exemplified in the deliberate human activity of creating new breeds of pigeons. It seems ironic that an explanation modeled on a purposeful human activity should come to be regarded as a challenge to purpose. Clearly, human beings have not created all of nature; the question is whether nature, by itself, has created everything about humanity. That question remains beyond the reach of a self-limited science.

"Blind chance is at the bottom of everything in nature."

Darwin's proposal of mechanisms for change in life-forms presupposed the existence of an initial life-form, but the problem of life's origin has stubbornly refused to yield to chemical investigations. After the initial production of amino acids in what was then accepted (in the early 1950s) as a model of the earth's primitive atmosphere, as a biochemist I expected much progress to be made toward an understanding of prebiological or "chemical" evolution. Over more than three decades, however, hundreds of investigations have produced competing hypotheses without leading to a clear understanding.

There is a certain irony in experiments set up to show that life was produced in small steps in an appropriate chemical environment by random molecular motions. In all such experiments, "pure" chance is "contaminated" by the purposeful intent of the researchers, who go to great lengths to control the variables in their experimental setups. If the "world" inside the flask serves as a model of the random processes of nature, what does the investigator "beyond" the apparatus represent?

The purposeful character of the scientific study *of* nature, illustrated clearly in such origin-of-life experiments, should be kept in mind when pondering the question of purpose *in* nature. Human beings are a part of nature but as even George Gaylord Simpson noted following his statement quoted above, it is "a gross misrepresentation" to say that human beings are *just* accidents or *nothing but* animals. A human being "happens to represent the highest form of organization of matter and energy that has ever appeared." (*Just* happens?) Our uniquely human status has led to a "new form of evolution," according to Simpson, requiring constant choice between different courses of action: "Man plans and has purposes. Plan, purpose, goal, all absent in evolution to this point, enter with the coming of man and are inherent in the new evolution, which is confined to him" (*The Meaning of Evolution*, pp. 344-45).

Simpson credited evolutionary science with "discovery" that life (apart from human beings and before our appearance) lacked any purpose of plan. For him that alleged discovery undermined all intuitive ethics or ethics based on divine revelation. In such a scientism, the existence of God is a sort of wishful thought by which most human beings have tried to comfort themselves in a world of merely human purposes. Such thinking may be as old as *Homo sapiens*, but that would make it a very late arrival, within the last million or so years of a 15-18-billion-year-old universe and a 4.5-billion-year-old earth.

One response to such a scientism is to recognize science itself as a sort of wishful thinking by which many human beings have tried to gain control over nature and thus to comfort themselves in a world they did not create. The quaint thought that purpose could be excluded by purposeful thinking has existed for only several hundred years of human life on earth, an idea so late in arrival as to occupy only the blink of an eye in the universe's long history.

What Darwin emphasized and what other scientists have established is that statistically random processes do play a role in creation (i.e., in the appearance of novelty). Anyone who has consciously engaged in some creative activity, such as writing a poem, can see that the act of creation can be analyzed as consisting of two distinct phases. A poet, for example, scans more or less randomly (in the equivalent of a scientist's "thought experiment") the possibilities for the next word or line, then selects the one that best fits the poet's creative purpose. To discover that creation is not associated with a consciousness *within* nonhuman nature says nothing about a consciousness *beyond* nature. Scientists and poets may not always be conscious of each step in their work, but they leave behind scientific publications and poems—evidence that creation has occurred.

Putting Science in Its Rightful Place

As science is presently defined, questions of overall purpose have no part in it. Some scientists with religious sensitivities are concerned that too much is being left out of science and want to put teleology back into "its rightful place" within science. I think it is better to leave science as it is but put *science* back into its rightful place, alongside other human endeavors of equal or greater importance.

Science is an extremely valuable way of answering certain types of questions, but we have no reason to assume that those are the most important questions. To overemphasize impersonal scientific knowledge could impoverish our views of human personhood and human society. As a way of knowing certain aspects of reality, science provides a gigantic and steadily growing "data base" from which many interesting and useful generalities have been derived. As the basis for modern technology, it offers those who can afford "high-tech" medicine, weaponry, etc., tremendous power to do good or evil—yet science eschews absolute moral categories just as it eschews teleology. The scientific enterprise has its own values and goals, but they come from the broader human perspectives of scientists, not from scientific methodology itself.

To put it plainly, my conviction that the universe is a purposeful creation is denied by an atheistic scientism, not by science itself. Indeed, scientific knowledge expands and expounds my understanding of how the Creator's purposes are worked out in the world I observe. Religious believers should not fear science—in its rightful place—but offer it wholehearted support. Much of what it leaves out, we have to offer.

I began this chapter with an illustration about purposeful communication. I will end it with another one, an experience I had at the Center for Theology and the Natural Sciences in Berkeley, California. Several years ago I participated in a CTNS seminar based on the work of a distinguished scholar, one of the contributors to this book. After reading one of his books, participants were to come together to discuss it with the author. As I made notes, I began to see what we were doing before the seminar as a kind of analogy for the scientific investigation of nature. We were free to analyze the object before us in any way we chose. We could explore patterns of relationships in its words and phrases, testing our hypotheses to see if they held up from one page or chapter to another. We could count word frequencies, establish hierarchies of significance of ideas by various criteria, propose scenarios of how early drafts had been changed by the editing process, and so on.

Yet none of the participants did such mechanical things. Instead we tried to follow the author's thoughts, inviting his response to our interpretations of what he had written. In that opportunity for personal interchange with an author, two points became clear to me. First, I saw that to concentrate on purely mechanical processes or on measurable properties would have kept me from asking truly important questions. Second, I saw that by a strictly "scientific" study I could have discovered facts that would have surprised even the author himself. To the author the message embodied in his work was what counted, not the mechanical processes of writing, editing, and publishing it. Even though he made use of them, those matters were not "on his mind." Indeed, by focusing exclusively on such processes, I could never have interacted with the mind of the author "in person."

As a scientist, I knew that the lifeless materials in the paper and ink obeyed well-established laws of physics and chemistry. Yet I intuitively grasped that the work as a whole was a purposeful creation. Why? Probably because of my own experience. I knew that material objects could be arranged to communicate, on purpose.

5

Robert John Russell

Cosmology: Evidence for God or Partner for Theology?

Science can purify religion from error and superstition; religion can purify science from idolatry and false absolutes. Each can draw the other into
a wider world, a world in which both can flourish. . . . We need each other
to be what we must be, what we are called to be.[1]

—John Paul II

I. Introduction

A. Purpose of Paper

The purpose of this paper is to explore a new and fruitful method to relate
a Christian theology of creation to contemporary cosmology. Its aim is a
creative interaction between two fields. It is based on the use of a common
methodology (drawn from the philosophy of science and introduced into
theological methodology) and it consists in a search for a philosophical bridge
between the fields by which the claims of both fields can creatively interact.
Through this interaction, it is hoped that each field can learn from the other

and undergo appropriate modification, one in which theology reformulates its central convictions in light of contemporary science and science brings to light and critically assesses its inherent philosophical and theological presuppositions.

This method is in sharp contrast to the two prevailing methods found in much of the literature on science and religion.[2] It is not an argument for God, for design or for purpose, based on science. Nor is it a strategy to so insulate theology from science that no exchange is possible (the "two worlds" approach). Rather it is an attempt to put in place a new method by which creative interaction can take place—for the benefit of both sides—but in which each field retains its own appropriate foundations.

B. Organization of Paper

In part II of this paper I summarize contemporary cosmology and the doctrine of creation. In Part III, I give arguments against the "evidence" argument and against the "two worlds" approach. I then suggest how interaction might work in general in part IV. Parts V and VII give specific examples of interaction by exploring two cases in particular: the "t = 0" problem and the anthropic principle. Although in this paper I must restrict my focus primarily to theological modifications, research is in progress on the scientific side of the interactive process. [3]

I hope this approach will show why I need to differ respectfully from what will likely be the positions adopted by some contributors to this volume. Indeed I hereby invite them to consider whether consonance is not a more fruitful and long-term method for showing the lasting value of scientific discovery to Christian faith—one that avoids outright conflict or repetitive arguments long since outmoded. The challenge to us all is critically important: Christianity stands to benefit greatly from a new period of creative interaction with science, as I also believe will science, and both parties will lose if old answers are rehashed or communication is lost. It is to the long-range goal of mutual creative interaction that I address this paper.

II. Brief Outline of Cosmology and the Doctrine of Creation

A. Brief Outline of Contemporary Cosmology[4]

The origin of modern cosmology lies in the theories of special and general relativity proposed by Albert Einstein early in this century. In 1905 Einstein published his theory of special relativity. It was soon given a decisive geometric interpretation by H. Minkowski, in which space and time were united into the four-dimensional geometry, space time. In 1915, Einstein extended this work to include gravity, the only fundamental force in nature of significance at cosmological scales. In general relativity, gravity is interpreted in terms of the curvature of space-time.

Einstein's theory was soon applied to the problem of understanding the structure and history of the universe. By the mid 1920s, E. Hubble's observations of distant galaxies suggested that they were receding from our galaxy at velocities proportional to their distance. G. Lemaitre, working closely with Hubble's observational program at Mt. Wilson, provided a theoretical model for Hubble's data. According to this model—which we now call "the Big Bang"—the universe as a whole is expanding in time! The expansion of the universe is surely one of the most astonishing scientific discoveries of our century, and it raises profound questions about the origin and destiny of the universe.

Actually there are three standard versions of the Big Bang. In the "closed" model, the universe is like the surface of a three-dimensional sphere, with a finite size. After expanding to a maximum size (perhaps one hundred billion years from now), the closed universe recollapses upon itself. In the "open" model, the universe is like the curved surface of a three-dimensional saddle, with an infinite size. The open universe will expand forever. In the "flat" model, the universe is borderline between open and closed. Its surface is like a four-dimensional plane, infinite in size. Like the open model, it too will expand forever. Today astronomers are still undecided about whether the closed, open, or flat model best describes the universe we live in. However, current evidence seems to favor the flat model—an infinitely large universe that will expand forever.[5]

Still, the staggering feature of *all* these models is that our universe has only existed for a *finite* amount of time! About 15-20 billion years ago, the universe must have "arisen" out of a "singularity"—an event that cannot be fully described by general relativity. If we imagine approaching this event by moving backwards in cosmological time t, the temperature and density of the universe would soar as the universe shrinks in size. Ultimately, at "t = 0"—what one might call the "beginning of time"—the density and temperature would go to infinity and the radius would vanish, signaling the breakdown of the model we're using—and possibly of the laws of physics themselves.[6]

What then are we to make of this initial singularity? On the one hand, it might indicate that the universe really did arise somehow out of an event that cannot be fully described by science,[7] thereby raising profound philosophical and theological issues beyond the competence of science to settle. On the other hand, the problems encountered at t = 0 *might* have more to do with Einstein's theory of gravity than with nature herself. With this in mind, alternative theories have been studied that seek to avoid the t = 0 problem. A notable example was the "steady-state cosmology" of H. Bondi, T. Gold, and F. Hoyle (1948), in which the universe had *no* beginning.[8] This model, however, was eventually eliminated by its inability to account for several factors, most notably the universal microwave background radiation discovered by A. A. Penzias and R. W. Wilson in 1965.

There are additional problems besides that of t = 0 that continue to plague the standard Big Bang model: (i) Why does there appear to be more matter than antimatter in the universe? (ii) What produced the clumping of matter into galaxies if the universe is symmetric in shape? (iii) How could separate portions of the very early universe have come to the same temperature and density at a time before they had interacted (the so-called horizon problem)? (iv) Finally, why does the universe seem to be flat, i.e, of all possible values for its curvature, why is it, apparently, precisely balanced between open and closed?

Underlying these problems is the need for a theory of "quantum gravity." Since the very early universe was subatomic in size, the correct cosmological theory will have to be consistent with quantum mechanics, the standard theory for subatomic phenomena. "Inflationary models" of the early universe, as developed by Alan Guth and others, are attempts in this direction. They appear to solve several of the problems besetting standard Big Bang cosmology, although they do not get around the issue of t = 0. Recently, however, J. B. Hartle and S. Hawking have begun to explore a speculative proposal dealing with quantum gravity. In their approach the universe has a finite past but no beginning, i.e. no singularity at t = 0![9] Another alternative has been proposed by R. Penrose, in which the universe develops spontaneously out of a background quantum field. Highly speculative and extremely hard to test, these proposals suggest the difficulty scientists have in dealing with the very early universe and the continuing challenge to understand its origin.

In sum. According to the standard Big Bang model, the universe began some fifteen to twenty billion years ago in an event that, given the assumptions of *this* model, has not physical precedent. As we trace back in time to the moment "t = 0" the density of the universe grows infinite along with its temperature while its size shrinks to zero. Since we cannot extrapolate the equations of general relativity back before t = 0, this event might well signify a kind of "absolute beginning" of the universe within the assumptions of this model. Is this the "beginning" that the Bible (e.g., Gen. 1:1) appears to describe?

B. Brief Outline of the Doctrine of Creation[10]

Does physical cosmology bear on the Christian doctrine of creation? This doctrine actually includes two related strands: *creatio ex nihilo* (creation out of nothing) and *creatio continua* (continuing creation). Each of these deserve attention in relation to physical cosmology.

1. Creatio ex nihilo

At its most basic level, *creatio ex nihilo* stands for the radical *contingency* of all that is, the utter dependence of all beings on a transcendent God as the sole source of their existence. As developed traditionally, this belief was expressed through a variety of interlocking arguments about creation. Theologians affirmed that God creates freely and with a purpose in mind, namely, to share the divine being with free moral agents. Hence *creatio ex nihilo* stood over against Platonic views of creation, in which the demiurge shaped preexisting matter while gazing upon the eternal forms. According to Christian theology, God's creative action is free of such prior logical and formal constraints, and matter itself, along with time and space, originate out of God's mysterious action and not out of any prior substance. In this sense, "creation out of nothing" really means "not created out of anything prior."

Creatio ex nihilo also implies that God transcends the world. This means that the world is not God, contrary to monism and pantheism; that the world is not a part of God's being as held by emanationism; that the world is not a divine being opposed to God, as against dualism; and that the world is not purposeless, as implied by nihilism. Instead creaturely existence is both contingent (ultimately dependent on God for its existence) and purposeful. In traditional language creation and providence connote God's sustaining both the existence and the order of the world; together with God's special, miraculous acts in nature and history, they form the spectrum of divine agency.

We must also recognize that *creatio ex nihilo* has often been heard by Christians in another way.[11] Along with the deeper philosophical sense of ontological dependence (that without God there could be no creaturely existence *per se*), creation has also been taken to entail a sort of religious historical cosmology. Genesis 1:1 in particular was frequently regarded literally as referring to the creation of the world at a finite time in the past.

Actually, most theologians before the nineteenth century held both views. St. Thomas, for example, argued that philosophy could demonstrate the contingency of the world but not its age; only by revelation could Christians know that the age of the world is finite.[12] Many twentieth-century theologians, including Langdon Gilkey, Paul Tillich, and Karl Barth, draw not only a sharp distinction between the two claims but argued that the cosmological interpretation should be dropped to avoid conflicting with science and causing philosophical confusion. In my opinion, however, the question remains unsettled; indeed it is the very question to which we must turn.

2. *Creatio continua*

Christian theologians also want to lift up God's ongoing action in the world in terms of creation. As immanent to the world, God acts continuously to create and sustain the world now and in the future. This part of the creation tradition rejects a deism in which God's only creative act was at the beginning of a static, deterministic world. Reality is not seen as complete nor the future entirely predictable; rather the world is in a process of becoming, of coming into being, and the future is open to God. The world is filled with novelty, and human choice counts in shaping the future, for God acts through nature and history. Ultimately God's faithfulness will bring all of reality to a just fulfillment at the end of the age.

Together *creatio ex nihilo* and *creatio continua* form complementary models of interpreting the central theological insight that God the Creator is both transcendent to and immanent in all of creation.

III. Evidence, Irrelevance, or Partnership?

How best might we relate cosmology and theology? I will focus on a specific topic—the "t = 0" problem—to illustrate why I *disagree* with the two ways people usually relate them (as "evidence for God" and as fully compartmentalized "two worlds"). I will then propose a third alternative, partnership through consonance.

A. ARGUMENTS AGAINST "EVIDENCE"

On the one hand many urge that we take the "t = 0" problem in cosmology as closely related to a literal creation of the world as described for example by Genesis 1:1 or as drawn from philosophical theology. This sort of position has surfaced to a varying degree by groups otherwise differing widely: evangelical and conservative Christians, religiously open scientists and educators, various denominational leaders and church spokespersons, mainline theologians, and so on.[13]

I am not entirely in disagreement with this position, especially in its more careful and nuanced handling; the real issue deals with the meaning of "evidence." Thus the question before us is how to address the relation between theology, philosophy, and science in such a way that we may obtain useful answers that in turn lead to further scholarly research rather than answers that reinforce previously taken, frequently abandoned, and, unfortunately, polemically argued divisions in the church.

In the case at hand we must therefore recognize that the meaning of "t = 0" is highly contextualized by the assumptions and limitations of Big Bang theory, including the philosophical and physical assumptions found in both general relativity and astrophysics. Many of these will change both as we learn more about the physical evolutions of the universe and as we move beyond the theory of general relativity into quantum gravity. William Stoeger[14] has written lucidly on these assumptions, which include:

(1) The "cosmological principle," that we do not occupy a privileged position in the universe. (2) The continuum assumption, that the universe can be represented by a continuum model consisting of a manifold (a four-dimensional surface, "space-time") with a metric (a distance function that represents curvature). (3) The nomological assumption, that physical laws and natural constants have universal validity. (4) The choice of a specific theory of gravity, either general relativity or a competitor. (5) The fluid assumption, that at very large scales, clusters of galaxies are uniformly distributed in the universe.

Moreover any scientific study of the universe whatsoever raises additional philosophical questions. (6) Can one scientifically study "the universe" if by the universe we mean "all there is"?[15] How do scientists study the universe "from within," i.e., if the universe includes the community of inquiry (the scientists) as part of the object of study? (7) Are there limits *in principle* to verification in cosmology? Surely the universe can never be observed in its entirety.[16] (8) There are highly restrictive *practical* limits to verification as well. Even observational data collected over thousands of years would disclose only a tiny fraction of the entire history and scope of the universe.

A different set of questions arises when we rely on scientific models in constructing a contemporary philosophy of nature. (9) Given that theories eventually get replaced, which features of the current theories should we take seriously as telling us something about the universe, and which features will be abandoned by future theories? *In particular, will the "t = 0" feature of Big Bang models recur in their successor theories,* such as quantum gravity? We have already seen how in the Hawking-Hartle proposal the universe may have a finite past but no initial singularity. Of course this a speculative idea that may not become widely accepted but it still demonstrates that such a model is at least mathematically possible.

Ultimately these and other scientific and philosophical issues[17] revolve around the more general and fundamental question of contingency: why does the universe exist? They are far removed from the specific idea of a "beginning" at "t = 0."

Finally, I would be very cautious about making *science* the starting point (i.e., the foundations) for *theology*. When in the past this point was shifted from Scripture and confession to science *per se*, the results were devastating for the church. Michael J. Buckley, for example, argues convincingly that atheism in the modern world arose in part out of the physics and metaphysics of René Descartes and Isaac Newton. Paradoxically, in their attempt to use the new science of mechanics as a *foundation* for religion, Descartes and Newton actually contributed the seeds for the growth of religion's adversary in the eighteenth century.[18] One can also raise strong theological objections to making a faith out of science, as neoorthodoxy and existentialist theology has so strongly emphasized in this century.

Of course if one starts with a theological position and looks to science to inform, critique, and expand its meaning, well and good, and in this sense "t = 0" might count as "evidence" for God. But if the foundations are switched from the data of religion to the data of science then I would be concerned about the resulting conclusions and their relevance to Christian faith. To the extent that it starts with science per se, I would resist following a path from science that purportedly leads to God (Exod. 20:4-6).

In sum. In general I would resist a close identification of the scientific case for "t = 0" in Big Bang cosmology with the theological claim that God created the universe "in the beginning." In particular I would be very dubious of an attempt to move directly from "t = 0" in science to the existence of God the Creator. It is hard to see how "t = 0" can count in *this* sense as "evidence for God" or "evidence for design." But this does *not* mean that I adopt the standard alternative, the "two worlds" approach (see below). Indeed as I will propose later, results from cosmology *can* count as a form of theological evidence, but only with a much more complex and carefully delineated understanding of what evidence means and how it helps articulate and apply, but not prove, a theory. First however I must outline my arguments against compartmentalization.

B. ARGUMENTS AGAINST "TWO WORLD" (COMPARTMENTALIZATION INTO IRRELEVANCE)

Many authors have argued for the strict compartmentalization of science and theology in recent decades. They believe that both the methods and the claims of these fields are entirely separable, and that to relate them is to misunderstand and even distort them. Support for this position comes from several sources: from Protestant neoorthodoxy, typified in the writings of Karl Barth, Reinhold Niebuhr, and in their earlier writings, Emil Brunner and Langdon Gilkey;[19] from the existentialist theology of Ruldolf Bultmann and others influenced by Kierkegaard and Heidegger; and from theologians such as George Lindbeck, who draw upon arguments in linguistic analysis.

I would resist attempts such as these to compartmentalize the scientific, philosophical, and theological concerns about creation and cosmology for several reasons.[20]

1. A move to compartmentalize the fields would ignore the actual *history* of the relations between them. Throughout its history, theology has been infused by the prevailing scientific worldviews and philosophical outlooks. Any attempt to understand theology in its present form must take into account the subtle and complex ways it has internalized these influences. One could even argue that the attempt to insulate theology from scientific or philosophical input represents one mode of its being affected by these fields. Moreover, if the possibility of such influences is denied, what influences do get through go unnoticed.[21] It is therefore essential that the possibility be recognized, if theology is to be critically reformulated in light of science and philosophy.

What may be more surprising is that the interaction goes *both* ways. History also records that philosophical and theological presuppositions were frequently woven, at least implicitly, into *science*. These presuppositions can be detected in the ways scientists construct, extend and defend their theories as well as in the historical origins of modern science, as seen in the writings of Galileo, Kepler, Newton, Bacon, and many others.[22]

In essence, the notion that one should *keep* theology and science entirely separate presupposes that they *are separate until related*, and this is itself part of the *myth* of modernity that needs to be "demythologized" for the sake of *both* fields.

2. Recent movement in the *philosophy of science* bodes well for a renewed dialogue between theology and science. Paul Feyerabend, Thomas Kuhn, Gerald Holton, Imre Lakatos, Michael Polanyi, Stephen Toulmin and others have pointed to the metaphysical themes inherent in science, the cultural factors in the choice between competing theories, and the incommensurability of meaning between succeeding scientific paradigms. These arguments have been picked up by *philosophers of religion* such as Janet Soskice, Mary Hesse, and Nicholas Wolterstorff, who have argued that scientific and religious language are similar in their dependence on metaphor, that faith plays a role in all forms of knowing, that theologians as well as scientists often adopt a critical realist position about their theories (doctrines), and that cultural and religious factors often influence science and theology in similar ways.

3. The *theological climate* is also shifting in favor of a renewed dialogue with science.[23] A growing number of writers are finding new and creative ways to relate science and religion, including such diverse thinkers from both the sciences and theology as Ian Barbour, Ralph Burhoe, P. C. W. Davies, Willem B. Drees, Lindon Eaves, George Ellis, Philip Hefner, Christopher

Kaiser, Nancey Murphy, Wolfhart Pannenberg, Pope John Paul II, Arthur Peacocke, Ted Peters, John Polkinghorne, William Stoeger, Thomas Torrance, and Howard Van Till, to name just a few. Though their theological proposals differ widely, they tend to agree that theology must in some way come to terms with the cognitive content of the sciences as well as with the importance of scientific method for theology.

Philosophy of science and philosophy of religion provide, for many writers, the bridge between science and theology, opening up the possibility of discovering theological issues in the limit questions of science, of reformulating doctrine and even of integrating views from both fields.[24] Recently Nancey Murphy has given a particularly convincing argument that theologians should adopt the methodology of scientific research programs as proposed by Imre Lakatos. This move would open theology to empirical evidence and provide theologians with rational criteria for claiming epistemic progress and for choosing between competing theological theories.[25]

4. Finally, the *scientific climate* is changing today. We know that science too has been affected—both in its historical origins and in its substantive development over the past three centuries—by the prevailing intellectual culture, including the forces of theological and philosophical thought.

What is only now being more fully appreciated is that such an interplay is a fruitful and vital part of scientific research, and not just an unfortunate intrusion of personal or cultural bias. Earlier on in this century, the founders of quantum physics were guided by sharply delineated philosophical assumptions about nature ranging from realism to positivism, pragmatism, and idealism. Similarly in constructing special and general relativity, Albert Einstein was guided by philosophical commitments reflecting in part the thought of Ernst Mach and Spinoza.[26] More recently, philosophical issues as well as technical problems in Big Bang cosmology have led to the development of inflation theories and to current proposals in quantum gravity. Today what may be most surprising is that scientists who have no explicit commitments to religion are inviting dialogue with religion—even if in many cases it is to challenge established religion with new religious views generated explicitly within the context of science. One need only read the popular books by John Barrow, David Bohm, Freeman Dyson, Stephen Hawking, Roger Penrose, Carl Sagan, Frank Tipler, E. O. Wilson, and many others—including many of the contributors to this present volume!—to find scientists raising theological issues within the context of their research.

In sum. Given the changing climate in scientific, philosophical, and theological circles today, I believe the time has certainly come to rethink *theological* doctrine in light of current science.[27]

IV. New Approach: Partnership with Theology

Is evidence (meaning "proof" as found in the classical design arguments) or irrelevance our only choice? How ought we to relate creatively cosmology and theology? How should we rethink theological doctrine in light of current science and analyze scientific theories for inherent philosophical and theological elements?

I believe that theological and scientific theories ought to have consequences for one another, both in their explicit affirmations and in the implicit ways they integrate elements of each field into the other both historically and in contemporary research. For theology the process will involve a subtle form of confirmationism by which scientific results can help critique, reshape, and assess theological assertions, and give new meaning to theological claims about God and the world. For science the process will involve an inspection of how the working assumptions in science affect explicit scientific theories and their interpretation of data, and how changes in these assumptions might creatively advance science.

My position is related to but distinct from that of "consonance." Consonance is a theme that has received increasing attention since it was put forward by Ernan McMullin a decade ago.[28] It has been picked up by several theologians, including Ted Peters,[29] Ian Barbour,[30] and Willem B. Drees,[31] and I have used it in several papers.[32] However in developing this notion with an eye toward *interaction*, I turn to philosophy as a bridge for actively relating claims between both fields. In particular, I first identify a general philosophical theme common to both fields, and see how each field shapes its meaning by its particular context. Through this first step a certain degree of consonance may be reached, though never total univocacy. Indeed, every relationship will contain both supportive and contradictory subclaims that shape the kind of consonance—or dissonance—between the two explicit positions being compared in theology and science.[33] Thus dissonance, too, plays a positive role since it indicates the need for change in at least one of the fields.

Next I study how the consonnance and dissonance change as scientific research progresses or as the domain of application in theology is expanded. If the initial consonance achieved through the philosophical bridge increases, this tends to confirm the relationship between these particular areas in theology and science. If increasing dissonance sets in, however, then this is evidence against either the particular form of the theological argument or against the implicit philosophical or theological issues in the scientific topic. There may be legitimate ways of reformulating the theological claim or the scientific theory to obtain a new degree of consonance. Ultimately, however, either side must be open to major revision or even refutation if moves to save either side are clearly *ad hoc* in the technical sense.[34]

The value to theology of this interactive method is that it allows us to work with a *particular* scientific theory and a *particular* theological claim *without* the *core* meaning of the theological claim being tied too closely to science and hence being *overly* vulnerable to scientific change, yet *also without* so insulating theology *as a whole* from science that no substantive relation exists. In working this way, we can make contact with science—not with the intent of proving a theological claim but of looking for confirmation. In the process we can let science reshape and constrain the meaning of theological language, purify it of outmoded scientific forms of thought, give it new meaning in the empirical context, and also possibly force its abandonment. In this way, "science can purify religion from error and superstition" as Pope John Paul II has recently proposed.[35] In other papers I hope to show the value to science of engaging in serious dialogue with theology and philosophy.

We now return to the problem of "t = 0" to illustrate the method in terms of this particular issue.

V. The "t = 0" Problem

For the "t = 0" problem I will choose *contingency as finitude* for the philosophical bridge between a model of the core theory in theology, that God is the Creator *ex nihilo*, and cosmology.

A. Relation to Cosmology

Finitude as a general philosophical category of being can be related to the meaning of finitude in the various empirical sciences and mathematics as well as to the theological doctrine of *creatio ex nihilo*. For example, in physics, finitude includes temporal and spatial finitude, and temporal finitude in turn involves both future and past temporal finitude. Now we can begin to make contact with cosmology, where the notion of past temporal finitude can be given a particular meaning—the age of the universe—when interpreted in terms of the Big Bang model of the universe.

B. Relation to Theology

We also make contact with a theological understanding of finitude since this occurs, as we have seen, in the doctrine of creation in which it is held that all created being is *finite* and that only God is *infinite*. One model of this core theory in theology is that creaturely finitude occurs in terms of the finite age of the world.

In this way we can initially relate the theological doctrine of *creatio ex nihilo* via the *philosophical* bridge of finitude to *empirical* claims about the universe having a finite age, marked with the limit condition "$t = 0$" in standard Big Bang models. In this sense, the theological claim about divine creation as entailing the contingency of the world can be said to be *consonant* with the empirical evidence for the beginning of the universe in contemporary cosmology.

This may sound like a good start, but what about the role of dissonance I have previously stressed? Actually our present problem is a particularly important example of how a mode of *consonance* reached in one area of the interaction between theology and science, might lead to problems of *dissonance* in other areas![36] Dissonance (as well as new forms of consonance) can arise in two ways: 1) as we expand the theological context keeping focused where we are in science, or 2) as we keep the theological focus on creation theology but turn to other cosmological models. We will study each of these ways next.

1. Expanded Theological Context

Recall that in the Big Bang model not only does the universe have a finite past, a finding that is "consonant" with creation theology. The model also tells us that the universe, if opened, is *infinite in size* and it will last forever: its future is *temporally infinite*. Thus it is *infinite in space and in (future) time*.

For many theologians this would seem to challenge the doctrine of creation's *fundamental* assertion that the universe is *finite* (as "$t = 0$" underscores in past temporal terms at least) since an open universe is *infinite now* (and expanding)! Moreover, the scenario for the far future of infinite time and unending cold challenges the meaning of *Christian eschatology* and the *doctrine of God*. In the latter, a key philosophical distinction is made between God as the only absolute infinity and creation as finite. As for the former, most Christians see history as moving toward a fulfillment that will take *time* itself up into the divine eternity. But an open universe will continue to exist forever. This means that while physical cosmology is *consonant* with theology in terms of the temporal past, if the universe is open[37] then cosmology is *dissonant* in terms of the temporal future and the spatial size with at least some expressions of the doctrine of God and Christian eschatology.[38]

Given this analysis we should focus more attention on these other key theological areas and inquire what precisely the dissonance is telling us. In this way, the dissonance is helpful in challenging us to obtain more clarity in our theological claims in light of the way cosmology uses these complex terms. I believe that dissonance as well as consonance is generally to be expected and that both are of value;[39] something is to be learned by the ways in which the consonance of one's theory is challenged by dissonant evidence and reshaped accordingly.[40] Of course the dissonance might grow so severe that radical changes in one or the other side would be forced. This is the cost of real relationship.

2. Changes in Science

Next we might track how consonance bears up to changes in science. The first point of contact was just studied: the consonance between standard Big Bang cosmology and *creatio ex nihilo* in terms of the philosophical category of finitude (or, more generally, contingency) expressed in terms of "t = 0." But Big Bang cosmology is currently being modified by inflationary cosmology; beyond this lie speculations about quantum gravity and their cosmological implications. How will these affect the "t = 0" problem?

Inflationary scenarios have been designed to resolve several of the problems that occur in Big Bang models, such as the matter/antimatter ratio, the horizon problem, global flatness, and so on. However, they retain the initial singularity; they only modify the standard scenario for a very short period of time *following* "t = 0." In this scene the consonance with creation theology is maintained as we move from standard Big Bang to inflation cosmology. However the situation becomes much more complex when looking at quantum gravity, where the research so far is extremely tentative and speculative.

One much-discussed proposal is the Hawking/Hartle model of the "quantum creation of the universe." [41] In this account the universe arises via a quantum tunneling process over Feynmann paths in superspace. According to Hawking, this quantum model of the universe has a *finite* past but *no* past singularity at "t = 0;" the universe is temporally past finite but unbounded.

One can think of some very rough analogies for this idea. A piece of string one inch long is finite in length and bounded by its ends. A circle one inch in circumference is finite in length but it is unbounded: it has no ends. Slightly closer to Hawking's model would be a mathematical line segment defined as all points between x = 0 and x = 1 but excluding x = 0 and x - 1 (i.e., the line segment 0 < x < 1). This line segment is finite in length, but it has no boundary. The two boundary points at 0 and 1 have been removed. This leads to the following curious fact: since no point is an end point, every point on the line segment has points to either side of it. No matter how close one gets to x = 0, there are still points closer to x = 0. To be a bit more accurate to Hawking's model we have to understand that the time variable loses its ordinary meaning as we consider events further and further in the past. Time ceases to have meaning near what would have been called the very early universe, and no event is left to correspond to the Big Bang singularity.[42]

Of course Hawking's proposal is highly speculative and will undoubtedly be replaced by other proposals. However we are not tied theologically to its future track record. Instead we should be able to learn something of value precisely in how Hawking's ideas challenge some of the assumptions in our standard theories—and this is in fact why we can work with tentative research proposals in science and not just "proven" theories. What then is to be learned theologically?

To me it seems that what has changed in moving from the Big Bang and inflationary models to Hawking's model is the *empirical* meaning of the *philosophical* category of *finitude* understood as past temporal finitude. With Hawking/Hartle the universe *is temporally finite* (in the past) but it does *not* have an initial singularity. In my view this does not disprove "design" or leave God "nothing to do," as Hawking and others occasionally suggest.[43] Rather this model changes the *form* of consonance from *bounded temporal past finitude* to *unbounded temporal past finitude*. It means that as we theologize about *creatio ex nihilo*, we should *separate out* the element of past temporal finitude from the *additional* issue of the *boundedness* of the past, and recognize that one *need not* have a *bounded* finite past to have a finite past.[44]

What we must understand theologically is that *creaturely finitude*, a fundamental category of the *ex nihilo* tradition, *need not entail boundedness*. What we have learned from quantum cosmology is that *we can claim that creation is temporally finite without necessarily claiming that creation had a beginning*. Thus our theological claim can entail more than merely *ontological finitude* since it also includes *temporal finitude*; yet it need not go so far as to identify temporal finitude with a *cosmic beginning*, let alone look to such a cosmic beginning as the foundation for faith in God.

I believe this is a tremendously important point for a Christian doctrine of creation, a point won only by our willingness to interact with research science and let it challenge (even falsify) our earlier theological stance, that *creatio ex nihilo* necessarily meant either "t = 0" ("identity") or nothing empirical at all ("two worlds"). Instead we can learn to live with partial truth and we can seek to correct partial error.

Thus Hawking's move does *not* bring on an overwhelming dissonance with creation theology, leaving God "nothing to do." Rather it in fact *enhances* our theological clarity, for it rids us of two unnecessary assumptions: 1) that temporal finitude must entail a beginning, and 2) that philosophical finitude can have no empirical context without one. It thereby removes both the "two worlds" solution (to 2) and the occasional (and disastrous) implication (to 1) that God only acts "in the beginning"—a far remove from the God of Jewish and Christian faith.

VI. Anthropic Principle: The Human Shape of Contingency

As a second example of consonance, I will turn to the now-famous "anthropic principle."[45] The anthropic principle actually has several versions that in one way or another try to relate the overall features of the universe with the evolution of sentient life. My method will be to start with the philosophical theme of contingency—not specifically in terms of finitude but now returning to the more general notion of *dependent being*. I will try to show that the *core* theological meaning of creation as expressed philosophically through contingency as dependence can be articulated in terms of the global contingency of the universe as pointed to by the anthropic principle. This approach is closely related to the perennial problem in philosophical theology: Is the sheer existence of the universe something in need of explanation? Does the existence of the universe lead to knowledge of God as various forms of "natural theology" propose?[46] I will try to distinguish my answers about the central theological problem from theologically peripheral "design" arguments while yet avoiding the move to compartmentalize theology from science.

First one can consider the universe as a *whole* and ask two questions: why does the universe exist (why does it display what I call *global ontological contingency*) and why does the universe exist with its actual global characteristics (what I call *global existential contingency*).[47] For example, under global existential contingency one might ask what accounts for the precise values of the natural constants, such as the speed of light, Planck's constant, or the fine structure constant.[48]

Secondly, one can ask about the *local* contingency of the processes and structures of the universe. Why, for example, does matter continue in a state of uniform motion if unaffected by forces, i.e., what are the philosophical assumptions that underlie the concept of inertia?[49] Indeed, what accounts for the continued existence and persistence in being of matter?

Such questions point to both the *local and global contingency* of the universe, in which the ongoing processes in nature raise questions that are grounded in science yet that move beyond the limits of science into philosophical and theological modes of analysis.[50]

Finally one can ask why the laws of nature take their actual forms. Again, do they arise as a reflection of the processes of nature or do they have an ontological status in their own right such that they actually govern natural processes. These questions and others fall under what I call the *nomological contingency* of the universe.

Now what I take to be a very exciting development in the field of science and theology is that contemporary cosmology is beginning to provide a means for relating these disparate senses of contingency through what has now become the well-known "anthropic principle." Although this principle takes several forms (weak, strong, cosmological, etc.), it starts with the observation that the evolution of life in the universe is very closely connected with certain highly exact global properties of the universe as a whole.

Of course most scientists presuppose that, given the right planetary conditions, including a stable orbit around a single star, the necessary thermal gradients, chemical mix and geological features, life will arise through the natural processes of Darwinian evolution. With the vast number of galaxies in the universe, where galaxies typically contain hundreds of billions of stars, these "right" conditions seem overwhelmingly bound to appear many times over.

But are there *global cosmological* prerequisites that make the development of galaxies and the evolution of life possible? Apparently there are. To see this, let us imagine moving progressively further back in cosmic time. We find in turn that 1) a sufficient distribution of second generation stars, 2) the right cosmic abundances of hydrogen and helium, and finally 3) a universe with just the right initial conditions are all prerequisites for life to evolve eventually within the unfolding history of the universe. Now the argument takes on a different tone: why does the universe as a whole have just those *global* characteristics such that life will *eventually* evolve in it?

Many writers see *evidence of design* here. In my opinion, however, what this train of thought has *actually* done is to *reshape the central theological meaning of contingency* by relating local existential contingency (why does life evolve on earth?) to global existential contingency (why is the actual universe one that is compatible with the evolution of life somewhere?).[51] I think this is a much more promising approach than a return to a form of deism in which natural theology functions as a substitute for revelation—or even for apologetics. On the other hand one can chose to start from faith and then, through the eyes of faith, to notice the "design" of a "fine-tuned" universe—but then this is *not* a design *argument* as much as an expression of personal piety (albeit expressed somewhat rationalistically).

Still we need to acknowledge that "design" is a standard response to the anthropic principle at this point. Actually there are two standard responses. For most scientists, the solution is essentially to reduce the problem to a tautology: the actual universe is "actual" *only for us*. There are *many* actual universes ("many worlds"); naturally, we exist in the one that is globally consistent with the eventual evolution of life. On the other hand, many Christians and other writers favoring design will argue instead that the actual universe is the *only* actual universe. If this be granted, then the striking fact that the only actual universe is also consistent with the highly fine-tuned requirements for the possibility of evolution and life leads to a form of "design" argument. In this way some theists (read *deists?*) today *do* attempt to warrant the existence of God based on the global, seemingly "fine-tuned" character of the universe. Like the "t = 0 supports creation" issue, this would be an instance of trying to base a specific theological claim (that a divine designer exists) on a "fact" of science (the apparently fine-tuned features of the universe).

I would resist both options—design or many worlds—since both are *precariously* related to science, philosophy, and theology. From a *specific* perspective, an infinity of actual, but empirically unobservable universes may seem implausible, thus lending support to the design alternative, but future research could reverse the picture. If, for example, the other worlds needed to explain our being in this universe are other *universes*—meaning in principle unobservable domains of existence—their existence would be almost by definition outside the realm of science. Yet there are already some preliminary suggestions about understanding our universe as a limited domain of an overwhelmingly vast universe; if the natural constants and perhaps even the laws of nature vary between domains, then our evolution in a domain compatible with life seems natural. Alternatively, the "fine-tuning" could be accounted for by new scenarios that explain the values of the fundamental constants.[52]

On the other hand and aside from their scientific merits, neither option seems to me conclusive for *philosophical* reasons. As I have argued elsewhere[53] even if one grants the many worlds option against design one can still argue for design at a more abstract level, say at the level of the laws of physics, and above that at the level of the laws of logic, etc. And yet at each of these levels one can also detect a "many worlds" type of counterargument—that there might be many laws of physics or kinds of logic, etc.! Clearly these are speculative arguments and they may *never* be conclusive, only *increasingly abstract*. But the upshot is that it is far from self-evident that the debate between design and many worlds must come to a full stop at the "first level" of the ladder.[54]

Ultimately, however, a "design" argument raises several profound *theological* tangles. First it begs the question whether the "Designer" one gets is worth the effort: is the Designer (and how is the Designer) substantively related to the biblical God? This is, of course, a variant of the perennial theological issue regarding the relation between the God of the philosophers and the God of revelation.

More pointedly, I am *very dubious* about theologians turning to scientific data for their *primary* evidence, abandoning religious data and seeking in scientific data the primary basis out of which to construct religious claims. These paths led historically to deism and, eventually, to the rise of atheism as a modern phenomenon.[55]

Should we therefore simply rule out the anthropic principle as irrelevant to theology and withdraw into a "two worlds" position in which the apparent fine-tuning of the universe for life is neither scientifically nor theologically germane at all? In my opinion there might exist other options.

For one thing, the anthropic principle leads us to recognize that in a very intricate way we humans are really at home in the universe. The universe need not be seen as inimical to life, nor does life need to be seen as an anomaly in an overwhelmingly barren universe. Of course from an evolutionary perspective nature can be seen "red in tooth and claw," and life the product of trial and error rather than *preconceived* purpose. But thanks to cosmology, when we cast our nets wide enough, a gestalt switch can happen, leading us to view our existence as a piece with the *universe* itself. This can be a deeply rewarding insight, with clear religious connotations. Seeing the cosmos as "home" and viewing nature with "trust" are important steps to healing the rift between our theological convictions about a loving Creator God and a world caught up in a pointless biological and cultural history of competition and carnage.[56]

Another way to approach the question has an even bigger payoff, for it goes to the heart of the intellectual task at hand: how to structure and interpret a theology of creation in light of our empirical knowledge of the universe. Though there is not space here to develop the approach in detail, let us return to the simplest case of "many worlds" versus "design." Suppose we reject *both* solutions; instead we shall assume that there is only one universe, but we will not try to use it for a design argument. What is left of interest to us theologically?

The answer lies in the fascinating way in which the cosmological fine-tuning shapes our theological language about the meaning of contingency as dependence. In essence it restricts our language about God's freedom to make separate, independent choices about the global and local character of nature and by relating our global and local modes of contingency. Thus if we work within the simple Big Bang model we will be led to speak more carefully, informatively, and precisely about *divine freedom in light of cosmology*.[57]

To see this, we focus on one of the natural constants, Planck's constant h, and its relation to *both* local and global contingency.

1) h and Local Contingency

Planck's constant is linked intimately to the uncertainty principle in quantum physics, and in turn to biological evolution, since one cause of variation is genetic mutation induced by radioactive processes. At another level it is arguable that quantum indeterminacy is a necessary (though clearly not a sufficient) factor in conscious life, including free will and the perception of the passage of time. Thus Planck's constant is linked to the phenomenon of life and sentience; it is thus a part of the existential contingency of the processes of a universe filled with sentient life.

2) h and Global Contingency

Planck's constant also characterizes the universe as a whole. During the first fractions of a second after the Big Bang the universe was governed by a single fundamental interaction;[58] the very early universe, being microscopic, was a quantum phenomenon. In this way the value of Planck's constant, as an irreducible part of quantum physics, is related to *global existential contingency*.

Theologians *must* then recognize that global existential contingency and local existential contingency *are not independent modes* in which the universe can be said theologically to be contingent. It may be, as Wolfhart Pannenberg asserts, that "the universe as a whole and in all its parts is contingent."[59] But *these two different types of contingency are mutually constrained by the fact that Planck's constant plays a key role in both domains of contingency.* Thus in this particularly simple example we seem forced to conclude theologically that *the action through which God creates the universe entails a dialectic of freedom and constraint.* There is a contingent, free element in nature, represented here by the precise value of Planck's constant. Yet this value determines both the global and the microscopic features of nature in a mutually implicative, mutually constraining way through the laws of physics.

This means that our core theological language about God will be influenced and constrained by, although not reduced to, our empirical knowledge of the universe. Granted that God might well be said to choose the values of the fundamental constants, including Planck's constant.[60] *Within this choice, however, the die is cast: God cannot independently choose the shape of local and global contingency vis-a-vis its relation to quantum physics* (any more than God can create a square circle, as the medieval scholastics pointed out). *The local and global contingencies of the universe are mutually empirically determining in a striking way.* God's freedom in choosing *ex nihilo* the value of Planck's constant and the laws in which it occurs *both allows* for the open character of the universe through which God can continually act *and conditions* the kind of universe to be one that requires billions of years of evolutionary struggle, suffering, and slow emergence to produce life, mind, and spirit.[61] Thus even from this simple, preliminary example I believe we can see that *science both gives meaning to, and critically shapes the meaning of, theological reflection on core assertions of Christian faith*, without preempting its *legitimate* basis in the religious experience of biblical and contemporary witnesses.

VII. Concluding Remarks

The theological task now before us is to relate the astonishing scientific discoveries of this century about the origin, nature, and future of the universe to the shifting patterns of theological reflection on Christian faith in the Triune God. In particular, we must come to understand God as acting as creator and redeemer both of and through the processes of nature as well as those of history. Our goal will be to show how our theology can appropriately be shaped, tested, fertilized, and potentially confirmed by contemporary cosmology even as theology critically challenges the myths being drawn out of science by a secular world and the philosophical and theological assumptions implicit in theoretical science. In the process, a new criterion for theory choice in theology might be whether a specific theological proposal can take account of, as well as participate in the scientific process of accounting for, nature in its empirical context. In this regard, the true test of a humble theology will be its willingness to put to the test, even in the domain of empirical science, its most carefully held views. Its strategy for engaging in such a process, however, will not be *naive* falsificationism but a resilient ability to evaluate what is at the core of our faith and what is expendable. It will entail recognizing the value of both consonance and dissonance in light of the changing contexts of new scientific theories and varying theological problems. It will involve a long-term research program, structured most fruitfully I believe along a Lakatosian-type methodology, through which theologians work together with scientists and philosophers in critically shaping the interaction of their fields with the hope that both will benefit and that our core theological doctrines will be potentially confirmed in the empirical context.

Such a process has already begun in relating theology and cosmology. As Ernan McMullin has pointed out, theology and science may indeed be in consonance, but it is a consonance that is constantly changing.[62] This short essay has sought to highlight some of the shifts in consonance and to suggest a method for "tuning the instruments" of theology so that consonance may be increased—a process that demands a solid understanding of the complexities and shifting patterns of contemporary physical cosmology and a critical engagement with the philosophical issues that are thereby occasioned. It is a research process now begun, and one for which there is every reason to anticipate a long and fruitful future.

6

Arthur Peacocke

Science and God the Creator

I. Introduction

No one today needs reminding that theologians can be deeply divided both on how to go about their task and on what they can and have established as a result of their activities. They, and many others in our culture, assume that scientists exhibit the very opposite characteristics. Scientists certainly agree about their methodology, insofar as this is common to the different sciences (and there *are* strikingly distinct styles in the various sciences), and they seem to be capable of coming to agreement—across international and cultural barriers—about what can be regarded as reasonably established knowledge concerning the natural world. But as soon as one asks about the philosophical and theological significance of their (seemingly agreed) findings, the citadel of apparent monolithic assent collapses. We have rightly come to be as suspicious of authoritative pronouncements of the "Science says . . ." kind, when what it is supposed to say has these wider connotations, as we have of the "The Bible says . . ." and "The Church/Tradition says . . ." varieties.

Thus we find Paul Davies, a physicist raising what he calls the "Big Four" questions of existence (Why are the laws of nature what they are? Why does the universe consist of the things it does? How did those things arise?

How did the universe achieve its organization?) and affirming that physics is uniquely placed to answer them. He continues: "It may seem bizarre, but in my opinion science offers a surer path to God than religion. Right or wrong, the fact that science has actually advanced to the point where what were formerly religious questions can be seriously tackled, itself indicates the far-reaching consequences of the new physics." [1]

He concludes the book with a reaffirmation of his "deep conviction that only by understanding the world in its many aspects—reductionist the holist, mathematical and poetical, through forces, fields, and particles as well as through good and evil—that we will come to understand ourselves and the meaning behind this universe, our home." [2]

However this concluding sentence certainly contains nuances that could just be the swallows that herald the coming of a summer in which scientists turn to theologians. This, too, seems to be the implication of a much-quoted remark by the astronomer Robert Jastrow who wrote: "For the scientist who has lived by his faith in the power of reason, the story [of the exploration of the beginning of the universe] ends like a bad dream. He has scaled the mountains of ignorance; he is about to conquer the highest peak; as he pulls himself over the final rock, he is greeted by a band of theologians who have been sitting there for centuries." [3]

So we have one physicist, Paul Davies, producing, no doubt, irritation in the "band of theologians," yet displaying some small signs of grace; and another, Robert Jastrow, instilling in them a sense of complacency—with an admixture of unease that perhaps he thinks theologians are committed to believing in "creation" as an act of God *in* time, at 15,000 million BC?

These quotations illustrate only too well the need for digging more deeply into the epistemology and claimed ontology of both science and theology when one has in purview this no-man's-land of the doctrine of creation across which, so one interpretation of this uneasy history has it, their battalions have fought inconclusively for centuries. So let me as a start make an inevitably brief incursion into this territory.

II. Science and Theology Today

"Critical" realism is the philosophy of science that I shall espouse here. It has the virtue of being the implicit, though often not articulated, working philosophy of practicing scientists who have the aim of depicting reality but know only too well their fallibility in doing so. The arguments for critical realism as a valid and coherent philosophy of science have been widely rehearsed elsewhere. [4] The position may be summarized thus, in the words of J. Leplin, "What realists do share in common are the convictions that scientific change is, on balance, progressive and that science makes possible knowledge of the world beyond its accessible, empirical manifestations."[5] Science is aiming to depict reality. The basic claim made by such a critical scientific realism is that it is the long-term success of a scientific theory that warrants the belief that "something like the entities and structure postulated by the theory actually exists."[6] A formidable case for such a critical scientific realism has,[7] in my view, been mounted based on the histories of, for example, geology, cell biology, and chemistry, which during the last two centuries have progressively and continuously discovered hidden structures in the entities of the natural world that account causally for observed phenomena.

Critical realism recognizes that it is still only the *aim* of science to depict reality and that this allows gradations in acceptance of the "truth" of scientific theories. It is a *critical* realism about entities, structures, and processes that figure in scientific theories (the "terms" of the theories), rather than about theories, as such. Critical realism recognizes that it is the aim of science to depict reality as best it may—and since this can be only an aim, the critical realist has to accept that this purpose may well be achieved by scientists with but varying degrees of success. Such a critical realism might more correctly be regarded as a *program* for the natural sciences and its success should be regarded as open to assessment in any particular case. For science can often be confident of the existence of that to which its theories refer, but at the same time accepting that its language and models concerning these claimed realities are always revisable and subject to change. This reminds us of the use of models and metaphor in science. "A model in science is a systematic analogy postulated between a phenomenon whose laws are already known and the one under investigation."[8] The deeply and irrevocably metaphorical character of scientific language does not detract from the aim of such language to refer to realities and entails an acceptance of its revisability in seeking to explore a world only partially and imperfectly understood.

Theology also employs models that may be similarly classified.[9] I urge that a critical realism is also the most appropriate and adequate philosophy concerning religious language and theological propositions. Critical realism in theology would maintain that theological concepts and models should be regarded as partial and inadequate, but necessary and, indeed, the only ways of referring to the reality that is named as "God" and to God's relation with humanity. Metaphor obviously plays an even wider role in religious language than in scientific. We have to distinguish between referring to God and describing him—this is crucial to a critical-realist stance in theology.

The metaphors of theological models that explicate religious experience can refer to and can depict reality without at the same time being naively and unrevisably descriptive—and they share this character with scientific models of the natural world. We may reasonably hope to speak realistically of God through revisable metaphor and models.

How, in theology, that which, the One who, is encountered in any particular experience is to be identified with what the tradition has named as "God" *should*, on this view, be by attempting to infer to the best explanation by application of the criteria of reasonableness that are used generally to assess ideas and, in particular, in appraising scientific models and theories—namely, fit with the data, internal coherence, comprehensiveness, fruitfulness, and general cogency.[10]

From a critical-realist perspective both science and theology are engaging with realities that may be referred to and pointed at, but which are both beyond the range of any completely literal description. Within such a perspective, it is therefore entirely appropriate to ask how the respective claimed cognitive contents of science and theology might, or should be, related. The history of theology shows that its development is intimately related to the understanding of the natural, including the human, world that has prevailed at different periods. More pertinently it behooves a critical-realist theology to take seriously the critical-realist perspective of the sciences on the natural world, for on that theology's own presuppositions, God himself has given the world the kind of being and becoming it has and it must in some respects, to be ascertained, be revelatory of God's nature and purposes. So theology should seek to be at least *consonant* with scientific perspectives on the natural world.

III. God and the Created World

We come now to our main task, namely, to inquire into the extent to which these concepts, models, and images of God that have been winnowed and refined in the Judeo-Christian tradition and have been critically analyzed philosophically can be illuminated by those impressive, at times intellectually vertiginous, perspectives on the world that the natural sciences now give us.

It is useful to express our scientific knowledge of the world in terms both of its being—what is there—and of its becoming—what is going on. Hence it might also be helpful to examine how the scientific perspective on the world might provide evidence for our understanding of both the "being" of God and of God's "becoming"—though fully recognizing, of course, that this distinction must be artificial, for the purposes of presentation only. Our concern, then, is with both divine being and becoming—with both static and dynamic metaphors. So we consider now some central strands in the concept of God and God's relation to the world—that is, themes relevant to the concept of God as Creator—and how they might be illuminated by new perspectives generated by the natural sciences.

A. DIVINE BEING

Ground of Being

The current scientific perspective does not substantially alter the nature of the philosophical debate or the status of the theistic claim but it does, it seems to me, highlight with greater intensity some of the issues at stake. Thus, what one might call the sheer apparent "givenness" of the world, with its cosmological, biological, and social history—its contingency—is enhanced by our newfound awareness of the regular lawfulness of its interconnectedness through space and time. Moreover the quantum field (the quantum "vacuum") in which those fluctuations are postulated as having occurred—at the start of the expansion of the present observed universe—is not, strictly speaking, simply "nothing at all." *Its* existence still calls for explanation of some kind, in the sense that it is contingent and need not have existed at all with its particular properties, namely, those represented by quantum theory.

Now the "Holy Grail" sought by the physicists is a "theory of everything" (TOE). This "TOE" would have to explain not only how our universe came into being, but also why there is only one set of physical laws. However there is increasingly also a recognition[11] of the impossibility of answering the question of why the laws of nature (in particular, those of quantum physics) *are* what they are—that is, to explain the existence of the laws whereby the original quantum field should have had the property of generating matter through its fluctuations. As Russell Stannard has put it, "For these reasons the goal of a complete theory of everything is unattainable, and the claim to have disproved the need of a Creator is false."[12] Hence the postulate of the existence of a "Ground of Being" continues to be plausible.

One

From a scientific perspective, the world exhibits an underlying unity beneath its remarkable diversity, fecundity, and complexity. The "best explanation" of such a world's existence and character, if any is to be found at all, cannot but be grounded in *one* unifying source of creativity, multiple though its expression and outreach might be.

Of Unfathomable Richness

But this underlying unity in the world that the sciences perceive was and is capable of giving rise to immense diversity culminating in the enormously varied richness of human experience and societies. As the creative source of all that is, *God must be a Being of unfathomable richness* to be able to bring into existence a cosmos with such fecund potentialities.

Supremely Rational

Twentieth-century science reinforces this experience of the inherent, yet always challenging, intelligibility and putative comprehensibility of the world's entities, structures, and processes. This cannot but render more probable than ever before inference to the existence of a suprarational Being as Creator as the "best explanation" of such a world's existence and character. The affirmation of the existence of *God as the supremely rational Creator* is strengthened and its truth rendered more, rather than less, probable by the increasing success of science in discovering the inherent, but in content ever-surprising, rationality of the cosmos.

Sustainer and Faithful Preserver

The natural sciences have led to such a revision of our concept of the nature of time that the relation of God to time needs to be reconsidered. First, we cannot now but be aware that *time* is an aspect of the natural order, being closely integrated in relativity and quantum theory with space, matter, and energy, and so, for theists, must be regarded as, in some sense, created. Second, the realization that time has a direction, in which there emerge new entities, structures, and processes, reinforces the idea that God is, as Creator, both the *Sustainer and faithful Preserver* through time of all-that-is and of all-that-is-becoming. If "God" is still to be their "best explanation," then God as Creator must be regarded as holding all in existence and maintaining the validity of all laws and relations throughout time. It should be noted that there is implied, if God is personal, a moral quality in the divine sustaining and preserving—that of faithfulness or "steadfast love," as the Old Testament calls it.

Continuous Creator

What the scientific perspective of the world inexorably impresses upon us is a dynamic picture of the world of entities and structures involved in continuous and incessant change and in process without ceasing. The new entities, structures, and processes display genuinely emergent properties that are nonreducible in terms of what preceded them and so constitute new levels of reality (for the critical-realist). Hence new realities come into being, and old ones often pass away, so that God's action as Creator is both past and present—it is continuous. Any notion of God as Creator must now take into account, more than ever before in the history of theology, that *God is continuously creating*, that God is *semper Creator*. Thus it is that the scientific perspective obliges us to take more seriously and concretely than hitherto in theology the notion of the immanence of God as Creator—that *God is the Immanent Creator creating in and through the processes of the natural order.*

Personal Creator of an Anthropic Universe

There are good general grounds for believing that God might be "personal," or "at least personal," or even, if one is more robust, "a person."[13] This belief, indeed experience, is basic and fundamental to the Judeo-Christian religious tradition. From the scientific "anthropic principle," we can infer that the world does seem to be finely tuned with respect to many physical features in a way conducive to the emergence of living organisms and so of human beings. We can also give reasons why living organisms might develop, through intelligible natural processes, cognitive powers, and consciousness as they increased in complexity and flexibility—and how the development of self-consciousness would involve awareness of pain, suffering, and death. The presence of humanity in this universe, far from being an unintelligible surd, represents an inherent built-in potentiality of that physical universe in the sense that intelligent, self-conscious life was bound eventually to appear although its *form* was not prescribed by those same fundamental parameters and relationships that made it all possible.

This now well-established "anthropic" feature of our universe has been interpreted in various and mutually inconsistent ways. For some[14] it renders any talk of a creator God more than ever unnecessary since we would not be likely, would we not, to be able to observe a universe that did *not* have the right conditions for producing us? Others[15] have seen in it a new and more defensible "argument from design" for the existence of a creator God. The whole debate is philosophically a very subtle and puzzling one,[16] depending, as it clearly does on the presuppositions and interpretative framework that one brings to bear on any assessment of the *a priori* probability of all the constants, etc.—all the "fine-tuning"—coming out just to have the values that could lead to life and so to us.

This is the point at which the truly astonishing character of this emergence of personhood can be properly emphasized. For, we may well ask, why did the world, before the emergence of living organisms, and *a fortiori* of humanity, not just go on being an insentient, uncomprehending mechanism—"merely the hurrying of material, endlessly, meaninglessly."[17] The fact is, it did not and it is indeed almost highly significant, as John Durant has remarked[18] that with all its impressive knowledge of the physical and biological worlds and of our human physical nature that science can tell us nothing about why we have the experience of subjectivity. There is a huge gap between what mechanism, and even organicism, can predict, and any plausible explanation of the presence of persons in the universe. The concept, and so actual instantiation, of personhood is the most intrinsically irreducible of all emerging entities that we know.

It seems, therefore, that the universe has through its own inherent processes—and there is no need to depart from this well-warranted assumption—generated a part of itself that, as persons, introduces a distinctively new kind of causality into itself, namely, that of personal agency. This scientific perspective therefore makes more urgent the questions concerning the significance of the emergence of the personal in the form: does not the very intimacy of our relation to the fundamental features of the physical world, the "anthropic" features, together with the distinctiveness of personhood, point us in the direction of looking for a "best explanation" of all-that-is (both nonpersonal and personal) in terms of some kind of causality that could *include* the personal in its consequences?

Since the personal is the highest category of entity we can name in the order of natural beings and since "God" is the name we give to this "best explanation," we have good reason for saying that *God is (at least) "personal,"* or "suprapersonal" and for predicating personal qualities of God as less misleading and more appropriate than impersonal ones—even while recognizing, as always, that such predications must remain ultimately inadequate to that to which they refer, namely, God. It is of the nature of the personal not only to be capable of bearing static predicates, referring to stabler settled characteristics, but also of predicates of a dynamic kind, since the flow of experience is quintessential to being a person.

For our models of God to be personal they must be dynamic as well as static. So it is appropriate to develop our consideration of the creative actions and activity of a personal God also under the heading of "Divine Becoming."

B. Divine Becoming

It is distinctive of free persons that they possess intentions and purposes and act so as to implement them. Hence it becomes proper to ask: Can we infer from what is going on in the natural world anything about what might properly be called the "purposes" of God as personal Creator acting in the created world? That is, can we discern the purposes of this personal God in any ways that are consistent with what we now know of the universe through the sciences? More broadly, is our understanding of God the personal Creator as the "best explanation" of all-that-is enriched by what science shows us concerning the natural world, including humanity?

Joy and Delight in Creation

The natural world is immensely variegated in its hierarchies of levels of entities, structures, and processes, in its "being;" and abundantly diversified with a cornucopian fecundity in its "becoming" in time. We can conclude only that, if there is a personal Creator, then the Creator intended this rich multiformity of entities, structures, and processes in the natural world and, if so, that such a Creator God takes what, in the personal world of human experience, could only be called "delight" in this multiformity of what he has created. *God has joy and delight in creation.*

Ground and Source of Law ("Necessity") and "Chance"

The interplay between "chance," at the molecular level of the DNA, and "law" or "necessity" at the statistical level of the population of organisms tempted Jacques Monod, in his influential book *Chance and Necessity* to elevate "chance" to the level almost of a metaphysical principle whereby the universe might be interpreted. He concluded that the "stupendous edifice of evolution" is, in this sense, rooted in "pure chance" and that *therefore* all inferences of direction or purpose in the development of the biological world, in particular, and of the universe, in general, must be false. In so arguing, he thereby mounted, in the name of science, one of the strongest and most influential attacks of the century on belief in a creator God.

But there is no reason why the randomness of molecular events in relation to biological consequence has to be given the significant metaphysical status that Monod attributed to it. This role of "chance," or rather randomness (or "free experiment") at the microlevel is what one would expect if the universe were so constituted that all the potential forms of organizations of matter (both living and nonliving) that it contains might be thoroughly explored.

The investigations of the Brussels school, under Ilya Prigogine, and of the Göttingen school, under Manfred Eigen, demonstrate that it is the interplay of chance and law that is in fact creative within time, for it is the combination of the two that allows new forms to emerge and evolve—so natural selection appears to be opportunistic.

The principles of natural selection involve the interplay and consequences of random processes (in relation to biological outcome) in the law-like framework of the rules governing change in biological populations in complex environments. These rules are what they are because of the "givenness" of the properties of the physical environment and of the already-evolved other living organisms with which the organism in question interacts. This givenness, for a theist, can only be regarded as an aspect of the God-endowed features of the world.

One might say that the potential of the "being" of the world is made manifest in the "becoming" that the operation of chance makes actual. *God is the ultimate ground and source of both law ("necessity") and "chance."*

On this view God acts to create in the world *through* what we call "chance" operating within the created order, each stage of which constitutes the launching pad for the next. However, the actual course of this unfolding of the hidden potentialities of the world is not a once-for-all predetermined path, for there are unpredictabilities in the actual systems and processes of the world (microevents at the "Heisenberg" level in nonlineai dynamical complex systems). There is an open-endedness in the course oí the world's "natural" history. We now have to conceive of God as involved in explorations of the many kinds of unfulfilled potentialities of the universe(s) he[19] has created.

There are, as we saw, built-in propensities—a theist would say "built in by God"—in the natural, creating processes that, as it were, "load the dice" in favor of life and, once living organisms have appeared, also of increased complexity, awareness, consciousness, and sensitivity, with all their consequences.

It seems that we now have to take account of: (1) this new perspective of God the Creator as acting through chance operating within the constraints of law, that is, of the God-given properties and propensities of the natural world; (2) a renewed emphasis on the immanence of God in the processes of the creative and creating world; and (3) our earlier recognition of the unpredictability of much of what goes on in the world.

These lead us to affirm that *God the Creator explores in creation.*

Self-Limited Omnipotence and Omniscience

Considerations such as these on the role of "chance" in creation impel us also to recognize more emphatically than ever before the constraints that God has imposed upon himself in creation and to assert that *God has a "self-limited" omnipotence and omniscience.*

The attribution of "self-limitation" to God with respect to his omnipotence is meant to indicate that God has so made the world that there are certain areas over which he has chosen not to have power. Similarly, the attribution of "self-limitation" to God in regard to his omniscience is meant to denote that God may also have so made the world that, at any given time, there are certain systems whose future states cannot be known even to him since they are in principle not knowable (for example, those in the "Heisenberg" range and certain nonlinear systems at the macroscopic level). If there is no particular point in time of which it could truly be said of those systems "this will be its future state," then it could not be known at any instant, by God or by us, what the future state of such systems will be. God's "omniscience" has to be construed as God's knowing at any time whatever it is logically possible that he know at that time.[20]

These considerations do not, of course, preclude God from knowing the probabilities of the sequence of events in such systems and so of knowing, and of influencing, the general direction of the history of natural events.

The Vulnerability of God

The conditions for the emergence of open-endedness in natural systems—and so, in due course, the experience of freedom of the human-brain-in-the-human-body—involve a subtle interweaving of chance and law, with consequences that are often not readily predictable in principle. If God willed the existence of self-conscious intelligent, freely willing creatures as an end, he must, to be self-consistent, logically be presumed to have willed the means to achieve that end. This divine purpose must be taken to have been an overriding one, for it involves as a corollary an element of risk to his purposes whereby he renders himself vulnerable in a way that is only now becoming perceivable by us. This idea that *God took a risk in creation* is not new but is now, I am suggesting, reinforced and given a wider context by these biological considerations.

A Suffering God

If God is immanently present in and to natural processes, in particular those that generate conscious and self-conscious life, then we cannot but infer that *God suffers in, with, and under the creative processes of the world* with their costly, open-ended unfolding in time.

There has been an increasing assent to this idea that it is possible, as Paul Fiddes has put it,[21] "to speak consistently of *a God who suffers eminently and yet is still God, and a God who suffers universally and yet is still present uniquely and decisively in the sufferings of Christ.*"

He points out that among the factors that have promoted the view that God suffers are new assessments of "the meaning of love [especially, the love of God], the implications of the cross of Jesus, the problem of [human] suffering, and the *structure of the world*" (italics added).[22] It is this last-mentioned—the "structure of the world"—on which the new perspectives of the sciences bear by showing how the world processes inevitably involve death, pain, and suffering if self-conscious sentient creatures are to emerge in a physical universe. An immanent Creator cannot but be regarded as creating through such a process and so as suffering in, with, and under it.

God and Time

The revived insight that God suffers in the processes of creation and, supremely, with suffering humanity, raises again the question of God's relation to time. For if God "suffers" with creation in some sense analogous to that of human suffering, God must be conceived as being changed through this interaction with the world.

Analyses of the question of the relation of God to time show that a number of important traditional attributes of God lose coherence and meaning if God is regarded as "timeless" in the sense of being "outside" time altogether. We have also had to recognize that, in some sense, God is also the Creator *of* the physical time that is so closely integrated with space, and so with energy, and so with matter, in the understanding that twentieth-century physics has given us. If God *creates* time, does he not "transcend" it in the sense of viewing the whole course of "our" time from the mountaintop, as it were, of another dimension—"above" or "outside" time so that our "before," "now," and "after" are spread out all for him to see?—and our talk of unpredictability has to be taken to refer only to human and not divine foreknowledge? Yet, we had to recognize that many events (at the subatomic ("Heisenberg") quantum microlevel, and possibly also the development of nonlinear dynamical systems) are unpredictable in principle. At best only the *range* of possible outcomes of such events is predictable in principle. This does not mean that God cannot have the most complete knowledge that is possible of the probabilities of the outcomes of these events, including the operation of our free will.

Our own sense of psychological time, the sense of succession of our conscious states, with which our own sense of personhood is so bound up, is closely related to created physical time. For we move freely from one to the other even though they seem, often, to proceed at different rates while sharing many interactions and running in parallel. This relationship can perhaps at least make intelligible to us how God's own inherent self-awareness of successive states (which must be attributed to God if God is to be "personal" in any meaningful sense) might be closely linked to physical, created time, while yet remaining distinct from it. On such a model, God would not be "timeless" and could be thought of as the Creator of every instant of physical time. Creation by God would be regarded as that activity whereby God gives existence to each instant of physical time, the "now" of the hand of the clock, and each instant has no existence prior to its being so created with all the entities, structures, and processes that fill it. On this interpretation, then, the future does not yet exist in any sense, not even for God—God creates each instant of physical time with its open, as yet not fully determined, outcomes, fecund with possibilities not yet actualized. If the future does not yet exist for God, any more than it does for us, there is no question of God's seeing ahead what the future is going to be, even though he can still have purposes to implement in that forthcoming future.

To summarize, we can affirm that: *God is not "timeless;" God is temporal in the sense that the Divine life is successive in its relation to us—God is temporally related to us; God creates and is present to each instant of the (physical and, derivatively, psychological) time of the created world; God transcends past and present time: God is eternal,* in the sense that there is no time at which he did not exist nor will there be a future time at which he does not exist.

God and "Imaginary" Time

The foregoing exposition has spoken of time as if it were meaningful to think of time as extrapolatable backwards at least as far as the "point" in time, the singularity, from which the expansion of our known universe began (the "hot, Big Bang"). However we must also consider now the speculative proposal of Hartle and Hawking who were led to the idea that the further one goes back along the ordinary "real" time scale the more it has to be replaced by a new parameter that includes also a mathematically "imaginary" component (i.e., one involving i, the square root of minus 1). According to Hawking[23] using this "time," involving an "imaginary" component, leads to the disappearance of the distinction between time and space. Furthermore, "space-time" (mathematical "imaginary" time unified with space) proved to be finite in extent and yet "have no singularities that formed a boundary or edge."[24] According to this, still highly controversial, speculation: "There would be no singularities at which the laws of science broke down and no edge of space-time at which one would have to appeal to God or some new law to set the boundary conditions for space-time. . . . The universe would be completely self-contained and not affected by anything outside itself. It would neither be created or destroyed. It would just Be."[25]

But the mystery-of-existence question still has to be pressed for, as Hawking himself has put it: "Why does the universe go to all the bother of existing? Is the unified theory so compelling that it brings about its own existence? Or does it need a creator, and, if so, does he have any other effect on the universe? And who created him?"[26]

We seem to have come full circle, for here we have the author of the most recent best-selling book by a scientist raising the very question that the astronomer Robert Jastrow believed the theologians, whom he anticipated the astronomers meeting at that mountaintop, were answering. Yet Hawking raises this question only with considerable ambiguity for, as we saw in the other quotation from *A Brief History of Time*, he toys with the possibility that the universe could "neither be created or destroyed. It would just Be."

IV. Conclusion

The trumpets of the scientists therefore give an uncertain theological sound and play a number of different tunes. But this does not, indeed should not, preclude the theologian from listening to their deliverances qua scientists, rather than qua novices in philosophy and theology. For *what* they have discovered and are discovering about the natural world affords late-twentieth century human consciousness with a vista that completely transforms the context to which theology has continuously to return, namely, the world, including the human world, which it affirms owes its origin to the will and purpose of a Creator God. That vista is overwhelmingly evocative and dazzling to the mind and spirit and constitutes a challenge of far greater significance and consequence than did the rediscovery of Aristotle for the times of St. Thomas Aquinas.

The sum effect, for me at least, of the cosmic panorama through space and time that the sciences now afford is to reinforce my conviction that without a creator God all-that-is (the "world") is without explanation both with respect to its very existence and with respect to the subtle, intricate, and ever-awesome rationality that it manifests increasingly as the sciences advance. These reflections also make even more urgent the need for a rebirth of images concerning the nature of God as Creator, the act of creation and the continuing nature of God's creative interaction with the world. There are, I believe, fruitful suggestions to be made with respect to all of these key matters—using especially the images of artistic creation, in general, and musical creation,[26] in particular. But that would be another exercise.

7

John Polkinghorne

A Potent Universe

The most obvious sign of purpose is an artifact, a contrivance constructed to fulfill a particular role. It is not surprising that those who first seriously used the insights of modern science to look for indications of the will of a Creator behind the pattern of the physical world sought to do so in those terms. This was the strategy of the physico-theology of the eighteenth and early nineteenth century: Paley's appeal from the watch to the watchmaker. With the benefits of hindsight we can see that this argument was too anthropomorphic in its character. It forgot that the Hebrew word normally used in the Old Testament for God's creative activity is the special word *bārah*, rather than the common word *āsāh*. Human beings can only manipulate the material at their disposal. God is the ordainer of the nature of the material. That is part of the meaning of the Christian doctrine that God creates *ex nihilo*. Unlike the Greek demiurge, he does not have to do the best he can with the raw material of preexistent brute matter.

There was another difficulty with Paley's idea of the Cosmic Craftsman. His credibility decreased with the growing realization that the world had a history. In the nineteenth century, first with the geology of the mountains and then with the paleontology of living beings, and finally in the twentieth century with the expanding universe itself, it came to be realized that the past had been radically different from the present. The universe as we know it had not sprung into being ready-made; rather it had made itself through a long evolving history. That would not have surprised St. Augustine who had written, in his great commentary on Genesis, that "in the beginning were created only germs or causes of the forms of life which were afterwards to be developed in gradual course"—words that are not far removed from those of Charles Darwin himself when he wrote: "There is grandeur in this view of life, with its several powers having been originally breathed by the Creator into a few forms or into one; and that . . . from so simple a beginning endless forms most beautiful and most wonderful have been, and are being evolved."

We know now that cosmic history is the astonishing tale of how initial simplicity has given rise to present multivarious complexity. What started as an expanding, almost uniform, ball of energy has become the home of life and self-conscious beings. It is the job of science to describe that marvelously fruitful process. There are many lacunae in our understanding, but we have every reason to believe that it is a continuous story that is to be told. It does not seem in the least likely that there are rifts in the web of process, discontinuities that could be bridged only by the supernatural intervention of a God of the gaps. Our knowledge of the biochemical pathways by which elementary life first came into being in the amino acid-rich, shallow waters of early Earth is almost nonexistent, but we have rightly become wary of assertions that only direct divine action could bring such life out of inanimate matter.

So has the image of a purposive Creator faded away like the smile on the Cheshire cat? Not at all! Rather, we have begun to look for signs of him where we ought always to have directed our attention, in the fundamental structure of the universe. After all, to a theist those regularities that we call the laws of nature are reflections of the faithful will of God. We must therefore expect that his purpose will be made manifest, not in the occasional abrogation of those laws—as if God were suddenly to change his mind—but in the very nature of those laws themselves. Their actual existence—that we live in a cosmos endowed with a fundamental order, transparent to our understanding and characterized by a profound rational beauty—is itself capable of being understood as the sign of a mind behind the flux of the world's becoming. The argument from intelligibility is an important insight of natural theology.[1] But we can go much further than that, for we have come to realize that the detailed and precise form that those laws actually take is a necessary precondition for the universe's fruitful history. This remarkable scientific insight, that a world capable of evolving beings like men and women is a very special world, is called the *anthropic principle*.[2] It seems that we do not live in "any old physical world" but in a potent universe.

One might feel surprised that one could arrive at something of signifi-cance just by thinking about the laws of nature. Are they not just the given ground rules under which our world operates, whether we like it or not? From the point of view of science that is the case. Every discipline has its necessary starting point, the given basis that it must assume in framing its explanations. For science, the laws of nature are what it takes for granted as the means of its understanding of what is going on. Of course, from time to time scientists have had to revise their notion of what these laws actually are, as our exploration of the physical world in regimes of ever-increasing largeness or smallness has revealed the existence of unsuspected new phe-nomena. I believe that this process is one of deepening and extension, rather than completely revolutionary replacement, so that one can understand the advance of physical science as one of increasing verisimilitude, a tightening grasp of an actual reality.[3] Our present (doubtless incomplete) knowledge of physical law can, therefore, be taken seriously. When one does so, it seems to me that a pressing *meta*-question, arising from science but going beyond the realm of the scientifically answerable, comes into the metaphysical agen-da. Science may be forced by its nature simply to take its laws for granted, but that does not mean that a wider search for understanding should do so. We have to ask what significance is to be assigned to the anthropic principle, that very precise "finely tuned" character of our natural law that has enabled the fruitfulness of cosmic history?

We are able to pose this question concerning the particular character of our actual world because we are able scientifically to imagine how things might have been different. Doubtless, the conceptual power of our minds to think of possible other worlds is pretty limited, but even within its con-fines we can see that an anthropic world, in the course of whose history we could have evolved, is a considerable rarity in a portfolio of conceivable universes. In the discussion that follows we can only illustrate the nature of the considerations involved. Exhaustive analysis would need more than the length of an article.[4]

Four requirements seem to be necessary for a potent universe:

(1) The Right Kind of Physical Law

It seems that fruitful process requires to be both reliable and yet open to a degree of variation. Consider, as an example, the transmission of genetic information through DNA. The copying process must be tolerably secure, otherwise the succession of the generations will be deleteriously chaotic, with no possibility of the orderly operation of a selection process. On the other hand, if copying were perfect, then there would be no variation on which selection could be brought to bear. It seems to me to be highly probable that a Newtonian universe, in which the deterministic laws of classical physics held sway, would be too rigid in its process for anything remotely lifelike to have evolved. Little massy particulate atoms, sticking together through contact or the interlocking of little hooks, would not have done the trick. Our world is, of course, *au fond* quantum mechanical. The celebrated indeterminacy of quantum theory introduces an element of chance, of the random exploration of possibility, into the development of the physical world, but it is also important to recognize that quantum mechanical discreteness (the limitation of possible outcomes compared to the infinitely variable possibilities of classical physics) at the same time introduces an element of stability. In fact, one of the earliest triumphs of quantum theory was precisely to explain why atoms are so stable, why they survive many collisions with their properties unaltered. Something like the subtlely flexible order of quantum physics would seem to be part of the specification of a potent universe. This thought of the anthropic necessity of quantum mechanics is capable of considerable expansion. For example, a consequence of quantum theory is a particular kind of behavior related to collections of particles of the same type. All electrons obey what is called "fermi statistics," which means that no two of them can ever be in exactly the same state of motion.[5] This exclusion principle is absolutely basic to the behavior of atoms, hence to chemistry, and so to the properties of matter that underlie all living systems. A Newtonian universe seems a conceptual possibility, but it could not have given rise to Sir Isaac.

(2) The Right Kind of Constituents

It is part of the fruitfulness of our world that it has various kinds of matter within it, which have differing properties in relation to the fundamental forces of nature. Thus there are protons and neutrons capable of being held together by the strong nuclear force to constitute nuclei, while there are electrons, which do not experience the nuclear force, and so do not get drawn into the nucleus but remain free to form atoms by encircling it under the influence of electromagnetic forces. It is conceivable, as modern elementary particle physics is prone to suppose, that this variety is the manifestation of an underlying grand unified theory, but at least that deeper theory has to have a richness of structure capable of sustaining such a variety of consequences. Again, one can imagine a universe in which that was not so. There does not seem anything inconsistent in a world with only photons and electrons in it,[6] but such a world would be rather boring in its history. Extended plasmas would seem to be the maximum richness of being to be expected from it. It is very remarkable that the almost infinite variety of our world arises (as the pre-Socratic philosophers had guessed 2 1/2 millennia ago) from a small number of kinds of basic stuff, but not any old collection of constituents would be apt to do the trick.

(3) The Right Srength of Forces

Once we know the kinds of forces present in the universe, we can go on to consider their intrinsic strengths. There are natural scales for measuring these, which are called coupling constants. It is not difficult to envisage them as being different from those that we actually experience. For example, gravity is a very weak force in our universe (its coupling constant is a tiny number, 10^{-39}), but we can conceive of worlds in which gravity was very much stronger. And similarly for electromagnetism, and the other basic forces. Very many considerations converge on the conclusion that these coupling strengths have to be very finely "tuned" to the kinds of values we actually observe, if the universe is to be anthropically fruitful. Let me give some illustration of why this is so.

A potent universe must have stars in it. They have two essential jobs to do. One is to provide the energy source for life. Virtually all the Earth's energy comes from the Sun, either directly or indirectly (through fossil fuels laid down millions of years ago). Therefore one must have stable long-life stars, providing a steady source of energy over the billions of years that it takes life to develop. We call these main-sequence stars.

Such stars perform a second vital task. They make the elements out of which all living beings will eventually be formed. In the initial Big Bang, only hydrogen and helium, the two simplest elements, are made. Life demands greater variety of chemical ingredients than that. The stars provide them, through the nuclear cookery taking place in their fiery furnaces. Every atom of carbon inside our bodies was once inside a star. We are all made of the ashes of dead stars. That process of synthesizing elements is a delicate business. It depends upon chains of nuclear reactions that must prove capable in their total effect of producing all the necessary elements in suitable abundances. And that is not the end of the story. Unless stellar history produces some stars that at the close of their lives explode as supernovas, all those elements so carefully produced would be left useless, locked up in the cooling core of a dying sun. Finally, to complete the critically sensitive tale of successful nucleosynthesis, it is only in the detailed process of those supernova explosions that the heavier elements can be made at all, for inside a star one cannot get beyond the most stable nucleus, iron.

All that sounds pretty complicated. It is, not only to understand and to describe, but also to bring about. Very small changes in the strengths of the fundamental forces would wreck the whole stellar program, making the corresponding universe sterile. The fulfillment of the requirement for steady energy sources is particularly sensitive to small variations in the strengths of electromagnetic and gravitational forces. The requirement of nucleosynthesis is particularly sensitive to the details of nuclear forces, both strong (holding nuclei together) and weak (causing various kinds of nuclear decay.)[7]

Stars began to form as galaxies condensed when the universe was about a billion years old. Their average life is about ten billion years. It is only in a "second generation" planetary system like our own that the chemical environment appropriate for life could come into existence. It then takes a few billion years for beings as complex as ourselves to evolve. It is no accident that we find ourselves living in an era when the universe is about fifteen billion years old. We could not have put in an appearance earlier.

The particular and delicate balances necessary for a potent universe are not only to be discerned in the circumstances of astrophysics. They seem to be present at all stages of cosmic and, eventually, terrestrial history. A very important requirement for anthropic fruitfulness is that there is an almost exact balance between the expansive effect of the Big Bang and the countervailing contractive influence of gravity. If expansion were to have had the upper hand by only a minute fraction, the universe would rapidly have become too dilute for anything interesting to happen in it. On the other hand, if gravity had been even slightly predominant, the universe would have collapsed before it could have had a fruitful history. Many believe that the exquisite balance between these two effects that has made our world potent, was achieved by a process called inflation—a kind of boiling of space—which took place before the universe was 10^{-30} seconds old. This is an era where the physics is controlled, not by the forces that we see today, but by the grand unified theory believed to underlie them. Only if that theory takes a specific kind of form would it yield an inflationary cosmic scenario, so even at that incredibly early epoch there had to be something special about the forces involved.

Returning to times when more everyday, and better understood, physics operated, there are many further constraints for anthropic fruitfulness. In the first three minutes of cosmic history,[8] the whole universe was the arena of nuclear reactions. When that era came to an end, through the cooling produced by expansion, the world was left, as it is today on the large scale, a mixture of three-quarters hydrogen and one-quarter helium. A little change in the balance between the strong and weak nuclear forces could have resulted instead in there being no hydrogen—and so ultimately no water, that fluid that seems so essential to life. A small increase (about 2 percent) in the strong nuclear force would bind two protons to form diprotons. There would then be no hydrogen-burning main-sequence stars, but only helium burners, which are far too fierce and rapid to be energy sources capable of sustaining the coming to be of planetary life. A decrease in the strong nuclear force by similar amount would have unbound the deuteron and played havoc with fruitful nuclear physics.

Turning our attention to local terrestrial matters, changes in chemistry and the properties of matter that would result from a variation in the intrinsic strength of electromagnetism (the controlling force for these phenomena) would be expected completely to alter the remarkable properties of the chemistry of carbon and the behavior of water, which seem to be crucial for the possibility of life.

This is just a selection of the considerations that encourage the view that a universe in which the force strengths differed only slightly from those that we experience would be one that was sterile in its history. Leslie has emphasized that often there are several quite different constraints, arising from distinct kinds of consideration, which concern the same coupling constant but yet are compatible with each other.

(4) The right cosmic circumstances

There are certain general aspects of our universe that are also necessary for its anthropic fruitfulness. One of them is its size. The cosmos is immensely big. Our Sun is just an ordinary star among the hundred thousand million stars of our galaxy, the Milky Way, and the Milky Way is nothing to speak about among the hundred thousand million galaxies of the observable universe. Sometimes we are tempted to feel dismayed by that immensity within which we are just the inhabitants of a speck of cosmic dust. We should not do so, for if all those trillions of stars were not there, we could not be here to be daunted by them. There is a direct relationship between cosmic size and cosmic age. Only a world as big as ours could have been around long enough for us to have appeared upon its scene.

Our universe is spatially three-dimensional. Again that is just as well. A two-dimensional world would have insufficiently complex possibilities in it (our alimentary canal would divide us into two separate halves, for instance!); a four-dimensional world could not sustain stable atoms or planetary orbits.

There are those who believe that a quantum cosmology, together with a "natural" boundary condition for the universe, might fix cosmic size and dimensions. Such notions are speculative in the extreme, but they might just conceivably reduce some of the conditions of this section to consequences of the conditions of section 2.

I have outlined the kind of considerations that lead us to think that our potent universe is not just "any old world," but extremely special—"finely tuned" is the metaphor that comes to mind—among the set of possible universes, in a way that has been essential for its remarkable fruitfulness. Two criticisms have been made of such a claim.

The first is that the range of cosmic choice is mistakenly assessed. It is suggested that a consistent universe *has to be* the way ours is. In a more sophisticated version of the argument (depending on notions of spontaneous symmetry breaking, the way in which the underlying unified force is thought to decompose, as energies decrease, to give the familiar forces of our world of direct physical experience) it is held that a universe would have to have large cosmic domains within it where the everyday circumstances would lie within anthropic limits. This notion has had a certain fluctuating popularity in contemporary physical thought, because of the great difficulty in combining quantum theory and general relativity in a self-consistent way. It is possible that there is an essentially unique way in which this can be done. Even if that were so, it is not clear that there is then also a unique way in which its symmetries can be broken. Even if one grants the maximum conceivable success to such claims, there still remain the considerations of sections (1) and (2). Why is the universe one that is both quantum mechanical and endowed with Einsteinian gravity? And is it not rather remarkable that a world that is consistent is also necessarily fruitful?

A more interesting counterargument is that we are in thrall to our limited imaginations. The considerations set out above mostly center round the conditions necessary for the coming to be of carbon-based life. Might there not be totally different ways in which a universe might be "fruitful," meaning by that give rise to systems of the immense complexity that surely must be required to sustain a phenomenon like consciousness? Could there not, after all, be immense "thinking plasmas," slowly pondering throughout their spatially extended complexity, or "civilizations" that rise and fall in the environment of neutron stars in less than a microsecond? Well perhaps . . . but those who make such suggestions are prepared to draw huge intellectual blank checks on totally unknown accounts. The human brain is far and away the most complex interconnected physical system we have ever encountered. Consciousness must be expected to require such extreme complication and it does not seem very likely that there are many intrinsically alternative routes to its achievement. It is impossible to be dogmatic about this— we understand so little of how mind and brain, the mental and the physical, relate—and if we were able to think of universes radically different from our own (rather than the kind of variations on present circumstance, which we have been discussing) then there might be possibilities of extraordinary kinds. In relation to this last point, Leslie has emphasized that it is an insight of considerable significance even if we can only say that our potent universe is extremely special in relation to hypothetical universes lying "near" it in the range of possibility. He calls this "the fly on the wall argument":[9] if I shoot blindfold and hit the only fly on the blank wall right in front of me, that is a remarkable occurrence, even if the wall behind me were to be crawling with flies.

I conclude that it is reasonable to hold to the view that there is something particular and finely tuned about a potent universe.

If that is so, what significance should we attribute to it? There have been a number of contrasting responses:

(a) Indifference

Some just shrug their shoulders and say, "That's the way it is, and there's an end of it." I am astonished at what seems to me to be an extreme lack of intellectual curiosity. The instincts of a scientist are to seek to understand things through and through, and I cannot treat the particularity of a potent universe as if it were a matter of posing no question of why things are this way. (Of course, if they were not I would not be here to ask the question, but "We're here because we're here" seems a pretty feeble argument.) A more sophisticated version of this attitude queries, "What can we learn from the single example of our universe?" Part of the reply lies in our ability, exemplified above, to conceive of many different possible universes, with which we can compare our actual one. When we do so, we are led to recognize our world's particular potency.

(b) The Weak Anthropic Principle

This acknowledges that a world of which we are inhabitants must satisfy the conditions that are consistent with our presence: carbon-based life, cosmic age of about fifteen billion years, etc. Although slightly better than (a), such mere acknowledgment seems to lack a necessary element of curiosity about what might be signified by the fine-tuning required.

(c) The Strong Anthropic Principle

Here we go to the other extreme and it is asserted as a kind of quasi-scientific principle that a universe *must* be anthropically fruitful and capable of producing observers within its history. It is very difficult to see why one should make such an assertion, just on its own, as if it were an almost self-evident truth. Frequently, attempts are made to link the SAP with quantum theory and the role of observers in bringing about consequences in that theory. I do not think this succeeds. First, still highly contentious is the degree to which quantum theory licenses any talk about "observer-created reality," [10] and second, the influence of observers is only relevant to the outcomes of interactions and not to producing the underlying laws of physics that control the phenomena (and which we were discussing above).

(d) The Moderate Anthropic Principle

This is my own stance. [11] It notes the fine-tuning of a potent universe as being an insight of significance that calls for some form of explanation. Since the *explanandum* is the laws of physics themselves—in other words, science's basic starting point for its discussions—we may expect the explanation to be of a metaphysical character.

John Leslie, who is given to discussing philosophical questions in a parabolic mode, puts the issue clearly in his story of the firing squad. [12] I am due for execution by fifty crack marksmen. As the sound of firing dies away, I find that I am still alive. Here is a fact that calls for explanation. It is not enough just to say, "Here I am, and that was certainly a close run thing." There are really only two kinds of rational explanation of my good fortune: either there were a very great number of such executions and by lucky chance mine was the one in which they all happened to miss, or the marksmen are on my side. These two lines of thought correspond to two ways people have sought to understand the particularity of our potent universe:

(1) Many Universes

If there were a great variety of different universes, each with its own physical law and circumstance, then it would not be very surprising if within that great portfolio of possibility, there should be one that just happens to satisfy the right conditions for anthropic fruitfulness. Of course, that is the one in which we live, because we could appear in no other. It is very important to be clear on what kind of explanation is being offered here. Although it is sometimes tricked out as if it were physical (by *illegitimate* appeal to quantum theory; see above), nevertheless, since we have adequate scientific motivation only to speak of the one universe of our actual experience, it is in fact a metaphysical hypothesis that is being proposed.

(2) Creation

A theistic understanding supposes there to be but one universe that is certainly not "any old world," for it is a creation that has been endowed by its Creator with just those finely tuned laws and circumstance that will permit its evolving history to be fruitful. The potency of the universe is seen as an expression of the purpose of God.

In relation to the anthropic principle alone, there might seem to be equal coherence in a (1) and (2). The latter gains much greater economy and persuasiveness when one takes into account that there are many other lines of argument that converge on the insight that behind the world of our experience there lies the fundamental Reality of God.[13] Moreover, the will of an Agent is a natural explanation for fruitful potency.

None of these considerations amount to a knockdown argument—there are no such arguments either for or against religious belief—but our scientific recognition of the special character of a potent universe finds deeply satisfying understanding within the intellectual setting of theism. A kind of anti-Copernican revolution has taken place. We do not live at the center of the universe, but the fabric of the world has written into it just those delicate balances that are necessary for us to have emerged from its history. If we have eyes to see, the anthropic principle will speak to us of the signs of God's purpose present in the remarkable potentiality with which our universe has been endowed in the basic ground of its physical process.

8

John C. Eccles

The Evolution of Purpose

I. Apparent Purpose

In its primary usage, purpose was understood as the meaning to do or to create something, or as the object for which anything is done or made. However, on that basis there have evolved a great variety of metaphorical usages. For example, when one surveys the cosmos from the time of the Big Bang there have been the creations of the whole range of natural elements from the original hydrogen and helium. Most remarkably there came into existence our solar system with its absolutely unique planet Earth. In my Gifford Lectures "The Human Mystery" I traced the great chain of contingency from the initiating "fireball" through the cosmic evolution to planet Earth. In some chapters of this book there can be discerned "purpose" in the most wonderful creations in the prebiotic world, which is the world of cosmology, of physics, of chemistry. We can interpret this creativity as leading "purposively" to the origin of life. I would suggest that up to this time we can speak of *apparent purpose*. In simple terms it can be called the fulfilling of the divine plan.

The prebiotic world had a material structure that was "poised" for the origin of life with the essential elements and molecules. From that still mysterious origin the way was open for biological evolution of the first living cells. There was a transformation in the survival process of these cells, which we can call *living purpose*.

II. Living Purpose: Teleonomy

As Monod states, "All living beings without exception [are] endowed with a purpose or project and so are distinct from all other structures or systems present in the universe . . . with this characteristic property, which we shall call teleonomy." Monod chose this term to avoid the concept of teleology, which savored too much of design for a purpose with the implication of a "designer" as Paley did surmise in his Natural Theology. All evolutionary biology is concerned with teleonomy. As Monod states, "The essential teleonomic project consists in the transmission from generation to generation of the invariance content characteristic of the species." Finally, Monod specifies, "the two essential properties that characterize living organisms, reproductive invariance and structural teleonomy."

Normally in cellular reproduction there is an accurate copying of the linear code written in the DNA, and hence there is stability in the genes from generation to generation, the reproductive invariance. However, very rarely changes called *gene mutations* do occur in the DNA code. There may be mistakes in copying with the replacement of one nucleotide for another, such as G for A, or there may be more radical changes with deletion or inversion of one or more nucleotide base pairs or even inversion of larger DNA segments. These copying errors may lead to the substitution of one amino acid for another in a protein. The effect of this may be negligible in the functioning of the protein. However, in the great majority, these exchanges are deleterious to the survival and reproduction of the individual, which consequently is eliminated in the process of natural selection.

Only on rare occasions is a mutation beneficial for survival and reproduction. Such a mutation will be transmitted to successive generations and will result in enhanced survival of the biological group sharing this mutation. So after many generations by *natural selection* this favorable mutation may come to be incorporated in all members of that species, which consequently reflect a slight change in genotype. Later another mutational selection may be added, and so on.

This is the essential basis of the modern version of Darwin's theory of *natural selection* or *survival of the fittest*. Favorable gene mutations are selected, whereas the unfavorable are eliminated. Hence by an initial process of pure chance, the gene mutation, there can be wrought by natural selection all the marvelous structural and functional features of living organisms with their amazing adaptiveness and inventiveness. As so formulated, the evolutionary theory is purely a biological process involving mechanisms of operations that are now well understood in principle, and it has deservedly won acceptance as providing a satisfactory explanation of the development of all living forms from some single extremely simple primordial form of life.

Can we use the term *living purpose* for this wonderful creativity of the evolutionary process? Granit suggests the term *immanent purposiveness* and speaks of an immanent teleology.

III. Conscious Purpose

These concepts of apparent purpose and living purpose can be regarded as types of purpose metaphorically related to "purpose" as defined at the outset, which involves meaning to do or create in a conscious performance. Thus there has now to be introduced the most significant concept of conscious purpose.

Much illumination of this theme is given in Granit's book *The Purposive Brain*. The title of the book is both a challenge and a paradox. The brain is a material structure with a basis of operation that by the neurosciences is being more and more reduced to physical terms—the immensely complicated anatomical arrangement of neurons with their action potentials, synaptic potentials, electrochemical gradients, etc. How can such a structure perform in a way that we are justified in referring to as purposive? The evolutionary process has given rise to organisms that are designed for efficient existence under a wide range of environmental circumstances. Survival requires control, adaptability, and learning. For these functions the purposive brain was evolved, and, as evolution prospered, the ever-increasing demands for these performances were met by nervous systems of progressively increasing complexity in both structure and function. Level upon level of development eventually resulted in the fullness of time in the human brain.

Throughout our whole waking day each of us in our inner world lives through experiences of the most varied kind: memories, imaginings, feelings, thoughts, sufferings, fears, hopes, desires; and in that rich tapestry there are experiences of our present interest, purposes, and meanings. All these experiences are encompassed in the concept of mind and are related in some manner to special activities of the brain. So discussion of conscious purpose leads inevitably to the mind-brain problem. How can consciously experienced purposes bring about purposive movements?

There are now techniques for studying the brain activity while precise purposive movements are being carried out by human subjects. In this technique radioactive xenon (^{133}Xe) is injected into the internal carotid artery through a canula that has been inserted for a clinical investigation. A battery of 254 Geiger counters has been mounted in a helmet applied over one side of the scalp. The brief injection causes a pattern of increased radioactivity, as observed by the counts of the Geiger assemblage. This increase in counts signals an increased blood flow (CBF), that in turn gives a quantitative measure of the subjacent cortical activity. The counts are done in the control resting situation and then during purposive movement, which was the carrying out of a complex learned series of movements, the motor sequence test (Roland et al., 1980). In fig. 2A there was a strong activation of the contralateral motor and sensory areas for the thumb and fingers (fig. 1), as would be expected, but there was just as strong an activation of the supplementary motor area (SMA) in the dorso-medial prefrontal lobe and that was bilateral. The primacy of the SMA is revealed in fig. 2B when during the radioactive Xenon test the subject was making no movement, but was carrying out the purposive movement mentally. A highly significant (about 20 percent) increase in neuronal activation was restricted to the SMA on both sides, and was nowhere else. The subject was at complete rest with eyes and ears closed. This rCBF increase is an index of an increase in primary neuronal activity of the SMA under the influence of a purposive mental intention by the subject. Evidently the purposive intention was bringing into action an immense ensemble of neurons, which of course would be essential if it is to cause the desired movement. We can ask, "How does the mental intention to initiate a purposive movement cause activation of selective areas of the brain—in the SMA? That question leads to the hypothesis that I have recently developed in relation to the ultramicrostructure of the mammalian cerebral cortex, where quantum physics may be expected to play a key role (Eccles, 1990).

A pyramidal cell of the mammalian cerebral cortex has on its apical dendrite thousands of excitatory spine synapses (fig. 3A). Each of these synapses operates through a presynaptic vesicular grid (PVG) of about thirty to fifty synaptic vesicles filled with the synaptic transmitter substance (fig. 3B). Each vesicle is poised on the presynaptic membrane (fig. 3B) for the emission of its transmitter molecules in exocytosis (fig. 3B, C, D). The apical dendrites of the pyramidal cells in laminae V, III, II bundle together as they ascend to lamina 1 (fig. 4) to form a neural receptor unit of the cerebral cortex of about one hundred apical dendrites plus their branches (fig. 3A) that is called a *dendron*, three being drawn in fig. 4 (Eccles, 1990).

In the hypothesis of mind-brain interaction (Eccles, 1990, p. 442) it is

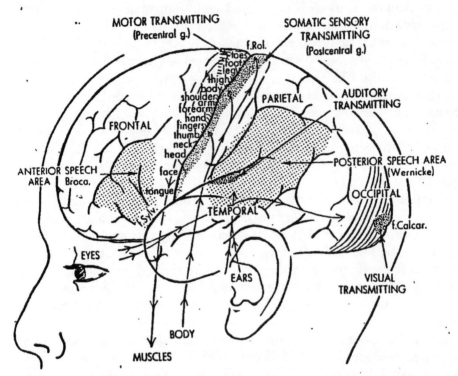

Figure 1. The approximate map of the motor-transmitting areas is shown in the precentral gyrus, while the somatic sensory-transmitting areas are in a similar map in the postcentral gyrus. Actually the toes, foot, and leg should be represented over the top on the medial surface. Other primary sensory areas shown are the visual and auditory, but they are largely in areas screened from this lateral view. Also shown are the speech areas of Broca and Wernicke. (f. Rol. = fissure of Roland or the central fissure; f. Sylv. = the fissure of Sylvius; f. Calcar. = the calcarine fissure.)

proposed that the whole mental world is microgranular, the mental units being called *psychons*. Ideally there would be one psychon for each dendron, as is shown in fig. 4 by the superposed patterns on each dendron of solid squares, open squares, and dots. It is further proposed that mind-brain interaction occurs for each psychon-dendron unit and that it can be accounted for by quantum physics because the exocytosis (fig. 3C, D) involves the displacement of a particle of only about 10^{-18}g, which is well within the range of Heisenberg uncertainty (Eccles, 1990, p. 443). There is an immense input to a dendron by thousands of synapses on the apical dendrite plus side branches of each pyramidal cell (fig. 2A), which gives tens of thou-

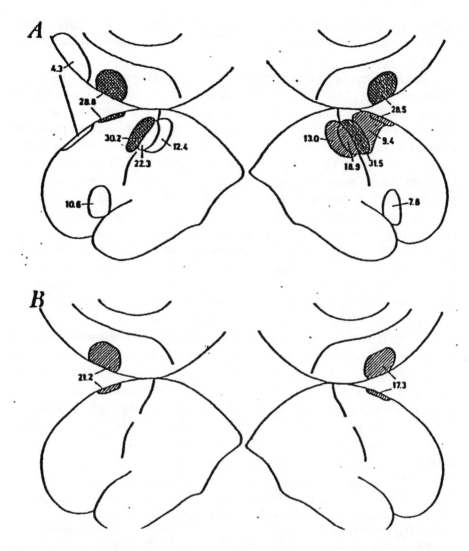

Figure 2.   A. Mean percentage increase of the rCBF during the motor-sequence test performed with the contralateral hand. Cross-hatched areas have an increase of rCBF significant at the 0.0005 level. Hatched areas have an increase of rCBF significant at the 0.005 level; for other areas shown the rCBF increase is significant at the 0.05 level. *Left*: left hemisphere, five subjects. *Right*: right hemisphere, ten subjects.
B. Mean percentage increase of rCBF during internal programming of the motor-sequence test. *Left*: left hemisphere, three subjects. *Right*: right hemisphere, five subjects. (Roland et al., 1980).

sands of synaptic vesicles on the PVG's, that are poised for exocytosis. Thus there are hundreds of thousands of poised synaptic vesicles on a dendron, which is a great biological amplifier.

In all mammals so far examined there is the same composition of apical dendrites of pyramidal cells arranged in dendrons (fig. 4). There may be as many as 40 million dendrons for the human cerebral cortex, but probably no more than 200,000 for the cerebral cortices of the most primitive mammals, the basal insectivores *(Tenrecinae)*. The cerebral cortex with the synaptic machinery of its dendrons can be regarded as a functionally effective neural design evolving in natural selection as a purely material structure for efficient operation of the cerebral cortex in conscious purpose.

Hitherto I have been concentrating on human purposive performances because this gives the primary meaning of purpose. It is generally recognized that the higher animals are conscious, though this cannot be established with the same degree of assurance as for human beings because humans have the subtlety of linguistic communication. Nevertheless we can speak of an animal as conscious when it is moved apparently by feelings and moods and when it is capable of assessing its present situation in the light of past experience and so is able to arrive at an appropriate course of action that is more than a stereotyped instinctive response. In this way it can exhibit an original behavior pattern, which can be learned and which also includes a wealth of emotional reactions and devoted attachments.

A good example of conscious purpose was given by Wolfgang Köhler in the 1920s. He had several chimpanzees in a large high room with smooth walls and there was a bunch of bananas hanging from the ceiling. As recounted by Thorpe (1978, p. 37),

> The chimps would at first try to reach the fruit by standing on their hind legs and by jumping, but all to no purpose. They would then appear dejected for a while and make no further attempts. At the start of the experiment a number of stout boxes or packing-cases had been placed around the floor, and sooner or later it would be noticed that one or another of the apes would glance first at one of the boxes and then at the coveted bananas. This would quickly be followed by the ape dragging the box underneath the bananas and standing on it, only to find that this did not bring him nearly high enough. Then another box would be fetched and placed, often precariously, on the first, again without a successful result. Only when a rather tottery pile of three boxes had been constructed was the chimp able to climb up and quickly snatch the fruit before the pile collapsed.

The overwhelming impression on observing such behavior is that the animal has worked out a new strategy in its mind, perhaps by a process of

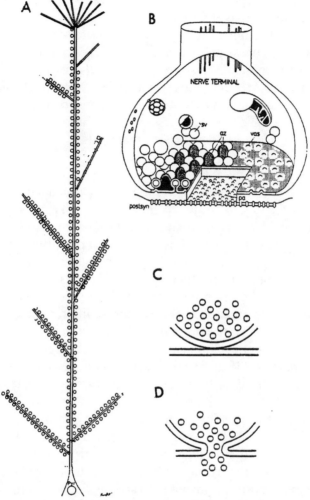

Figure 3.   A. Drawing of a lamina V pyramidal cell with its apical dendrite showing the side branches and the terminal tuft studded wtih spine synapses (not all shown). The soma with its basal dendrites has an axon with axon collateral before leaving the cortex.
B. Schema of the mammalian central synapse. The active zone (az) is formed by presynaptic dense projections spacing synaptic vesicles (sv). Pa = particle aggregations of postsynaptic membrane (postsyn.). Note synaptic vesicles in hexagonal array, and the vesicle attachment sites (vas) to the right. Further description in the text by Akert et al., 1975.
C, D. Stages of exocytosis with release of transmitter into the synaptic cleft (Kelly et al., 1979).

mental trial and error, and then put it into action—the whole performance being strongly suggestive of purpose.

Such purposive movements would be expected in our nearest animal relative with a large brain as illustrated in fig. 5. But as noted above there is good evidence for consciousness in other mammals. In fig. 5 well-developed cerebral cortices are seen for monkey, cat, and even for the rabbit and opossum. We can assume that appropriate investigations could discover evidence for consciousness and conscious purpose in all mammals. Consciousness is of course most evident in domesticated mammals.

Thorpe has reported (1978) performances of some birds that give evidence of conscious purpose. He reports a strong impression of true purposiveness in birds at feeding time where the food is suspended on threads that are too fine for the bird to be able to cling on. In such cases some individuals of certain species (such as tits and crows) will learn to pull up the string or thread by a series of tugs, holding the loops of pulled-in thread with the feet. When this happens it can often be noted that this new behavior is by no means stereotyped but that there are a number of variations in the pulling-up strategies so that the same overall action of securing the food is seldom accomplished in precisely the same way on different occasions. This is the kind of behavior that has often been described as "Insightful."

How far down our evolutionary origin can we recognize some evidence for conscious purpose? If all mammals exhibit conscious purpose, its evolutionary origin can be as early as 200 million years before the present (BP) (Jerison, 1990).

Then comes the question about the reptilian origin of mammals (Jerison, 1990; Ulinski, 1990). However, there seems to be no good evidence that reptiles experience consciousness and hence participate in conscious purposes. Thorpe (1974) reports on the behavior of amphibia and reptiles, but does not mention conscious purpose. All actions can be regarded as instinctive and this has to be assumed also for still-lower vertebrates, the fish. So conscious purpose came into the mindless world of biological evolution with the origin of mammals. Animals would not experience gleams of consciousness until the mammalian cerebral cortex with its microsite neuronal structures (fig. 3, 4) had evolved with the propensity for relating to another world than the matter-energy world. So conscious purpose has entered the hitherto mindless world.

In order to discuss further the influence of conscious purpose on the supplementary motor area (fig. 2B) it is necessary to introduce the dualist diagram of fig. 6. The whole world of conscious experiences or mind is labeled World 2 and is sharply separated from the brain in the materialist

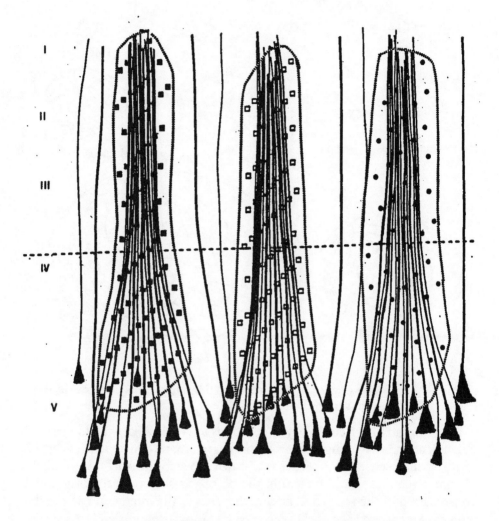

Figure 4.   Drawings of three dendrons showing manner in which the apical dendrites of large and medium pyramidal cells bunch together in lamina IV and more superficially, so forming a neural unit. A small proportion of apical dendrites does not join the bunches. The apical dendrites are shown terminating in lamina I. This termination is in tufts that are not shown. The other feature of the diagram is the superposition on each neural unit or dendron, of a mental unit or psychon, that has a characteristic marking (solid squares, open squares, solid circles). Each dendron is linked with a psychon giving its own characteristic unitary experience.

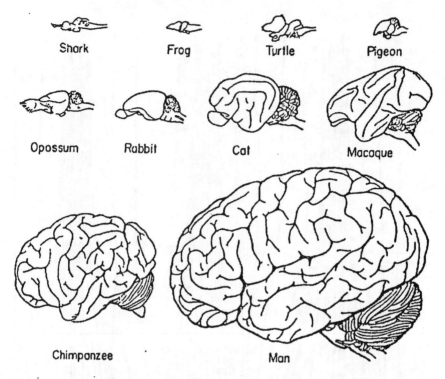

Shark   Frog   Turtle   Pigeon

Opossum   Rabbit   Cat   Macaque

Chimpanzee   Man

Figure 5. **Brains of vertebrates drawn on the same scale (Courtesy of Prof. Jan Jansen, Sr.).**

World 1 by an interface. All psychon actions in World 2 have double arrows. Neural actions have single arrows. For diagrammatic convenience World 2 with its outer sense and inner sense is drawn above the liaison brain in World 1, but actually it would be within the cortex, as shown by the origin and termination of the reciprocal arrows that signify the interaction across the interface between the two Worlds. A conscious purpose is an intention to cause some action, and so in fig. 6 it is diagrammed as double arrows from conscious intention in Inner Sense to dendrons of the SMA. The excitation of the SMA, as illustrated in fig. 2B, activates the appropriate area of the motor cortex as seen in fig. 1 and in fig. 2A for bringing about conscious purpose. The diagram of fig. 6 would obtain also for the conscious purpose of mammals. The postulated conscious purpose of birds (Thorpe, 1978) would require illustration on a bird cerebral cortex, but there is as yet no information about any psychondendron organization in the bird brain.

Much of human conscious purpose is in carrying out practical actions, which have no discernible moral implication. An example is the motor sequence test illustrated in fig. 2A, B. Much of our life is lived in that ordi-

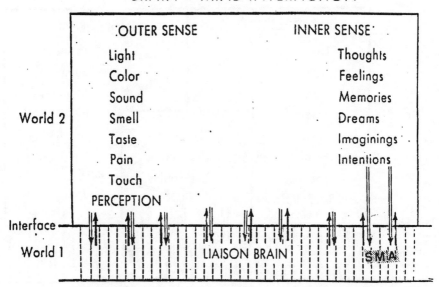

Figure 6.   Information-flow diagram for brain-mind interactions for non-human mammalian brain. The two compnents of World 2, Outer Sense and Inner Sense, are diagrammed with communications shown by arrows to the Liaison Brain in World 1. It will be noted that mammals are given a World 2 corresponding to their consciousness. Neural actions are shown by solid arrows. Mental actions by psychons are shown by arrows with double stems. Note psychon arrows from intention to the supplementary motor area.

nary level, in our work and in most of our household responsibilities. It is the world of practical affairs. Such human conscious purposes are not fundamentally different from nonhuman conscious purposes and both are diagrammed in fig. 6.

Such conscious actions can be carried out with great precision. The question arises: How can the mental intentions in fig. 6 effectively bring about skilled purposive movements? The answer is that our skills in conscious purposes are the consequence of incessant practice. It starts with a baby a few months old practicing hand movements incessantly, that are visually observed and progressively perfected. So in carrying out a conscious purpose the mental intention is directed to the precise neurones of the SMA that project to the motor cortex appropriate for that movement. All conscious purposes are brought about as a consequence of motor learning, both

BRAIN⇌MIND INTERACTION

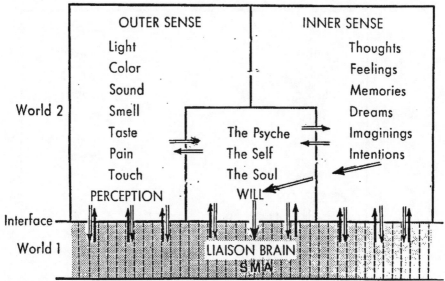

Figure 7. Information-flow diagram for mind-brain interaction in the human brain. The same conventions as in fig. 6. The Psyche, Self, or Soul are diagrammed with their communications shown by psychon arrows. Note the psychon arrows from Intention to Will and then to the SMA of the Liaison brain.

for humans and other mammals. There is no doubt that much of this motor learning is in the brain, the cerebral cortex, and the cerebellum. However, learned skills are also known in the mind, else our intentions in fig, 6 would be "blind" and conscious purpose would fail.

IV. Self-Conscious Purpose

At this state I have to introduce an important caveat. The hypothesis for the origin of consciousness in Darwinian evolution would not account for the highest levels of consciousness in *Homo sapiens*, which are the unique experiences of human selves. These are illustrated diagrammatically as the central World 2 structure in fig. 7. In fig. 7 there is a central core of conscious experience that is labeled the psyche, the self, or the soul. These names relate to the same entity, which may be discussed in psychology, in philosophy, and in theology.

There are two primal certainties: first, that one exists as a unique self-conscious being; second, that the external world exists, including one's body and brain. The uniqueness of our experienced self has not been given an

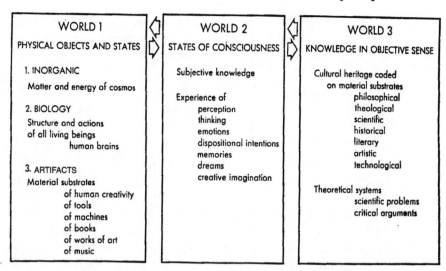

Figure 8. Tabular representation of the three worlds that comprise all existents and all experiences as defined by Popper and Eccles (1977).

acceptable materialist explanation (Eccles, 1989, p. 237). The proposed genetic uniqueness leads to a fantastically impossible genetic lottery and cannot account even for the uniqueness of identical-twin selves. The proposed environmental differentiations do not determine one's uniqueness, but merely modify its ontogenetic expression. Since materialist solutions fail to account for our experienced uniqueness, I have proposed (Eccles, 1989, p. 237) that it is necessary to postulate a supernatural creation for each human self, which is a mystery beyond science. In self-conscious purpose we as selves relate to the world, including other selves.

The mirror-recognition test detects the most primitive level of self-recognition. Human babies can first do this at about 18 months (Amsterdam, 1972). Gallup (1977) reported mirror recognition by a chimpanzee after training, but it was not possible even with any other nonhuman primates. By contrast, as a baby matures into childhood, there is an overwhelming development of selfhood. Thus hominid evolution eventually led to *Homo sapiens* with indubitable self-recognition and so with self-conscious purpose. The reality has been vividly expressed by the great evolutionist, Dobzhansky, (1967) for the emergence of human self-consciousness or self-awareness as he calls it:

> Self-awareness is, then, one of the fundamental, possibly the most fundamental, characteristic of the human species. This characteristic is an evolutionary novelty; the biological species from which mankind has descended

had only rudiments of self-awareness, or perhaps lacked it altogether. Self-awareness, has, however, brought in its train somber companions—fear, anxiety and death awareness. . . . Man is burdened by death-awareness. A being who knows that he will die arose from ancestors who did not know.

Self-conscious purpose in hominid evolution can be identified at a primitive stage in the ceremonial burial customs that were carried out by Neanderthal man about 80,000 YBP.

From that primitive beginning cultural evolution has eventually given *Homo sapiens* the whole of human culture and civilization that is very inadequately listed in fig. 8 as the World 3 of Popper. It gives our cultural heritage and should prescribe the moral basis for our self-conscious purposes throughout our life as civilized beings. Each human person is dependent on its educational opportunities for being able to participate in the richness of World 3. Linguistic and moral education are essential for all, as also are selections from the other World 3 disciplines. Our present societies throughout the whole world are in grave danger because of the deficiencies in basic education. So life is often lived without meaning or purpose.

Self-conscious purpose must be considered with reference to the diagram of fig. 7 and the problem of free will. In fig. 6 the intention to act is seen as double arrows to project directly to the SMA (fig. 2B) and thence to the motor cortex (fig. 2A). It is the pathway for *conscious purpose* as described in section 3. A quite different situation is shown in fig. 7 for *self-conscious purpose*. It differs from fig. 6 because there is a central core of Self and Will. Will is operative on any voluntary movement in which the moral consequences are evaluated by the self.

Thus the "Willed" self-conscious purpose entails a moral responsibility. In order to illustrate this diagrammatically, the double arrows from "intentions" in fig. 7 are drawn through Will to the Liaison Brain (SMA) and not directly, as would be the case for conscious purposes that are devoid of moral considerations, which is always the case for nonhuman mammals and very often also with humans (fig. 6). Moral responsibility is not for nonhuman animals. Although they may carry out voluntary movements (fig. 6), they do not "will" them, which means to evaluate their consequences for good or ill. This is an essential feature of self-conscious purpose, as is illustrated diagrammatically in fig. 7 by the double arrows that signify an action by psychon communication.

It should be recognized that there is superb design of the dendrons (figs. 3A, B; 4) for their receptive function both neuronal and psychic. It must be accepted that all mammals are conscious beings with some purposive control of their actions, as illustrated in fig. 6. The human situation is a further development with the coming of self-consciousness and self-conscious purpose in which it can be conjectured that psychons may exist apart from dendrons in a unique psychon world, which is the world of the self, and which is shown centrally in fig. 7. There are great unknowns in this conjectured world of psychons. Their very nature is to give experiences, and we can only indicate their existence diagrammatically by the site of their dendron interaction, which is shown as an ensheathing in fig. 4.

The transmission of psychon to psychon could explain the unity of our perceptions and of the inner world of our mind that we continually experience from moment to moment—that is, for all of the World 2 experiences illustrated in fig. 7 above the interface and listed in fig. 8.

Hitherto it has been beyond explanation by any mind-brain theory that multifarious neural events in our cerebral cortex can from moment to moment give us global mental experiences that have a unitary character such as in landscape vision. We feel central to our experiential world (World 2). It raises a fundamental question. Are the intimate experiences of the self also composed of unitary psychons in the same manner as for perceptual and other experiences (fig. 4)? We have conjectured above that there may be a category of organized psychons not linked to dendrons, but only with other psychons forming a great psychon world apart from the brain, as is indicated in the central locus of fig. 7, the psyche, self, or soul. The uniqueness of the experienced self has led to the hypothesis of its supernatural creation. From this central location in fig. 7 it could control the cerebral cortex by self-conscious purpose that acts by psychon communication as diagrammed by the double arrows in fig. 7.

With self-conscious purpose a person has a great challenge in choosing what life to live. On the one hand one can choose to live dedicated to the highest values, truth, love, and beauty, with gratitude for the divine gift of life with its wonderful opportunities of participating in human culture. One can do this in accord with opportunities. For example, one of the highest achievements is to create a human family living in a loving relationship. I was brought up religiously under such wonderful conditions, for which I can be eternally grateful. There are great opportunities in a life dedicated to education or science or art or to the care of the sick. Always one should try to be in a loving relationship with one's associates. We are all fellow beings mysteriously living on this wonderful spaceship planet Earth that we should cherish devotedly, but not worship.

Unfortunately in this very imperfect world the great virtues also are matched by great evils. These are also brought about by self-conscious purposes (fig. 7). I do no more than list some of these well-known evils that afflict our society and that are based on hate: aggression at all levels, lying, cheating, torturing, killing, child abuse, selfishness, pride, the cult of ugliness.

What self-conscious purposes can be developed to counteract evil? It is urgently necessary to have a renaissance in religion together with a transcendent value system, else we can be moving into a future with a moral vacuum. Evil will triumph over good as can be seen in the tremendous drug degradation. The future could then be for human persons existing with meaningless, selfish pleasures and vices and an ultimate fate of misery and suffering.

V. Epilogue

Sherrington (1940) in his great book *Man on His Nature* develops a theme leading up to purpose. Mother Nature, as exhibited in biological evolution, apostrophizes man:

> You are my child. Do not expect me to love you. How can I love—I who am blind necessity? I cannot love, neither can I hate. But now that I have brought forth you and your kind, remember you are a new world unto yourselves, a world which contains in virtue of you, love and hate, and reason and madness, the moral and immoral, and good and evil. It is for you to love where love can be felt. That is, to love one another.
> Bethink you too that perhaps in knowing me you do but know the instrument of a Purpose, the tool of a Hand too large for your sight as now to compass. Try then to teach your sight to grow.

The aim of this article is to "teach" in that manner in relation to an inquiry into purpose. It has been treated in an evolutionary manner. Biological evolution gives place to cultural evolution with the creation and development of values. So we have purpose at four levels with at the end a plea for a renaissance in religion.

There are two fundamental religious concepts. One is God the Creator of the cosmos with its fundamental laws, beginning with the exquisite quantitative design of the so-called Big Bang and its aftermath—the Transcendent God in which Einstein believed. The other is the Immanent God to whom we owe existence. In some mysterious way, God is the Creator of all the living forms in the evolutionary process, and particularly in hominid evolution of human persons, each with the conscious selfhood of an immortal soul. On this transcendent vision we have to build our lives with self-conscious purpose.

9

Daniel H. Osmond

A Physiologist Looks at Purpose and Meaning in Life

Darwinism in the minds of many, eliminated purpose in any form and implied that animal evolution, including that of man, was the result of blind chance.[1]

Now the history of scientific advances has shown us clearly that any appeal to Divine Purpose, or any supernatural agency, to explain any phenomenon, is in fact only a concealed confession of ignorance, and a bar to genuine research.[2]

The universe troubles me, and much less can I think that this clock exists and should have no clockmaker.[3]

The great majority of the most famous developers of the mechanistic world model—Newton, Boyle, Faraday, Maxwell, Compton, Eddington come to mind—were believers in God. Their belief gave them all the greater confidence in the worthwhileness of studying nature.[4]

Human souls are in this view the purpose and end of the whole story, so far as the world is concerned—not merely the servants of the species and not even mere means to some other mundane end.[5]

The Lord is my shepherd, I shall not be in want. He makes me lie down in green pastures, he leads me beside quiet waters, he restores my soul. He guides me in paths of righteousness for his own name's sake. . . . Surely goodness and love will follow me all the days of my life, and I will dwell in the house of the Lord forever.[6]

Introduction

The topic of "purpose" is not within my areas of expertise in a formal, academic sense, but of great relevance to my life as a working scientist who also believes in God. Like millions of fellow Christians, I *experience* the love and guidance of the Good Shepherd in my life whose Spirit infuses it with purpose, meaning, and hope. I believe such religious experience to be valid, not hallucinatory, and therefore have a keen interest in examining how it can be integrated with scientific experience. I believe in the God of the Judeo-Christian Scriptures who created all things and who reveals His purposeful acts in human history, most fully in the life, death, and resurrection of the historic Jesus who came in the fullness of time to redeem those who accept Him.

There is an enormous body of historical, textual, legal, and experiential evidence to substantiate such belief, which is too lightly set aside by many scientists who have never examined it or tried to reconcile it with their scientific perspective on life.

One reason for such neglect is that the evidence is not in the category of "test-tube" data, so much beloved of laboratory experimentalists. But it is manifestly foolish and irresponsible to disregard other categories of evidence that are appropriate to the experience of faith. Here, as in the realms of history, literature, law, and personal and interpersonal relationships, proofs that are not of the test-tube variety are common currency, and, indeed, more appropriate. We all rely on such evidence for areas of our personal and collective lives that lie outside the scientific laboratory.

As an active researcher and educator in physiology who is accustomed to handling "test-tube" evidence, I wish to discuss my view of purpose, which, I believe, is not incompatible with the scientific side of my life. I have long since rejected the view that it is necessary to be an atheist or agnostic in order to be a respectable scientist or that it is more scientific to believe in a world of CHANCE than in a world of DIVINE PURPOSE. I gratefully acknowledge the encouragement and insights provided by my four collaborators.†

Purpose: What Is It?

Purpose has to do with ends, "that for the sake of which a thing (person) exists." One can ask about the purpose of the universe, or of the world, of animate beings generally, or of humans specifically. And, in relation to humans, several levels of purpose can be identified, ranging from the basic requirements for physical survival and gratification to the ultimate and most searching intellectual and spiritual issues of life. Sooner or later, thoughtful people ask, "For what sake (purpose) do I exist?" They do so when crises confront them, if at no other time, but, of course, the purpose of one's life should no more be contemplated only in times of crisis, than the purpose of one's automobile should be pondered only in times of traffic accidents.

Levels of Purpose and Changes in Purpose

At the most primal level, human purpose can be defined as individual and group survival and perpetuation of the race. In order to survive, one must eat, drink, seek shelter, companionship, etc. Beyond that are various other needs, desires and ambitions such as enjoying a good career, or having fun, or doing good science, or working for the benefit of humankind, or helping to fulfill God's purpose on earth. Or, one might aspire to various combinations of these, and other options as diverse as the people who make such statements and the circumstances in which they make them. Purpose can range in scope from a primal fight for survival to the highest levels of intellectual and spiritual aspiration and attainment. And it can change with the circumstances of life, which implies that some people may unwisely make do with an inadequate purpose at one stage of their lives only to discover that they need something more satisfying later on. It is worth discovering "true purpose" for the whole of our lives, if such a thing exists.

Thus, an ebullient teenager, feeling "on top of the world," may look at purpose differently before and after suffering a crippling accident, as might a business tycoon before and after losing his fortune, or his loved ones. Many so-called atheists, or agnostics, change their minds when facing danger or death, as expressed by the old adage, "there are no atheists in foxholes," or, if you will, "there are no purposeless people in foxholes." History demonstrates that there have been marked changes in the prevailing climate of opinion concerning divine Purpose (henceforth designated Purpose). Its present rejection by many scientists should be viewed against a backdrop of millennia of previous acceptance and in relation to future possibilities in a blind world where millions of people, including thousands of erudite scientists, have first embraced atheistic Marxism and then abandoned it within an interval of seventy-five years.

One Purpose has lasted for millennia. It is proudly embraced by countless well-informed people whose lives are motivated for good by it. There are good reasons for believing in such Purpose, better reasons, I believe, than the reasons for believing in "blind chance," which, after all, is the main alternative.

Purpose: Intellectual and Theological Imperatives

Belief in Purpose cannot simply be a matter of "head knowledge," though it surely must have a firm intellectual foundation. Nor is it a matter of wishful thinking or "blind faith." Rather, for me, it is rooted in a vital experience of having been reconciled to a God who is very real and active in working out His Purpose on earth.[7] This experience is not merely subjective, but conforms with the tenets, provisions, and imperatives of the historic Christian faith: God has made known to those who are His "the mystery of His will according to His good pleasure which He Purposed in Jesus Christ." And, "We are God's workmanship, created in Christ Jesus to do good works, which God prepared in advance for us to do."[8]

Our knowledge of God's Purposes is limited, but one thing is abundantly clear from the Judeo-Christian Scriptures and is authenticated by the best understanding of the historic Christian Church: God calls His people to Purposeful involvement in the world. Claiming divine authority, Jesus Christ commissioned His disciples to be engaged with Him wholeheartedly in praying for, and working out divine Purpose, "Your kingdom come, your will be done on earth as it is in heaven,"[9] and "Go and make disciples of all nations."[10] The coming of Jesus Christ has unavoidably divided humankind into those who believe in His Lordship and Purpose, and those who do not. I write this as a believer, not only because I believe, but also because, having tried to write with "studious objectivity," I found that I could not do it and had to drop the mask. For all of us, there may be time, but not much room, between belief and unbelief. The issue is whether belief is reasonable and whether Purpose is real and vital and motivates us to do good.

Purpose: Beliefs and Actions

Throughout Judeo-Christian history, strong belief in biblically inspired Purpose has translated into life-changing action. Such actions have been an outflow and manifestation of belief, not incidental to it. The value of the beliefs has been tested by the quantity and quality of actions they have produced and by their perserverence in the face of obstacles. It is one thing to do good things now and again: it is something else to *initiate* good things and to keep on doing them against the tide of popular opinion. Men and women of Purpose have a proud record in terms of initiating and maintaining good works in the face of apathy, ridicule, and opposition. Having proved their worth and gained popularity, some of these works have eventually been copied or supported by others, but the pioneering was done by those who knew Purpose clearly and strongly enough to shed blood for it. There is a strong connection between knowing Purpose, glimpsing a vision of the "celestial city" and working hard to build a better world in the here and now.

Over the years, much has been made of the failures and misdeeds in the so-called Christian West and too little of the vast amount of good that has been done, and continues to be done, by those who espouse Purpose. Cynics disregard the obvious fact that not all nominal Christians in the West understand the faith, or adhere to its precepts, and that many reject it altogether. But for all its foibles, the West has achieved standards that continue to act as an irresistible magnet for millions of would-be immigrants and refugees from other countries that have not been shaped by a Christian heritage. There must be something right about the West and it became "right" over a long period of time for very good reasons. It did not just happen: countless people of Purpose made it happen.

Sir Frederick Catherwood, a former industrial adviser to the Ministry of Economic Affairs in Britain has written:

> In fact, a country like Britain owes to Christianity much more than it will now acknowledge, and a good deal of what is best in the moral code of British society has been the working out of Christian morality in practice. In particular, respect for the dignity and responsibility of the individual has been a feature of our society which stems directly from Christian teaching and has been worked out in terms of universal suffrage, universal education and individual liberty. This view of the individual must therefore be part of any Christian view of industrial society.

> The British tradition which appears to reflect the Protestant ethic most strongly is the code of the professional man. In our law, our medicine, our civil service, our armed forces, we have a tradition of professional competence, public duty, disinterested service and financial integrity which it is difficult to better anywhere else in the world. It may seem too much to claim such a close correlation between Christian faith and standards of professional conduct, but it is in the Christian and Protestant countries that these standards are most commonly found, and every Christian who is a professional man will agree that his faith and his professional standards go hand in hand.[11]

Other easily recognizable examples of Christian influence in society are the Salvation Army and many social benefit organizations in almost every major city in the West. Behind each endeavor, now taken so much for granted, stand historic figures (like General William Booth of the Salvation Army) whose clear vision of their Purpose in life sensitized them to the problems they saw, inspired them to tackle these problems, and motivated and empowered them to overcome all obstacles in pursuit of their goals. While others slumbered or turned a blind eye, the beliefs and actions of these Purposeful people were joined powerfully together to achieve worthwhile ends for the benefit of humankind.

It has been well said that when Lord Shaftesbury (1801-85), the great social-industrial reformer of nineteenth-century Britain, prayed:

> . . . your kingdom come . . . he was quoting no idle petition but rather was he renewing his covenant with God, to strive afresh for justice in human relationships, for peace and good will among men. . . . In contrast with Marx's materialistic and inexorable laws of economics, Shaftesbury's whole philosophy of life was spiritual, and in his religion he found his inspiration for social endeavors . . . to enthrone the spirit and ethnic of the Man of Galilee in all human relationships—personal, social, national and international. . . . Indeed, the fact confronts us on every hand that Shaftesbury's work can never be understood apart from his faith. . . . Therefore, if we would breathe the atmosphere in which his lifework was accomplished, we must needs have patience first to study the faith that dominated his career . . . (giving him) his rightful place as the British Abraham Lincoln—the Emancipator of Industrial England.[12]

In 1877, British prime minister Disraeli declared: "The name of Lord Shaftesbury will descend to posterity as the one who, in his generation, worked more than any other individual to elevate the condition and to raise the character of his countrymen." [13]

The range of social conditions Shaftesbury addressed in Britain is truly staggering, and included the treatment of "lunatics," problems of health and sanitation, lodging houses, popular education, the "Ragged Schools" and the nation's outcasts, industrial slavery in the collieries, opium and liquor traffic, and the working conditions of chimney sweeps, workers in factories, agriculture, brickyards, etc. He also worked tirelessly for the abolition of slavery in America and for better working conditions for the masses in India, which, at that time, were truly appalling.

To quote Bishop Stephen Neill:

> It is necessary to insist a little on the practical contribution of Christian idealism to the well-being of men, since in modern times history is one of the great instruments of propaganda, and a veil of mythological distortion has been spread over all the events of the day before yesterday.

> When Elizabeth Fry began her great work for the reform of the prisons, visitors to Newgate (prison) were astonished to see the rabble of women prisoners sitting quiet and spellbound as Mrs. Fry read to them from the Bible in her wonderful voice. . . . She was, in fact, a timid, shrinking woman

... but driven to carry out her incomparable work only by the compelling power of the love of Christ.

One of the great spheres in which the great service rendered by the Church is today most readily forgotten or denied is education. The first general Education Act for England was passed only in 1870. Up till that date, education had been wholly in the hands of voluntary bodies, among which the Churches were vastly the most considerable.[14]

Be they great men and women, or not, past or present, Christians cannot escape the biblical precept that all Christians are called to Purpose.[7] Christians without a sense of Purpose are a contradiction in terms because our identity and partnership with the God of Purpose harnesses us, individually and collectively, to fulfill His Purpose through us in a needy world that cries out for the saving, healing and motivating love, justice, and power of God. Every age, in every place, in every sphere of human endeavor needs, and produces, men and women of Purpose, like Lord Shaftesbury and Elizabeth Fry. They are the salt of the earth.

Purpose: An Ongoing Discovery

The axiom that all Christians can, and should, experience and implement Purpose in their lives does not exempt them from the hard work of discovering the full dimensions of that Purpose on a daily basis. It is one thing to know that we are inheritors of Purpose: it is another matter to know exactly what the daily specifics of it might be. Frequently, the outworkings of Purpose are recognized more clearly in hindsight, but whether it be as a flashing light to the rampaging Saul of Tarsus on the road to Damascus[15] or as a gentle whisper to the discouraged prophet Elijah on Mount Horeb,[16] a sense of Purpose can, and must, be the experience of those who belong to God.

Rejection of Purpose: Living in Two Solitudes

The experience of Purpose in one's personal or communal life of faith clashes sharply with its systematic exclusion, or rejection, in the scientific environment. I can recall no significant, explicit discussion of Purpose in my thirty years as a science student and faculty member at two major universities. The climate of opinion is indifferent, if not strongly opposed, to it. As Mascall acknowledges in his discourse on Christian Theology and Natural Science: "There is, at any rate, a prima facie antagonism between the outlook and discoveries of science on the one hand and the outlook and dogmas of orthodox religion on the other." [17]

While writing this chapter, I tested the waters again by bringing up the subject in the faculty lounge, during successive coffee breaks. Blank expressions and no takers!

Thus, Christian scientists often find themselves straddling two solitudes: a world espousing faith and Purpose that they share with fellow Christians who are mostly nonscientists, and a world of science from which such faith and Purpose is excluded. In the immediate sense it is done by neglect, or in the name of scientific objectivity, but, underlying that is a widespread secularism that rejects ultimate Purpose and cherishes only temporal, pragmatic, scientific goals.

But the solitudes need not continue to exist and bridges have already been built by many individuals and organizations. Among these are the American Scientific Affiliation,[18] its sister organization, the Canadian Scientific and Christian Affiliation, and Christians in Science, and the Victoria Institute in Britain. All testify to the fact that good scientists can be Christians without compartmentalizing their faith, or their science, and that solid answers exist in response to genuine questions about the validity of faith and Purpose. Unfortunately, too many are unaware of such bridges.

Purpose: The Point of Contention in Debates on Science/Faith?

Between the solitudes of "Purpose" and "no Purpose," periods of uneasy truce are broken by outbursts of intense debate, such as those concerning creationism/evolutionism, behaviorism, or sociobiology. From time to time, there are high-profile legal conflicts, usually involving school textbooks or curricula. The best known of these is undoubtedly the "Monkey Trial" of 1925, in which a young Tennessee teacher, John Scopes, was brought to court for teaching evolutionary ideas in high school, but there have been many, more recent, lower profile equivalents, especially in North America.

It would be fair to say that, whatever the immediate, contributory causes for such debates or legal conflicts might be, at any given time, the fundamental philosophical contention is the same: acceptance or rejection of a worldview that accepts a God of Purpose, who created the world for a Purpose, which God's people knowingly (and others unknowingly) are to help fulfill in every age and every arena of life, including scientific endeavor. Whether stated, or not, this point is implicitly present.

Relationship of Causality, Purpose, and Meaning

The terms causality, purpose, and meaning are used in somewhat overlapping fashion in the literature, probably because, in practical terms, causation implies purpose and the purpose behind that which has been caused imbues it with meaning. Discovery of Purpose in the creative activity of God can become the source of Meaning in life, defined in terms of "the sense conveyed, or intended, by something that is said or done," [19] as to the Purpose of my life.

In Judeo-Christian terms, creation bespeaks causation: God caused the world to be, by whatever mechanisms He chose. The fact that such mechanisms can be described by scientists can no more deny creatorship than a verbal description of a great painting by an art critic can deny the role of the unseen painter who painted it.

Few people have difficulties with the primal levels of purpose, i.e., that humans live to eat, drink, enjoy, work, serve, create, and procreate. The difficulties arise at higher levels of consideration, especially spiritual levels, involving issues such as, "Did God create this world with a Purpose in which humans can also participate?" Or, more simply, "Does God have a Purpose for my life that I can know?" In essence, if God caused our world to come into being for a Purpose, which is related to His creatorship and ongoing activity in this world, including human life, then the discovery, pursuit, and accomplishment of this Purpose in each persons' life is what infuses it with ultimate Meaning.

Dr. Victor Frankl on Purpose and Meaning

Not infrequently, the existence of suffering, injustice, hunger, disease, and death is adduced as an argument against Purpose. A good God of Purpose would not allow such things to happen, therefore, either He does not exist or He is not good. This complex subject has been dealt with by many writers, including C. S. Lewis.[20] Suffice to say here that much of the evil in the world is directly attributable to human beings of free will, who choose to do evil against the expressed will of God. Such evil cannot be blamed on God, or used properly as an argument against Purpose.

The point made here is that purpose and meaning, as well as Purpose and Meaning, are experienced not only when life is good but also when it is bad. The psychiatrist Victor Frankl experienced and observed this while in the depths of horrible deprivation and suffering. Frankl writes: "Man's search for meaning is the primary motivation in his life and not a 'secondary rationalization' of instinctual drives. . . . That is why I speak of a *will* to meaning."[21] ". . . Our contention is that there is a meaning of life—a meaning, that is, for which man has been in search all along—and also that man has the freedom to embark on the fulfillment of this meaning." [22]

Frankl's view of a fundamental human need for meaning and an inherent ability to seek for it and achieve it (by act of the will), if taken seriously, would further underscore the view that Purpose is not merely an interesting philosophic topic but "a pearl of great value," which, when discovered by a discerning merchant (to use a New Testament parable) will cause him to sell everything that he has to raise the money required to buy it.[23]

Frankl questions authorities who contend that meanings and values are "nothing but defense mechanisms, reaction formations and sublimations." He writes: "I would not be willing to live merely for the sake of my defense mechanisms, nor would I be ready to die merely for the sake of my reaction formations. Man however, is able to live and even to die for the sake of his ideals and values!" [21]

Frankl cites a French opinion poll demonstrating that 89 percent believe humans need "something" for the sake of which to live. Moreover, 61 percent concede that there is something, or someone, in their own lives for whose sake they were ready to die. Frankl also cites a survey of 7,948 students at 48 American colleges, conducted by social scientists from Johns Hopkins University of whom 78 percent say their goal is "finding a purpose and meaning to my life."

The fact that humans claim to experience a profound spiritual Purpose in life, even in concentration camps, suggests that attainment of such Purposefulness is possible in the depths of life, and, indeed, that its attainment makes the most difficult circumstances more bearable. No one need give up on Purpose if Frankl, from his experience of unspeakable horror, can write movingly of "a spiritual freedom—which cannot be taken away—that makes life meaningful and purposeful." [24] In a context of utter hopelessness he affirms Nietzsche's words: "He who has a *why* to live for can bear with almost any *how*." [25]

And, about the days immediately after his liberation from the jaws of death, once again hearing the joyous song of the larks in the sky, Frankl writes: "I stopped, looked around, and up to the sky—and then I went down on my knees. At that moment there was very little I knew of myself or of the world— I had but one sentence in mind—always the same: 'I called to the Lord from my narrow prison and He answered me in the freedom of space.' " [26]

Even if all purpose and meaning in Frankl's context of observation does not refer to ultimate Purpose or Meaning in a spiritual sense, it would be rash for any cynic to underestimate the spiritual tone of Frankl's own personal experience or to deny the supreme value of such experience in all circumstances of life—good or evil.

Support for Frankl on Purpose and Meaning

Another psychiatrist, Carl Jung has written: "During the past thirty years . . . among all my patients in the second half of life—i.e. over thirty-five—

there has not been one whose problem in the last resort was not that of finding a religious outlook on life. It is safe to say that every one of them fell ill because he had lost that which the living religions of every age has given their followers, and none of them has been really healed who did not regain his religious outlook."[27]

Norman Giesler has used a somewhat physiological argument to make an important philosophical point. He points out that to argue against purpose is to imply that there is a strong human need for something that does not exist—a rather unphysiological concept—and which automatically condemns humans to a perennial state of deprivation.

Giesler summarizes several telling expressions of man's need for the transcendent:

> Sartre was not alone in expressing man's need for God . . . . Samuel Beckett's *Waiting for Godot* reflects a craving of contemporary man to hear from God. . . . The novels of Franz Kafka express man's unsuccessful attempts to be in communication with some meaningful cosmic otherness beyond oneself. . . . Walter Kaufmann points to, "Man being the ape that wants to be god. . . . Religion is rooted in man's aspiration to transcend himself . . . whether he worships idols or strives to perfect himself, man is the God-intoxicated ape. . . . Even Nietzsche found life unbearable without God and finally went mad. . . . Speaking of Dante and Spinoza, he wrote, "Of course, their way of thinking compared to mine, was one which made solitude bearable; and in the end, for all those who somehow still had a 'God' for company. . . . My life now consists in the wish that it might be otherwise with all things that I comprehend, and that somebody might take my truths appear incredible to me. . . ." In short, Nietzsche found his atheism unbearable. Sartre, too, complained of the seeming unlivability of his position, declaring that, "atheism is a cruel and long-range affair."[28]

> The experience of these atheists is reminiscent of the skepticism and agnosticism of Hume and Kant. Hume confessed that when he could no longer bear his own skeptical thoughts he would leave them for a game of backgammon. Schopenhauer found his release in art. Immanuel Kant, after he had allegedly demonstrated the impossibility of arriving at God rationally, found it practically necessary to postulate a God to make sense out of his moral life."[28]

> Basic human expectations and experience lead men to believe that if men need water, then there is water somewhere. If men need food, then there is food to be found. And even though some men die of thirst and hunger, history has demonstrated that water and food do exist to fulfill man's needs. . . . Some men may *think* that there are real but unfulfillable needs, but few men (if any) will really *believe* it, and no man can consistently *live* it. We may conclude therefore, that what men really need really exists . . . that there really is a God or Transcendent. For believers and unbelievers . . .

there is a sense of contingency and dependence, that need for transcendence within man that cries out for fulfillment. . . . To believe otherwise would conflict with both human expectations and human experience. . . . The fulfillment of the need for God in some men indicates that an experience with this God is actually achievable.[29]

Judeo-Christian Perspective on Purpose and Meaning

The Judeo-Christian Scriptures are so impregnated with this perspective that almost no part of them can be said to exclude it. Be it the creation account in Genesis, the lives of the early patriarchs, the delivery of Israel from Egypt, the ebb and flow of political powers on the national or international scene, the coming of the Messiah in the fullness of time, or the calling of the church to fulfill God's will "on earth as it is in heaven"—all deal with the outworkings of God's Purpose on earth. Nothing is without Purpose, not even, it would seem, the painful days of Israel's slavery in Egypt,[30] or her agonies in the Babylonian Exile.[31]

Israel's slavery in Egypt was a prelude to her redemption from Egypt, which has been celebrated ever since in the Feast of the Passover. Concerning this, Rabbi W. Gunther Plaut has written:

> It is precisely the aspect of redemption that is a major skein in both religions (Judaism and Christianity). Although both have grown apart in their observance, redemption—the possibility of human transcendence—remains the common theme. It has spoken powerfully in the past and does not cease to address us in an age in which human prowess has reached a new peak of exaltation. . . . God is the motive power in history. . . . He stands over and against creation, including humankind.[32]

Christopher Dawson also comments on a grand panoramic scale, as follows:

> All the great religions of the world agree in expressing this truth—that there is an eternal reality beyond the flux of temporal and natural things which is at once the ground of being and the basis of rationality. The Christian faith goes much further than this. It, and it alone, shows how this higher reality has entered into human history and changed its course. It shows how a seed of new life was implanted in humanity by setting apart of a particular people as the channel of revelation which found its fulfillment in the Incarnation of the Divine Word in a particular person at a particular moment of history. It shows how this new life was communicated to a spiritual society which became the organ of divine action in history, so that the human race may be progressively spiritualized and raised to a higher spiritual plane.[33]

Impact of Christian Purpose upon Western Civilization

Few unbelieving scientists today seem to appreciate the heritage they enjoy in the West because of its Judeo-Christian heritage. As Dawson puts it:

> The Greeks and the Romans had been prepared for Christianity by centuries of ethical teaching and discussion. Plato and Aristotle, Zeno and Epictetus and Marcus Aurelius had familiarized men with the ideas of man's spiritual nature, the immortality of the soul, divine providence and human responsibility. But the barbarians knew none of this. Their moral ideals were still derived from the primitive heroic ethics of tribal society: virtue was military valor and loyalty, justice was revenge, religion was an instinctive veneration of the dark forces that manifest themselves in the life of the earth and the fates of men and peoples. Thus, the main effort of the Church had to be directed towards moral education, to the establishment of a new order resting on a faith in divine providence and on the spiritual and moral responsibility of the human soul towards God. . . . The Latin Grammar followed the Gospels into the forests of the North and the remote islands of the western ocean. This new Latin ecclesiastical culture found its center in the monasteries which almost from the beginning were schools of Christian learning as well as schools of the Christian way of life. . . . Christianity was not an archaic survival of a dead culture but a vital process which was capable of giving birth to new forms of culture. And this process extended far beyond the limits of formal education into the underlying stratum of native barbarian society where it gave birth to a new art and a new vernacular of Christian literature.
>
> As Toynbee himself has shown, Western civilization is inseparable from Christian civilization, and the latter is the more fundamental and intelligible unit. . . . But if we begin our study with Christian culture we immediately discover the sources of the moral values of Western culture, as well as the sources of the intellectual traditions that have determined the course of Western education. . . .
>
> The activity of the Western mind, which manifested itself alike in scientific and technical invention as well as in geographical discovery, was not the natural inheritance of a particular geographic type; it was the result of a long process of education which gradually changed the orientation of human thought and enlarged the possibilities of social action. In this process the vital factor was not the aggressive power of conquerors and capitalists, but the widening of the capacity of human intelligence and the development of new types of creative genius and ability.[34]

In other words, scientific development in the West cannot be divorced from the educational system of the West, whose roots lie in its Christian heritage and institutions, founded and sustained by Christian men and women of Purpose. The evolution from paganism and barbarism to enlightenment has been very rough in places and characterized by many lapses in individual and collective behavior. Certainly, the wartime experiences of Dr. Victor Frankl represent a tragedy of monumental proportions. But, a light has always illumined the darkness, and strong homing instincts toward higher moral and spiritual ground have always manifested themselves. This is seen in the Reformation and Counter-Reformation, during many other religious revivals and by the establishment and growth of numerous churches and religious movements representing the daily striving of millions of "ordinary people" who quietly aspire to higher spiritual standards and Purpose in their lives. Herbert Butterfield writes:

> One of the most fundamental of the differences between people must be the question whether they believe in God, or not; for on that depends their whole interpretation of the universe and of history—on that depends their answer to so many questions. . . . The virtues of Western Society in modern times were in reality the product of much education, tradition and discipline, they needed centuries of patient cultivation. Even without great criminality in anybody—merely by forgetting certain safeguards—we could lose the tolerance and urbanities, the respect for human life and human personality, which are in reality the late blossoms of a highly developed civilization.[35]

Roots of Science in Western Civilization

Objections to Purpose are frequently justified on scientific grounds. It is suggested that science has displaced the need for belief in Purpose as well as provided proofs against it. At an undergraduate level especially, the juxtaposition of the words *science/faith* implies antagonism and the need for a choice to be made between the two antagonists. It is one, or the other, but not both. And, since science is so manifestly valid and valuable, faith cannot be, thereby implicitly ruling out Purpose.

In reality, there is good historical evidence that modern science cannot only coexist with faith and Purpose but owes much of its early growth and impetus to it. Science grew in the West because of the prevailing Judeo-Christian perspective in the West. Far from being antagonists, science and Purposeful faith were nursed in the same bosom. Prominent incidents, such as the conflict between Galileo and the ecclesiastical establishment of his day, are not at all symptoms of fundamentally irreconcilable differences, but are rather attributable to temporary misunderstanding, political pressures, and other complications (see below). Thus, Hooykaas writes: "One has to recognize as a simple fact that 'classical modern science' arose only in the western part of Europe in the sixteenth and seventeenth centuries . . . metaphorically speaking. Whereas the bodily ingredients of science may have been Greek, its vitamins and hormones were biblical." [36]

And Coulson, quoting the historian Sprat in a discussion of Christian influence on the Royal Society of Britain, founded in 1646, writes: "I do here in the beginning most seriously declare that if this design (of the Royal Society) should in the least diminish the reverence that is due to the doctrine of Jesus Christ, it were so far from deserving protection that it ought to be abhorred by all the political and prudent, as well as by the devout part of Christiandom." [37]

Coulson further states: "Practically all our older schools (in Britain), as well as the greater part of Oxford and Cambridge, are religious foundations . . . and, as people like Herbert Butterfield and A. N. Whitehead have shown convincingly, science grew up within a Christian tradition: and for many years it was in no sense distinct or separate." [37]

Much the same applies to the older schools and universities of many parts of Europe and North America.

Dawson continues:

> Seen from this angle, the modern progress of science and technology acquires a new meaning. The technological order which today threatens spiritual freedom and even human existence by the unlimited powers which it puts at the service of human passion and will, loses all its terrors as soon as it is subordinated to a higher principle. Technology that is freed from the domination of individual self-interest and the mass cult of power would then fall into its place as a providential instrument in the creation of a spiritual order. But this is impossible, so long as our society remains devoid of all spiritual aims and is intent only on the satisfaction of its lust for power and the satisfaction of its selfish desires. . . . The more science a culture has, the more religion it needs.[38]

Positive Contributions to Science of Judeo-Christian Theology

The Thomistic Synthesis of Christian theology with Aristotelianism contributed the beliefs that the universe is ordered and that this order is intelligible to humans. Such beliefs are essential because the arduous lifelong task of investigating nature demands the belief that the universe is comprehensible. This belief was based on a biblical understanding of a noncapricious Creator who establishes regularities in His creation: "As long as the earth endures, seedtime and harvest, cold and heat, summer and winter, day and night will never cease." [39]

As Stanley Jaki expresses it:

> Science found its only viable birth within a cultural matrix permeated by a firm conviction about the mind's ability to find in the realm of things and persons a pointer to their Creator. All great creative advances in science have been made in terms of an epistemology germane to that conviction

and whenever that epistemology was resisted with vigorous consistency, the pursuit of science invariably appears to have been deprived of its solid foundation.[40]

And again:

Great cultures, where the scientific enterprise came to a standstill, invariably failed to formulate the notion of physical law, or the law of nature. Theirs was a theology with no belief in a personal, rational, absolutely transcendent Lawgiver, or Creator. Their cosmology reflected a pantheistic and animistic view of nature caught in the treadmill of perennial, inexorable returns. The scientific quest found fertile soil only when this faith in a personal, rational Creator had truly permeated a whole culture, beginning with the centuries of the High Middle Ages. It was that faith which provided, in sufficient measure, confidence in the rationality of the universe, trust in progress, and appreciation of the quantitative method, all indispensable ingredients of the scientific quest.[41]

To be sure, many scientists today are able to do science without necessarily believing in a Purposeful Creator. But in order to do so, they must implicitly accept an ordered universe that can be known. This view they owe to their scientific forebears who believed, without giving them credit. Such scientists are able to function scientifically as though they believe in an intelligent Creator without actually doing so! Purpose lies outside their domain of scientific discourse much as the roots of a tree lie outside the trunk. In each case the latter cannot stand without the former though the former is hidden from view.

Hawthorne has pointed out that the assumption of an ordered universe is not readily deduced from Nature because scientists often make progress by the observation of *irregularities* in Nature. Scientists also assume that their senses and minds are trustworthy enough to provide them with a true picture of the universe as a result of their observations.[42] Hence the applicability of Lewis's comment that a strict materialism manages to refute itself:

A theory which explains everything else in the whole universe but which made it impossible to believe that our thinking was valid, would be utterly out of court. For that theory itself would have been reached by thinking, and if thinking is not valid, that theory would, of course, itself be demolished. It would have destroyed its own credentials. It would be an argument which proved that no argument was sound—a proof that there are no such things as proof—which is nonsense.[43]

The critical issue is that of a scientism that claims for science more than the tools of science can provide. Assumptions that are fundamental to the conduct of scientific endeavor do arise from a worldview that is shaped from beyond the laboratory, a worldview that should be recognized and respected rather than ignored or downgraded.

As Owen states it:

> Since the scientific method begins and ends with observation, science can concern itself only with that kind of reality which is observable; and the kind of reality which can be observed is physical reality. Science also aims at mathematical exactitude and therefore restricts its investigations to that kind of reality which is measurable; and the kind of reality which can be measured is quantitative. We can measure, for example, the size, but not the beauty, of a picture; we can observe the physiological aspects, but not the goodness of a human action. The quantitative principle is a limiting principle which states that as long as science is true to its method it must confine its studies to the observable and measurable aspects of reality.[44]

Malcolm Jeeves has discussed limitations of the scientific method that usually escape notice: "The popular view of science also portrays it as being based always and solely upon precise observation, so that the scientist is supposed to deal with 'pure facts,' which will then yield indubitable, objective and impersonal knowledge. But of course there are no such things as uninterpreted facts." [45]

The key is to understand how much of reality can be investigated by science and what realities lie outside its capability. Science can either give us truth about the WHOLE of reality or it gives truth (total or partial) about those realities with which it is competent to deal.[46]

Recognizing the legitimate bounds of science is essential. Just as religion should not be thrust into the scientific domain, so science (scientism) should not usurp competence outside its legitimate domain. Nor should reductionists assume too lightly that explanations at "micro" levels of organization can be extrapolated satisfactorily to "macro" levels of organization.

In speaking of "domains," MacKay reminds us that we should not think of a flat field with a fence down the middle labeled "Religion only: science keep out!" on one side of which are scientists and on the other, theologians.[47] He suggests that no part of this world of observable events lies outside the boundary of scientific study. Rather, the limitations of "domains" will show up in the restricted kinds of descriptions that the language of theology or science will allow to make of the events studied.

For instance, an electrician's language about electrical circuits and lights in a big advertising sign is quite adequate to describe the electrical aspects of it but *inadequate* to describe the message being advertised, such as, "Bongo is good for you!"

MacKay: "If you come to the advertisement prepared to describe it only in electrical terms you will see nothing but lamps and wires. If you come to it with a different state of readiness, prepared to *read* it, you will see the advertisement. . . . Once you understand the language of each description, what is there to be described in each is a matter of fact." [47]

In short, empiricism has overreacted: because it is not competent to deal with the language of Purpose, it behaves as though Purpose does not exist.

Purpose and "a Society Devoid of . . . Spiritual Aims"

If modern science grew up in Christian soil, how may one explain the widespread rejection of Christian Purpose so evident in the modern scientific era? Why are the "gurus" of modern science so entrenched and outspoken in their unbelief?

I suggest that one major explanation is historical and hinges specifically on the issue of purpose, as propounded by the ancient Greek thinkers, notably Plato and Aristotle. In essence, the tension developed because of a faulty understanding of purpose and, especially, because of its misuse at the scientific level. In addition, Greek concepts of God and the world became intertwined and Judeo-Christian concepts and entrenched in the ecclesiastical structures of the day, thereby creating dissonance in an unfortunate mix of faulty science, faulty theology, and complex ecclesiastical politics.

It cannot be emphasized enough that what was being sorted out in those early days of conflict, and continues to be sorted out today, was/is not so much the validity of historic faith/Purpose on the one hand, and the validity of science, on the other, but rather the proper domains and boundaries of each. In other words, the authority and language of theology should not intrude upon the domain of science, whose authority and language should not, in turn, usurp the domain of faith/Purpose.

To suppose that Galileo's conflict, for instance, proves that Science and Christianity are enemies locked in deadly battle, and that it is the duty of all good scientists to continue the fight, is to oversimplify to the verge of utter folly.

In order to understand this, and move closer toward the goal of correcting this unfortunate situation, it would be helpful first to review some pertinent history very briefly.

Purpose in the Writings of Plato and Aristotle

Plato and Aristotle developed ideas about God, creation, and purpose (causality) that shaped Western thought for the best part of two millennia. Their immense influence is, on the one hand, proof of their greatness, and on the other, the source of the problem. It is worth examining the essence of their thoughts in order to appreciate their incompatibility with the historic Christian faith, as well as with advancing science.

Plato's views (427?-347 B.C.) laid the foundation for Aristotle. He proposed a "Demiurge" as a sort of detached intelligent creator whose shaping of the world was restricted in two respects. He had to follow not his own plan but the model of the "Eternal Ideas" and he had to put the stamp of these Ideas on a chaotic, recalcitrant matter that he had not created himself.[48] Plato used the term *physis* for the world soul (the moving and animating principle of the universe) as well as for the "Ideas." Other thinkers of his time used *physis* for the "visible things of the world." For Plato, these visible things were the products of Intellect and Design.

Hooykaas[49] points out that, at first glance, Plato's Demiurge seems to be similar to the biblical Creator, but that, in fact, "he" is very different.

First, Plato's Demiurge creates by bringing together two existing things, material and plan, the one resisting the perfection of the work, the other restricting the freedom of its design. In contrast, the biblical Creator creates *de novo* both in material and design, according to His sovereign will.

Second, the Demiurge leaves the *sustaining* of the universe to the "world soul" and he even delegates the construction of living beings, humans included, to him, because he considers it beneath his dignity and beyond his power to do this. On the other hand, the biblical Creator considers the creation of man to be his crowning act.

Third, for Plato, man is made by the secondary gods after the image of the universe—a mere image of the image of god. The biblical Creator creates man in His own image and for purposes that are both physical (stewardship of Nature) and spiritual (doing the will of God on earth).[50] This perception of Purpose is radically different from Plato's.

For both Plato and Aristotle the essential aspect of anything is its form, not the matter from which it is formed. Matter is not the "real being" but a negative and passive potentiality that acquires specific existence only when actuated and determined by form.[51] Accordingly, the causes of "form" assume special importance, as seen also in the works of Aristotle.

Aristotle (384-322 B.C.), was probably the greatest collector and organizer of knowledge in the ancient world.[52] He produced an encyclopedia of information within a system of thought that molded the mind of the Western world for centuries. This system combined both science and philosophy since it sought to explain natural phenomena ultimately in terms of cause, meaning, and purpose.[53] As will become apparent, such a combination proved to be increasingly unsatisfactory.

The tension that surrounds the Aristotelian concept of cause and purpose can be understood in terms of its basic content and limitations that eventually served to constrain scientific progress, and provoke a negative overreaction against all varieties of teleology.

For Aristotle, God is the unmoved Mover of the universe. He is the sum and goal of all purpose in nature, the First and Final Cause. God is not the creator of the material world but the cause of all order and motion in the universe. God is not love, but pure thought, a rational soul contemplating and knowing itself alone, ignorant of the universe of which He is the final cause but not the efficient cause (see below).[54]

Without going into detail, some of these concepts are partly in line with biblical views, while others, (e.g. God is not the Creator of matter, and not Love) are in direct contradiction. As stated, for Aristotle, God was not so much the *efficient* cause of the world (i.e., the agent that produced it) as its *final* cause (i.e., its goal).[55] This too is not consonant with the biblical view. To understand this better, Aristotle's four causes are summarized briefly.

The Four Causes of Aristotle

In the Greek, the word for *cause* is synonymous with *why* construed as a noun, and *reason* as in "the reason why." Aristotle's four causes were used as explanatory principles, or building blocks, for understanding physical phenomena.

Thus, according to Aristotle, "We do not understand a thing until we have acquired the WHY of it."[55] An explanation of it is complete only if four fundamental questions are answered. For instance, a complete account as to why a marble statue is the way it is, might be as follows. A statue is produced by a sculptor (its *efficient* cause) by his imposition of changes upon a piece of marble (its *material* cause) for the purpose of possessing a beautiful objects (its *final* cause), the marble thereby acquiring the form and distinctive properties of a stature (its *formal* cause).

Difficulties with Aristotle's Four Causes

First, there are ambiguities as to the distinctions among, and the significance of, the four causes. For instance, it has been argued that a final cause (e.g., possession of a beautiful statue) can be viewed as being no more than the inevitable consequence of an efficient cause (the completion of a piece of work by a sculptor).[56]

Second, from a modern scientific perspective, a major difficulty in Aristotelian thinking was the belief that the form of a thing can be equated with its final cause, or purpose,[53] and that by discovering purpose, one can deduce what a thing is made of and how it works.

As Owens has pointed out, to know that the eye is meant for seeing (the why of it) contributes little to a detailed scientific understanding of its basic form and function.[56, 57] It is true, for instance, that knowing that an eye is meant for seeing can help to pinpoint the first logical approaches to a proper scientific investigation of the anatomy and physiology of vision but, beyond that, knowledge of *purpose* does little to illumine detailed scientific knowledge of *structure* and *function*. Indeed, speculations based on purpose are liable to distract attention from more informative experimentally based knowledge. Historically, this is exactly what happened.

Third, as Butterfield states it:

> The Aristotelian universe was one in which the things that were in motion had to be accompanied by a mover all the time. . . . It was a universe in which unseen hands had to be in constant operation and sublime intelligences had to roll the planetary spheres around. Alternatively, bodies had to be endowed with souls and aspirations, with a disposition to certain kinds of motion, so that matter itself seemed to possess mystical qualities. The modern law of inertia, the modern theory of motion, is the great factor which in the seventeenth century helped to drive the spirits out of the world and opened the way to a universe that ran like a piece of clockwork.[57]

Thus, the downward motion of a falling rock is better explained scientifically in terms of physical laws and principles of cause and effect than in terms of the essence of the rock or the final cause of all motion.

Fourth, as Gilson points out, Aristotle is often reproached for his anthropomorphism, i.e., for his unsatisfactory habit of considering nature from man's point of view:

> We say that Aristotle imagines nature as a sort of artist who deliberates and makes a choice among appropriate means toward the end which he proposes to himself. To the question, "How does nature produce beings made up of heterogeneous parts?" Aristotle responds with another question, "How does man fabricate objects made up of such parts?" Art imitates nature; it must be then that Nature proceeds in a manner analogous to that of art.[58]

Fifth, as pointed out by Hooykaas,[59] Aristotle did not shake loose from the Platonic view that "a science founded on observation could not be a true science." In spite of his admission that all knowledge begins through the senses, he developed his physical system largely upon deductive reasoning.

These brief examples should suffice to illustrate that, noble as it was in its ancient context, Aristotelian thought was severely limiting when considered in the light of either well-informed historic Christian theology or of an emergent empirical science.

Domination and Extension of Aristotelian Influence

Aristotelian thinking dominated the centuries that witnessed the disintegration of the Greek Empire and the rise of Rome. Within its framework, Hipparchus and Ptolemy developed their astronomy that placed the earth as the center of the universe around which the sun, moon, and planets revolve.[53] Between A.D. 1200 and 1225, when the complete works of Aristotle were recovered and translated into Latin, their influence was renewed among new generations of medieval scholars, extending it to the seventeenth, even eighteenth century, and certainly well beyond their useful life.

Blending of Aristotelian Philosophy with Christian Theology and Ecclesiastical Authority

A major compounding of the problem resulted from Thomas Aquinas's (A.D. 1225-74) undertakings to synthesize Aristotelian natural philosophy with Christian theology.[60] Aquinas argued that philosophy (human reason) and theology (divine revelation) must be compatible. He developed his system within Aristotle's philosophical framework in which logic professes to give rigorous proof from accepted premises. This method supported the view that knowledge is derived from intuitive axioms as well as from theology, which, in turn, was under ecclesiastical authority.[53] This arrangement wrapped science in the same package with philosophy and theology and undoubtedly interfered further with the free investigation of nature by empirical experimentation.

In varying degrees, since at least the thirteenth century on, the alliance between Aristotelian philosophy, science, and theology gained such strength that any questioning of Aristotle could be construed as an attack upon the church. This set the stage for the struggles of Galileo Galilei (1564-1642) that epitomize the fight for freedom of scientific thought, based on observations, from ecclesiastical restrictions based upon dogma.[61]

Classical Physiological Example of Blending Faulty Aristotelian Thinking with Emerging Scientific Empiricism

William Harvey (1578-1657) is credited with the great discovery of the circulation of the blood. His work is a superb example of careful empirical observation that is still referred to in modern university physiology courses. Yet Harvey had not expunged Aristotelian influence from his thinking. For instance, he was sufficiently moved to associate his brilliant observations with the cosmic theories of his master Aristotle in these words: "The motion of the blood may be called circular in the way that Aristotle says air and rain follow the circular motion of the stars. . . . So the heart is the center of life, the sun of the Microcosm, as the sun itself might be called the heart of the world." [62]

This prompted Leake, translator of Harvey's "De Motu Cordis," to comment:

> Harvey is here somewhat behind the times, neglecting the prime discoveries of the preceding century, of Copernicus, Kepler, and his onetime teacher Galileo.[63]

> One must admit that the farther Harvey strayed into cosmic philosophy, the less his genius was displayed.[62]

It appears that such Aristotelian perspectives maintained their hold for longer in some branches of science (e.g., biology) than in others (e.g., physics and astronomy), despite the impact of great biological breakthroughs such as those of Andreas Vesalius (1514-64) in anatomical studies and of Harvey in regard to circulation of the blood.

Having outlined some negative consequences of Aristotlelian thought and of its interweaving with Christian theology, as root causes of tension with emergent science, it is now necessary to demonstrate how early and clearly many of the "greats" had grasped the problem. In essence, many of them recognized that the problem was not so much belief in purpose (or Purpose), but the unnecessary intrusion of such teleology into purely scientific domains.

Early Recognition of the Misuse of Aristotelian Teleology

It could be argued that the seeds of opposition to such teleology were sown centuries earlier by the Atomists Leucippus and Democritus of the fifth century B.C., but that it did not gather force until the time of the "mechanical philosophers of the seventeenth century A.D.[64]

But, very early, Roger Bacon (c. 1214-94), pointed out that "the introduction of such (i.e., Final) causes into physics has displaced and driven out the investigation of physical causes, making men rest in specious and shadowy causes . . . to the great detriment of science. And this I find to be true not only of Plato, but also of Aristotle, Galen and many others who frequently sail upon the same shallows."[65]

Later, René Descartes (1596-1650) distinguished sharply between mind and matter.[66] His call for the abolition of "wonder" by "understanding" voiced the confident conviction that nature contains no unfathomable mysteries and that she is transparent to reason. The effect of Descartes's dualism of mind and matter was "to excise every trace of the psychic from material nature with surgical precision, leaving it a lifeless field." [66]

Other "mechanical philosophers" of the sixteenth and seventeenth centuries including scientists like Robert Boyle (1627-91), also emphasized reductionism. Boyle believed that since a machine was made up of atoms and could be understood mathematically, so Nature itself could be understood mathematically without allusions to final causality.[67]

Further, Isaac Newton (1642-1727): "I scruple not to propose the Principles of Motion . . . they being of very general extent, and leave their causes to be found out." [68]

In the beginning of the seventeenth century, Francis Bacon, a major advocate of empiricism, essentially believed, as indicated by Hooykaas, that

> the root of all evil in science is the violation of the truth of nature by rationalistic prejudice. And, further: . . . again and again Bacon criticized the intellectualism of the Greeks, their neglect of experiments and their premature construction of theories on too narrow a basis of facts. Only contact with the reality of the world of phenomena would, in Bacon's opinion, force our minds into soberness and modesty: "when the mind of man works upon nature, the creatures of God, it is limited thereby, but if it works upon itself or upon a too small part of material things, it spins out laborious webs of learning." That is, the restoration of science required first of all the collecting of more facts . . . only after that would it be time to start theorizing afresh.[69]

Further, Michael Polanyi: "The . . . approach of Aristotle and Aquinas aiming at the discovery of a divine purpose in the phenomena of nature has been abandoned and theology forced to withdraw everything that it had taught of the material universe." [70]

Purpose as a Pursuit of Scientific Investigation versus Purpose as a Prerogative of the Scientists

Concerning the overthrow of Aristotelian teleology, Coulson writes: "All this does not mean, as John Baillie has pointed out, that there are no Final Causes, but only that natural science has no business with them: they are not yet discoverable by empirical methods. And, as Bacon goes on to say: this treatment of causes does not cast any doubt on the providential ordering of nature; rather does it exalt it." [67]

In other words, Final Causes (and Purpose) had not been disproven in the least, but rather, the crucial principle had been established, that much more could be learned from nature by asking different sorts of questions and by relying on direct observation, than by relying on philosophical presuppositions.

Coulson again: "We need to remember that Laplace, asserting that he 'had no need of that hypothesis' (God), and Descartes, crying 'Give me matter and motion, and I'll construct the universe,' were both professing Christians; and within certain limits, they spoke correctly.[72]

In essence, Laplace and Descartes were not dismissing "Final Cause" but simply excluding Him from the scientific level of empirical discourse in which He did not belong.

> We need to cultivate the restraint of Galileo, who left the world of angels and spirits until the time should come when it could be explored. . . . It is that self-control—the voluntary restriction to the task of extending knowledge outwards from the observed to the unobserved instead of imposing imagined universal principles inwards on the world of observation—that is the essential hallmark of the man of science, distinguishing him most fundamentally from the nonscientific philosopher.[72]

New Version of Galileo's Idea and Vision

Stillman Drake, a leading authority on Galileo, has made a penetrating analysis of the widespread and traditional view that there was an "eternal and inevitable conflict between Galileo and the Church, and more generally, science and religion."[73]

Galileo was indeed persecuted, but it was a unique, political affair that was not entirely representative of any larger, ongoing conflict between science and religion. In an open and well-publicized letter to the grand duchess of Tuscany, Galileo wrote: "It seems to me that in disputes of physical science, the Bible should be reserved for the last place." Which Drake rephrased as: "Reading and explanation of the Bible being the most difficult and exacting of all, other spheres of secular pursuit should be exhausted before the Bible enters into it." It is not impossible, Drake suggests, "that Galileo was punished for being of uniquely valuable service to the very Church which punished him. That service was to mark clearly . . . a line dividing the authority of scientific inquiry from the authority of religious principles."

Drake further suggests that the Christian church, at least her so-called mainline denominations, had substantially learned her lesson. By and large, she was wise enough to avoid repeating the conflict of the 1600s in the later context of Charles Darwin's theory of evolution in the 1800s and Einstein's theory of relativity of the 1900s.

The same cannot be said for science. It appears that a substantial reversal of roles has occurred. In the past, the Church had wrongly incorporated an extraneous, pagan metaphysical outlook that had not only corrupted and distorted its theology, but had provoked severe tensions with emergent science. Now it seems, science has implicitly incorporated a secular, materialistic metaphysic that places it in an adversarial position with respect to the historic Christian faith experienced and enjoyed by countless millions of well-educated and uneducated people alike.

The Secular Metaphysics of Modern-Day Science (or Scientism)

Michael Polanyi has alerted us to this issue: "I shall re-examine here the suppositions underlying our belief in science, and propose to show that they are more extensive than is usually thought. They will appear to co-extend with the entire spiritual foundations of man, and to go to the very root of his spiritual existence. Hence, I will urge, our belief in science should be regarded as token of much wider convictions." [74]

With respect to "the religion of Evolution," Mary Midgley states: "And today, a surprising number of the elements which used to belong to traditional religion have regrouped themselves under the heading of science, mainly around the concept of evolution. . . . Evolution is the creation myth of our age." [75]

And Bernal: "Now the history of scientific advances has shown us clearly that any appeal to Divine Purpose, or any supernatural agency, to explain any phenomenon, is in fact only a concealed confession of ignorance, and a bar to genuine research." [76]

It is interesting, in light of the discussion above that the substance of this statement may not be in line with its intent. In other words, it is quite appropriate to suggest that divine Purpose should not enter into purely scientific descriptions of natural phenomena. It may not be as appropriate to imply that divine Purpose has become irrelevant, or inaccessible to human experience, if, in fact, this is being implied here.

The evolutionist George Gaylord Simpson has claimed, in the name of science, that "man is the result of a purposeless and materialistic process that did not have him in mind. He was not planned." [77]

And Stephen Hawking has suggested: "It is a bit like the well-known horde of monkeys hammering away on typewriters—most of what they write will be garbage but very occasionally, by pure chance, they will type out one of Shakespeare's sonnets. Similarly, in the case of the universe, could it be that we are living in a region that just happens by chance to be smooth and uniform?" [78]

But, of course, one would not have a Shakespearean sonnet from the typewriting monkeys' productions unless there was a creative intelligence who could pick it out from among all the other sequences of letters they had typed! With such an intelligence present, there would be no need to depend on the monkeys!

Richard Dawkins states: "We are survival machines—robot vehicles blindly programmed to preserve the selfish molecules known as genes. This is a truth which still fills me with astonishment." [79]

In a more subtle vein, Edward Wilson offers that: "The concept of an active, moral God who created the world is even less widespread. The concept most commonly arises with a pastoral way of life. The greater the dependence on herding, the more likely the belief in a shepherd god of the Judeo-Christian model." [80]

I say subtle, because belief in a God of Purpose is matter-of-factly reduced to statistics, at the level of a public opinion poll that reveals that faith is more common among herdsmen.

Nowhere is this secular metaphysic more bluntly expressed than by the Nobel laureate French biologist, Jacques Monod. In his much-publicized book, *Chance and Necessity*,[81] Monod proposed that,

> Chance alone is the source of every innovation, of all creation in the biosphere. Pure chance, absolutely free but blind, is at the very root of the stupendous edifice of evolution. This central concept of biology . . . is today the sole conceivable hypothesis, the only one compatible with observed and tested fact. All forms of life are the product of pure chance. . . It is impossible to accept any system . . . that assumes a master plan of creation.

Note the CHANCE has become CAUSE and, by inference, PURPOSE as well. For, if human beings are the products of blind CHANCE, they cannot, and should not, expect, or hope for, Purpose, anymore than a rolling tumbleweed driven by the wind across a field can lay claim to purpose. The tumbleweed simply tumbles and humans simply live.

Inadequacy of Purposeless Scientism

Etienne Gilson asks: "What is it then that the modern biologist wishes to say by declaring that it is *scientific* to exclude final causality from the explanation of organized living beings?" [82]

He points out that such exclusion must have a scientific basis in order to be valid, but it does not: "This pure mechanist in biology is a man whose entire activity has as its end the discovery of the 'how' of the vital operations in plants and animals. Looking for nothing else, he sees nothing else, and since he cannot integrate other things in his research, he denies their existence. This is why he sincerely denies that existence, however evident, of final causality. . . . He is not trying to deceive others: he simply deceives himself."

Gilson continues:

> A sort of intellectual asceticism alone allows the scientist to deny the evidence which each moment of his life as a man, and even of his activity as a

scientist (savant) does not cease to confirm. One can, moreover, doubt that the most resolute adversaries of finalism can succeed in eliminating it from their mind. The occasions for coming back to this point are numerous. . . . It is difficult to speak of the *function* of an organ or tissue without danger-ously brushing against the idea of a natural teleology. To say of a machine . . . that it functions implies the notion that it functions as it ought to func-tion and as has been foreseen that it would function. The same is true in biology and particularly in medicine. . . . When an organism ceases to func-tion as it should . . . it ceases to exist.

Chance as a Creative Force and an Alternative to Purpose

Coulson states: "It is nothing less than tragic that this (the fact that scien-tists do not realize how laden they are with presuppositions) is so widely misunderstood. The greater part of our schoolboy's acceptance of science and rejection of religion springs from his unexamined belief that science accepts no presuppositions and must therefore be superior to a Christianity which is overloaded with them." [83]

There is absolutely nothing in science that does, or can, deny the ex-istence of a Purposeful Creator. Most of the scientists I have met are even singularly unaware of the philosophical arguments for or against the exist-ence of God. Yet many of them operate from the presupposition that Pur-pose is to be rejected. In this case, the main alternative is Chance, as espoused by Monod (above).

But, as pointed out by Donald MacKay, on whose thoughts this entire section depends:

the advocates of chance have fallen into the trap of confusing the scientific and mythology concepts of chance. "Chance" in science is not the name of a thing or an agent, least of all a cause or source of anything; it stands for the *absence* of an assignable cause. To personify chance as if we were talking about a causal agent, "free but blind" . . . is to make an illegitimate switch from a scientific to a quasi-religious mythological concept. To pro-ceed to claim scientific authority for describing this as a "central concept of biology" is to compound confusion. To dress up the result as if it were "observed and tested fact" that was at odds with all concepts of divine immanence in natural events is little short of dishonest.

Monod's astonishingly ill-supported argument is probably not to be un-derstood apart from his declared hatred of all forms of religion, which he scorns as "rooted in animism, (existing) outside objective knowledge, out-side truth and . . . strangers and fundamentally hostile to science, which they are willing to use but do not respect or cherish." [84]

By definition, chance has to do with happenings, or events that have no cause that can be ascertained, foreseen, or controlled. MacKay points out that rolling a die produces a random sequence of numbers, purely in the sense that it is the product of a random process.[85] Even if an orderly sequence such as 9-9-9-9-9 were to turn up, after many trials, it would still be a random sequence. If only *disorderly* sequences were desired, sequences such as 9-9-9-9-9 and 1-2-3-4-5 might be useless because, although random, they have a discernible order. Such disorderly sequences are better obtained from a preprinted table of well-scrambled numbers (sometimes also called random numbers) from which unwanted orderly sequences have been carefully weeded out.

When the word *random* is used, we have to ask ourselves whether it refers to a PROCESS (rolling of a die) or to the PRODUCT of that process that could be orderly or disorderly. Thus, if we are referring to the PRODUCT of the process, random #1 can mean having no determining cause while random #2 can mean having no discernible order.

Obviously, the world is not random #2: it may be the product of a random process, but, like the orderly sequence of 1-2-3-4-5, it has a discernible order. Scientists rely on Nature's orderliness and regularity in the pursuit of their studies. Without it, the results of their experiments could have been nonreproducible from day to day and the scientific "laws" based upon them impossible to formulate or sustain.

This leaves us with the question of random process. Monod's implicit assumption is that if the process by which we came into being is random, the biblical view of Purposeful creation is ruled out.

At issue in this argument is the question, "Random with reference to whom—us, or God?" In order to tackle this question we must deal with concepts of determinacy and indeterminacy and predictability and unpredictability.

Determinacy/Indeterminacy and Predictability/Unpredictability

Science specializes in determination, even prediction, according to precedent. For instance, eclipses of the moon are considered "physically determinate" events because their timing can be specified from existing data about the solar and lunar systems. Eclipses of the moon are predicted in almanacs as events whose specification is determined according to the rules of verifiable precedents. Eclipses are not *guaranteed* to happen in the sense that they are *caused or controlled* by the specifications. They are only predictable by these specifications, according to precedent.

If the specifications were unavailable, we would not be able to predict the eclipses, *but they would still happen*. Predictability says something about the state of our science, rather than about the moon or its eclipses. The determining causes of eclipses and the eclipses would exist just as much whether we could predict them or not.

To speak of an event (creation of the world) as indeterminate, is to say that it had no prior specification—that no prior specification existed, unknown to us, which we would have been correct to believe and mistaken to disbelieve if only we had known it. Such a statement, neither Monod, nor any other scientist can make with authority.

Donald MacKay and Ockham's Razor: Is Purpose beyond Necessity?

William of Ockham (c. 1300) gave special focus to a principle that became known as Ockham's razor. He expressed it in various ways, notably:

> Entities are not to be multiplied beyond need, or,

> A plurality (of entities or causes or factors) is not to be posited (or assumed) without necessity, or,

> It is vain to seek to accomplish or explain by assuming several entities or causes what can be explained by fewer.[86]

Ockham's razor can be applied in many situations and it has been applied against God's creation Purpose, using the logic that is "beyond need," or "without necessity," because it adds an unnecessary entity (Purposeful creation) to an existing explanation, i.e., or origin by blind Chance.

The problems with this view are that it assumes the primacy and adequacy of the one explanation (Chance) and of the method by which it was derived. This method is assumed to be scientific in an empirical sense and that sufficient credence can be placed in Chance as to obviate the need for an other explanation, i.e., Purposeful Creation.

In his recorded lecture on "Economy vs Nothing Buttery," MacKay has pointed out that a scientific explanation is only complete when a complete chain of cause and effect is available, as in the working of a simple, mechanical clock. When the function and interaction of every part of the clock's mechanism are fully understood, no other explanation is required and Ockham's razor becomes fully applicable.[87] However, virtually all branches of science have not advanced to the level where such complete explanations are available. In the absence of full knowledge, there remains room for the formulation of new, scientific, working hypotheses: such addition of new scientific entities is both commonplace and appropriate.

The question arises whether there are areas of knowledge and personal experience, in matters of causality, Purpose, and meaning, which are not only incomplete, but which also require categories or entities of a nonscientific nature, because they are NECESSARY.

To illustrate such necessity, MacKay gives two illustrations.

ILLUSTRATION 1: DOTS VS MESSAGES

A series of 35-mm photographic slides is projected on a screen, at progressively longer viewing distances. The first slide is a magnified close-up view that reveals a large number of rather fuzzy-edged black dots. They can be counted, measured, and otherwise subjected to mathematical or physical scrutiny, perfectly adequate for dealing with dots. No other entity need be introduced. The next slide, at lower magnification, shows that the dots make up the letter S, as it might appear in newsprint, or dot matrix. Clearly another category of evidence is beginning to emerge—a letter of the English alphabet. This is borne out by the next slide that shows that the letter S is part of a word that is grouped with other words in portions of sentences. The next slide confirms that the original S is part of a newspaper article about politics that is embodied in a large letter X cut out of a newspaper.

The final slide shows that the cut-out letter X is one of several big letters cut out of the same newspaper and that have been arranged in a sequence to spell the word EXIT. It transpires that all four letters were cut out of newsprint by the organizer of a meeting to put together a temporary exit sign for a lecture hall, presumably in order to fulfill some local fire-safety regulation aimed at protecting the public in case of a fire.

Obviously, at the level of dots (first slide) no hypotheses beyond mathematical and physical ones appear to be necessary. But, when the letter S appears, questions can be raised about other entities. By the time the X and the other cut-out letters appear to spell the word EXIT, it becomes obvious that scientific analysis at the level of dots alone is inadequate. A message in English is in view that *demands* the attention of other entities. Entities *have* increased, but with *necessity*. In case of a fire, being able to locate the EXIT would be more important than knowing all about the black dots of which the EXIT sign was made up! The purpose and meaning of EXIT could become more important and appropriate than the mathematics and physics of dots.

ILLUSTRATION 2: BOULDER FALLS DOWN A HILLSIDE AND KILLS A MAN

A boulder perched on a hillside was anchored by a rope to prevent it from rolling down a hill and hitting a man in his flimsy hillside hut. One night, the boulder broke loose, rolled down the hill, and killed the sleeping man. The simplest, most direct explanation was that the rope had frayed as a result of ongoing friction and had broken spontaneously.

However, examination of the broken edges of the rope by the investigators of this tragedy revealed straight, regular ends, as though they had been cut. A path to the boulder was discovered and witnesses were located who testified that a man had been observed walking along that path quite frequently. The man turned out to be an enemy of the man living in the hillside hut.

The police now get involved and the issue shifts from a scientific problem focussing on the law of gravity, the size, weight, and geometry of the boulder, the soil conditions of the hillside, and the strength and condition of the rope, to policemen, lawyers, courts, witnesses, and juries. These new categories NEED not have been introduced at the outset but mounting evidence soon made it NECESSARY to introduce them. The entities were not multiplied BEYOND necessity but because of it. We readily accept the new entities as appropriate to the case.

MacKay points out that Ockham's razor is not violated in either illustration and that the principle of economy, or parsimony, can be protected at every level of consideration be it dots vs messages or gravity vs crime. At each level of consideration, entities need not be multiplied beyond necessity *but as many entities should be considered as are appropriate to the multiple levels of valid investigation.* To the relatives of the dead man in the hillside hut, apprehension, legal trial, and sentencing of the alleged murderer who cut the rope is most assuredly valid and important. They would not be satisfied with learned discussions of the law of gravity.

By inference, Purpose would not need to be considered if it could be demonstrated that Chance offered a sure final explanation of causality. But, as mentioned, there is no sound empirical method for deriving Chance. Nor is there a sound empirical basis for excluding Purpose; indeed there are many reasons for retaining it, as we have seen. Thus, Ockham cannot be used to argue that scientific minds should content themselves with Chance and not consider entities such as Purpose.

A graphic statement has come from Goudge, with respect to the incompleteness of knowledge concerning evolution. The theory of evolution, as the major explanation for biological origins by Chance, has assumed the stature of an incontrovertible law in many minds. One would think that here, of all places, Ockham's razor should apply and that other entities should not be multilplied. We should not be looking for other hypotheses or explanations since we already have all that is necessary. In fact, there are such enormous gaps in our knowledge that a wide-open mind on the matter would be highly advisable.

Thus, Goudge outlines the state of affairs that would have to exist if evolution were "fully explained" and there was no need for additional explanations of any kind. All the following would have to be fully comprehended:

(1) the detailed historical course of evolution; (2) historical explanations of all those single, non-recurrent events which were transitional episodes of major significance in (1); (3) systematic explanations involving generalizations or laws of the various evolutionary patterns or recurrent events in phylogenesis; and (4) the precise manner in which (2) and (3) are to be combined in an over-all theory, such that it will account for (1) regarded as a single, complex historical process with large-scale features of its own. It is fairly apparent, even without further analysis, that available knowledge on all four points is nothing like complete.

With regard to (1) the largest gap in our knowledge occurs at the beginning of life's history, because of the scarcity of Pre-Cambrian fossils. This gap may actually embrace as much as three-quarters, and almost certainly embraces half, of the total history of life, for the first living things existed on the earth at least 1,000 million years ago (probably longer), whereas only since the Cambrian period is the fossil record reasonably adequate. Yet significant blanks in the record occur during the past 500 million years, so that although we know the outlines of the story, we remain ignorant about unnumerable details.[88]

I do not wish to employ a "God of the Gaps" argument built upon gaps in evolutionary knowledge. This would be dangerous because science has a habit of filling gaps, sooner or later. Nor would I wish to predict that, because these particular data are either unavailable or very difficult to obtain, evolutionary gaps will never be filled and use this prediction to argue in favor of Creatorship and Purpose. My point is simply that, in the presence of such huge gaps in knowledge concerning their most important theory pertaining to biological origins, all scientists should exhibit a more realistic, humble attitude. With such huge gaps staring us in the face in the empirical domain, we should refrain from usurping other domains, not accessible to empirical study, with an air of arrogance or superconfidence.

To reiterate, Chance is a philosophical, not a scientific, concept. It is a word that explains nothing about causality. In a strict sense, it does nothing more than allude to the ignorance of those who use it, because Chance is not a casual agent. It refers to the absence of an assignable cause according to precedent. To say "by Chance" is to say, "I don't know why," or "I don't have the data, according to precedent, for explaining the cause of this event."

In contrast, Purpose claims the Creator as an assignable cause, belief in Whom is an experience claimed and enjoyed by millions of responsible people, including many scientists, with salutary consequences in life. Purpose is no more derived by empirical means than is Chance, but both its presence and absence in human experience produces effects that have been documented by psychiatrists, psychologists, and other observers of the human condition. There is much to support a Purposeful life based on the accumulated wisdom of the ages found in the Judeo-Christian Scriptures. These are a source of evidence worthy of any scientist's attention.

Evidence of Purposeless Lostness in Present-Day Society

In the literature already cited, as well as in the media on a daily basis, I see ongoing evidence of human malaise and a frightening sense of "lostness." People have "come of age" in rejecting the God of Purpose but they seem to be far from satisfied with the alternatives. Here is but one recent sample:

> Instead of God, we now have gods. Instead of the word, we have the image. Instead of content, we have form. Instead of knowledge, we have information. Instead of love, we have sex. Instead of values, we have interests. Instead of absolute truth, we have political correctness, changing with the seasons. In this "doleful" world," writes Nobel laureate poet Joseph Brodsky, "What's said is, "I agree," not "I believe." [88]

As Butterfield puts it:

> An historical religion, by the terms of its very existence, implies a certain conception of God, a certain view of the universe, a certain doctrine about human life and a certain idea concerning the course of things in time. By its fundamental assumptions it insists upon a God who stretches out His arms to human beings presumed to be groping in grave distress and blind bewilderment. It asserts that eternity is brought into relation with time, and that in the supra-terrestrial realm, the kingdom of the spirit is not locked away, for it is here and now, and the two planes of existence intersect. . . . The Word was made flesh. . . . Matter can never be regarded as evil in itself.

> On this view there can be no case of an absentee God leaving mankind at the mercy of chance in a universe blind, stark and bleak. And a real drama—not a madman's nightmare or a tissue of flimsy dreams—is being enacted on the stage of all human history—a real conflict between good and evil is taking place, events do matter, and something is being achieved irrespective of our apparent success or failure. [89]

Summary and Conclusion

As a physiologist who believes in Purpose I have referred to the Judeo-Christian Scriptures as presenting a Creator of Purpose who calls those who believe in Him to share in fulfilling this Purpose for the benefit of humankind. Jesus Christ calls His disciples to Purpose: "Thy will be done, on earth as it is in heaven." Dedicated men and women heeding this call over the ages have contributed immense benefits to their societies in the West, as well as to other countries beyond.

However, many scientists exist in a philosophical solitude that rejects Purpose in favor of "Blind Chance." They seem not to appreciate that this philosophical position is no better supported by science than is Purpose. They ignore experiential evidences of Purpose in all circumstances of life, as well as historical evidence of its impact on many aspects of life in the Christian West, including the nurture of science.

Some historical root causes for the rejection of Purpose are identified, notably the faulty use of Aristotelian teleology in scientific explanations. Such misuse aggravated the conflicts of the sixteenth and seventeenth centuries, including the best-known conflict between Galileo and the ecclesiastical authorities of his day concerning the motion of the Earth.

Many scientists and philosophers astutely recognized the source of tension and themselves remained believers in Purpose while seeking to rid Theology of Aristotelian metaphysics on the one hand, and Science of primitive teleology on the other.

The main alternative to Purpose is Blind Chance, an ill-founded philosophy that has been roundly exposed by MacKay. Thus, a strange crossover of historical roles is occurring: in Galileo's day, the church adopted a philosophy and a science it could neither absorb nor defend. Today, science is adopting a particular, ill-founded philosophical position (Chance) as an implicit part of itself, but cannot defend it.

Purposeless existence is not a neutral state of being but rather one that can, and undoubtedly will, spawn a variety of harmful consequences, judging by much of what is experienced in the scientific miliu or observed in daily life.

To speak of an event (Purposeful creation of the world) as a Chance event is simply to speak of the absence of an assignable cause—i.e., to say, "I don't know why." Belief in Chance says more about the ignorance of the one who believes than about how we got here. Science alone cannot answer all questions at all levels. Scientists must be open to other sources of knowledge, just as an electrician repairing an electrical advertisement must realize that it is both an electrical device and the source of a message that transcends the device. Neither Purpose nor Chance are at the level of "electricity," which can be profoundly investigated by empirical science. Both are at the level of "message," as real to those who can read, understand, and experience it as an electric shock would be to the electrician. Purpose is the messenger and the message: "Light has come into the world . . . for a Purpose."[90]

10

David Wilcox

How Blind the Watchmaker?

The Meaning of Purpose

Since time began, we have looked at the stars and the world around us, and wondered. We exist. Why? Might there be an intelligence, a designer, behind the world of our experience? How can we know? This primordial sense of wonder has not deserted us. We look into the labyrinthine architecture of the cell, examine the numbing diversity of the rain forest, or plumb the unfathomable depths of the human brain. Awe rises within us, and the breath of a designer seems warm on our neck. But, a sense of wonder is not proof of design. Is there any (or indeed, can there be any) evidence that the living world has some purpose? In more esoteric terms, have boundary constraints for life been placed on the cosmos by some outside agency?

In any such complex and critical matter, we must begin with definition. To consider the evidence for *purpose*, we must define the meaning of *cause*, for purpose is final cause, one of the four types of cause distinguished by Aristotle.[1] Final cause is the intended purpose of the maker of an object. Formal cause is the maker's plan or blueprint for the object. Material cause is the raw material from which it was made, and efficient cause is the force applied to the raw material that actually produces the object. A full causal explanation for any object will thus involve a description in four dimensions. For instance, in defining biological causality, Rieppel ties material and efficient causes to ontogeny ("embryonic" development), and formal and final causes to phylogeny ("evolutionary" development).

An intelligent designer is, of course, not the only answer to the question of biological "final cause." The answer of G. G. Simpson (1967) stands in stark contrast: "It is already evident that all the objective phenomena of the history of life can be explained by purely naturalistic, or in the proper meaning of a much abused word, materialistic factors. . . . Man is the result of a purposeless and natural process that did not have him in mind.[2] As an "antiteleologist," G. G. Simpson clearly viewed the material cosmos itself as an adequate and autonomous final cause. Humanity *can* have no purpose to its maker, for its maker (autonomous matter) has no intentionality. (Notice that even a materialist cannot deny meaning to the *question* of purpose, for that would imply that the materialist's own negative statements about purpose are meaningless nonsense.)

Clearly, *efficient* causes (applied forces) have brought about aardvark and rose, human and sequoia. But that is not a necessary denial of purpose. Applied forces have also produced *human* artifacts such as lawn rakes and orbital shuttle craft. When we humans make tools, the shaping forces (*efficient* causes) act upon the raw materials (*material* causes) under the direction of our (hopefully) intelligent design or blueprint (the *formal* cause) for the tool we intend to make (the *final* cause). For objects produced in "nature," efficient causes also act on material causes under the "direction" of formal causes—although the formal cause may simply be the surface of a crystal or the sequence of a parental strand of DNA. In both human and natural causality, formal causes act as *boundary conditions* to constrain/direct the force of the efficient cause.

The idea of purpose or ultimate design therefore does not deny the reality or importance of the material and efficient causes studied by science, but it does suggest that intelligence might be the source of the *formal* causes in nature, the natural boundaries that shape the direction taken by nature's efficient causes. A convinced "teleologist," Princeton theologian B. B. Warfield,[3] expressed it thus, "Some lack of general philosophical acumen must be suspected when it is not fully understood that teleology is in no way inconsistent with—is rather necessarily involved with—a complete system of natural causation. Every teleological system implies a complete 'causo-mechanistic' explanation as its instrument." Which view does the evidence support? The argument started long before Warfied and Simpson.

The History of Debate

Certainly, the debate is not a product of modern science. Indeed it predates Christianity. In 45 B.C. Cicero (100-43 B.C.), arguing for the Stoics, stated, "When we see a mechanism such as a planetary model or a clock, do we doubt that it is the work of a conscious intelligence? So how can we doubt that the world is the work of the divine intelligence?" To the Stoics, the beauty, uniformity, intelligibility, and evident purpose of both animate and inanimate nature implied an intelligent and beneficent creator.[4] On the other hand, the Atomists (Epicureans such as Lucretius, 99-55 B.C.) argued that the world, and all its forms, was a product of undirected natural processes, a random concourse of adherent "atoms" that was, in part, badly designed. Thus, no intelligent source for final cause needed to be postulated. The intrinsic characteristics of the atoms themselves would suffice.[5] It all sounds very familiar.

Leaping millennia, it is well known that the concept of perfect local adaptation as the "natural" purpose of living things was a central issue in the debates surrounding Darwin's theory. That, however, was a view of purpose that differed sharply from the earlier view of seventeenth-century scientists such as John Ray. In Ray's view of final causation, the "ultimate purpose" of the biotic world was the revelation of the glory of God. Such "general revelation" was God's intent *behind* all adaptations, patterns, etc.[6] The debate took a sharp turn when Archdeacon Paley identified living things with industrial machines, and thus equated their biotic functions with their ultimate purposes.[7] This "Newtonian" view embedded the final purpose of biological entities (as created machines) in the natural order. Such local adaptationism was the core of the arguments for design used by the British natural theologians such as Darwin's mentor Adam Sedgwick.[8] (However, the view of biological final cause as perfectly designed local adaptations did not necessarily mean that the natural theologians excluded material, formal, and efficient cause from their theoretical work.)[9]

The radical "materialists" of London such as Knox and Grant, followers of the "higher anatomy" of Etienne Geoffroy Saint-Hilaire, also collapsed all causes into matter itself.[10] Matter was considered to be aware, self-shaping, and self-realizing. Biotic patterns were thus necessary products of the material cause.[11] They followed Lamarck in viewing adaptation to the happenstance of present circumstance as an unimportant interference in this material self-realization.

Reacting to the materialists, idealists of the Naturphilosophie school such as Richard Owen viewed formal cause (boundary conditions) as immaterial structural blueprints.[12] Efficient (material) cause was shaped primarily by that governing "archetype," not "by any known properties of matter." Typically, they considered man as the intended purpose (final cause) that archetypically guided the natural order from "the first embodiment of the Vertebrate idea under its old Ichthyic vestment, until it became arrayed in the glorious garb of the Human form."[13]

According to Rieppel,[14] the positivistic materialists (or naturalists) of Huxley's circle[15] wished to reduce all causation to efficient cause. Thus, the final cause would be simply the product projected backward. Especially with Darwin's theory (or metaphor) of the environment as the creative source for biological form, selection was viewed as both efficient and formal cause, the logical equivalent of the purposes of commercial breeders. Material cause (new variation) was simply assumed to be adequate and plastic enough for natural selection to mold.

However, the debate over whether the material cause (raw material) or the efficient cause (process-selection) set the boundary conditions for biological change (formal cause) continued. NeoLamarckians opposed natural selection as the source of order, suggesting instead either an intrinsic order found in the material itself or some directive immaterial source for new material variations, which selection merely realized or modified.[16] Such views retained natural selection as a minor boundary constraint on evolutionary change, but termed the major constraint, new variation, "intrinsic" evolution. Darwin responded by placing production of new variation under environmental direction as well (Pangenesis).

That debate continues today, and so does the confusion. The formation of the Modern Synthesis in the 1940s can be viewed as a victory for the idea of environmental selection as dominant "formal" cause. It relegated mutation to an amorphic clay sculpted by selection, a material cause ineffective in constraining the efficient causes that produce new biological types. "Natural selection is a creator, it builds adaptation step by step."[17] On the other hand, the importance of the material being shaped is currently making a comeback, for instance in the concepts of the "structuralists"[18] and in hierarchy theory.[19]

A Few Clarifications

Before proceeding, let us eliminate a few red herrings. One rather decayed specimen is the idea that an extracosmic intelligence is (only) an alternate *efficient* cause. Teleological hypotheses do not concern an agent that acts in gaps *between* natural processes, but rather, one who *directs* them. Of course, an event without physical cause would clearly support the existence of an immaterial entity able to act as a cause, but a "miracle" in that sense is not a proof that the "whole show" is governed.

A second fishy suggestion is the identification of final cause with "vitalism." Clearly, the hypothesis of some sort of "elan vital" can be an alternative nonmaterial *efficient* or *formal* cause, but if it lacks intentionality or purpose, it is simply an extramaterial analogue of an autonomous material universe. Thus, the question of ultimate purpose would remain unanswered.

A more important consideration is the question of how we recognize "purpose" in an object. Clearly, we do not recognize anything without mental templates or remembered images. In the case of human artifacts, we recognize purpose against a backdrop of natural "purposeless" events. In most cases, this is a matter of simple probability. We deduce complex formal causes from complex effects, which we detect against a background of alternative simple effects with greater probability. If some complex effect seems to lack a sufficiently complex formal cause, we look for an additional and sufficient source of those boundary conditions. But how do we know the probabilities of background events? In 1990, a Xerox machine is a sufficient causal boundary for an exact copy of a complex document, and therefore we do not make the necessary 1490's assumption that it was copied by hand. But, how well do we know the universe?

Further, we recognize intent in artifacts by seeing them as components of larger mental templates. Without templates, we see no utility. A camera examined by a Stone-Age Einstein might suggest a complex formal cause (technology) but would not reveal its final cause (purpose). On the other hand, since we *do* have such mental templates, we may see final causes that are not there. For instance, are our categories for Mousterian (Neanderthal) tools (burins, hand axes, sidescrapers, etc.) due to our own mental templates, or to theirs?

But how can we see purpose (or its absence) in the "whole show"? A cosmic final cause could completely determine material causes as well as formal causes. As Darwin[20] responded to Asa Grey, "On the other hand, an omnipotent and omniscient Creator ordains everything and foresees everything. Thus we are brought face-to-face with a difficulty as insoluble as is that of free will and predestination." Ultimate final cause *does* shape the whole show, whether it is an intelligence or not, and thus there is nothing left to produce a contrasting background of probabilities. Can we therefore perceive design or its absence with any certainty? If we cannot, is one vision of reality more rational than the other? Where do individuals obtain their foundational mental templates? "Faith is the substance of things hoped for, the evidence of things not seen."

The Exploration of Genetic Phase Space: or, Dr. Dawkins's Amazing Technicolor Gene Machine

If ultimate final cause of the Biosphere is beyond us, can we possibly detect an intelligence in its formal cause? Does not the evident complexity and mutual adaptedness of living things indicate intelligence? On the basis of the neo-Darwinian concept of accumulative selection, Richard Dawkins[21] argues that such an intelligence is not needed. In brief, all living things are the products of specific genomes, which are blueprints written in the same language (describing protein structure) upon the same medium (DNA). This means that any genome could be turned into any other by just changing (mutating) the right DNA bases (letters) (as *cog* becomes *dog* if the *c* is "mutated" to *d*).

So, all possible genetic messages (genomes) are points in a single multidimensional probability space, which has been called genetic phase space, "GPS."[22] Since random change or movement can be used to search such a probability space, all that is needed to move (evolve) from worm to Einstein is to chance upon, and then accumulate, the right base changes. Neo-Darwinism states that mutation randomly throws up new sequences and environmentally based selection accumulates those that are useful. In this way, the cosmos itself can act as a "blind watchmaker," and no exterior blueprint is needed as formal cause. (Which does not exclude the possibility that such a blueprint shaped the whole cosmos at its beginning.) How effective is this argument? Let us consider Dawkins's illustration of the process.

To show the power of such accumulative selection, Dawkins wrote the "Biomorph" computer simulation. In Biomorph Land, trees "evolve" as guided by the user's choice of variants on the current type, producing a wide variety of visual images, suggesting insects, machines, etc. This is, of course, closer to domestic breeding than to *environmentally* directed evolutionary change, but that was, after all, Darwin's metaphor. The environment was viewed as breeder. (Incidently, this aspect of Biomorph Land demonstrates the possibility of extramaterially guided environmental selection.) Biomorph Land, however, has more serious difficulties as a model for morphogenesis.

As every casino owner knows, the success rate of random searches is less a matter of possibilities than of probabilities. Outcomes (and his profit margin) depend entirely on the characteristics of the probability space being searched. A rigged game (or a formal cause!) can be deduced because of its excessive string of low-probability outcomes. Biomorph Land can generate an accumulating visual complexity by following possible trajectories. But, is Biomorph Land an adequate model for GPS? How likely is the payoff? Are the probability characteristics of genetic phase space more like Biomorph Land—or more like a roulette wheel? There are four significant difficulties; the size of the probability space, the size of the exploratory probe, the viability of the outcomes (locations), and the source of the boundary conditions.

First, the size of the matrix: GPS, the probability space of all possible genomes,[23] has an information content of 2^n bits where n is the number of bases. Biomorphs, on the other hand, are described by a sixteen-digit number. Thus Biomorph Land has a probability space of only 10^{15}, whereas the GPS of genomes of mammalian size, (2.5 billion bases), contains around $10^{1,000,000,000}$ binary bits of information.

Second, the fraction of the probability space made available to selection each generation is much smaller in genetic systems. No matter how many offspring are generated, they clearly represent (search) a much smaller fraction of the GPS than the equivalent set of Biomorph "probes." Further, Biomorph "probes" show all possible offspring each time, whereas mutation reveals only a vanishingly small fraction of possible mutants. This means that finding the next step in a possible trajectory in GPS will be far harder, even if it exists—in some cases next to impossible.

Third, the viability of variants in Biomorph Land is completely unlike reality. *No* Biomorph necessarily dies without offspring, since it may be chosen by the intelligent "selector" who is using the program. Thus, in the Biomorph probability space, no trajectory is impossible. But most mutant organisms die, thus GPS *does* have impossible trajectories. However, the acceptance of nonintelligent formal causes for biological morphologies depends on the existence and the likelihood of viable trajectories across GPS, reasonably probable trajectories that depend on the accumulation of *minor* sequence changes. But, *isolated* viable spots in GPS may exist, sequences that would involve so many simultaneous specific point mutations to reach, that an intelligent formal cause would be the simplest explanation. How can we know whether some existing creatures are or are not of that sort? Do we always have evidence for intermediate forms and gradual change?

Fourth, the rules that control Biomorph morphology (formal causes) are exterior givens. A particular sixteen-digit number *means* a specific Biomorph due to the Biomorph program that defines it. DNA sequences also have meaning only if they are defined. However, biological definitions are themselves encoded on the genome, and thus also part of GPS. So, the definitions must be explained by the same formal causes (search mechanisms) as sequences they define. But, how can the successful search of a stable defined matrix of possibilities lead to an understanding of how that matrix was constructed? Understanding morphogenesis means to explain the rules, not what they govern.

The Biomorph model of evolutionary change shows that neo-Darwinian mechanisms will indeed work—if an intelligent formal cause is responsible both for constructing the rules of morphology (which determine the probability matrix), and for determining the direction of selection. But, that is a bit less than it was intended to show. One must also demonstrate that both formal and material causes are adequate in the *absence* of intelligence.

To distinguish directed and undirected formal causes in the biosphere, one must know the probability matrix of the unfathomably large GPS. But, we cannot deduce that pattern from observed patterns of genetic change, for we can not simultaneously deduce two dependent probabilities—*both* the pattern's probability if not directed, *and* the probability that it *was* being directed. One must be known to calculate the other. Thus, neo-Darwinian logic cannot easily rule out the involvement of intelligent formal cause in the appearance of new biotic morphology.

If we knew the contours of GPS, we could state which morphogenetic trajectories would be likely in fossil history, and thus deduce the likelihood of intelligent guidance. But, we do not know if viable locations in GPS are uniformly distributed, contiguous networks, or clumped and isolated. In our ignorance, we assume a structure for GPS. We project back onto the vast and misty canvas a map of the structure of reality that will support our view of cosmic formal cause. If we reject intelligent cause, we assume GPS is rich in linked viable probabilities. If we hold to intelligent cause, we realize that the GPS *might* be much poorer. The statement that GPS *must* have a structure that would allow gradual and undirected emergence is based on worldview assumptions, not on observations. The GPS becomes our "field of dreams," its contours a projection of our metaphysics.

Revising the Topography of Genetic Phase Space

But is GPS really terra incognita? As mutation accesses portions of GPS and selection assesses them, the pattern of change should at least reflect the local structure of GPS. Neo-Darwinism expects gradual change, for it assumes that GPS is a rather uniform plain with few obstacles, a malleable array of variation molded by the environment. Has that assumption been either fruitful or reasonable? Rieppel objects, "The attempt of evolutionary theory to capture the biological world in a single and unified causal explanation rests on a reduction of the four Aristotelian causes to one (efficient)—a heritage of the Enlightenment, which . . . hampers a full understanding of the complexity of living systems." [24]

Recall that even in Biomorph Land, the nature and distribution of possible Biomorphs are set by the program, not the user. This concept—that the genetic information (the "program" encoded in the DNA) is the major determinant of the evolutionary process—is termed *structuralism*. It represents a return to the central idea of NeoLamarkianism concerning formal cause. Evolution was thought to be shaped by *intrinsic* material cause rather than by *extrinsic* neo-Darwinian environmental shaping (efficient cause).

Rieppel states, "According to the atomistic perspective, organisms were formed by an aggregation of parts of particles. . . . As these parts were in principle interchangeable, organisms were conceived as fundamentally variable. . . . What is therefore required is a 'generative structuralism' governing not only the invariance of structures, but at the same time their generation and transformation." [25] The boundary conditions are the rules of the genetics program. For several lines of research, the key idea is *coherence*—genetic programs are holistic, error-checked, cybernetic systems.

In developmental biology, Wagner argues for individuation or entity formation in organogenesis. The genetic description is a goal-seeking blueprint, error-checked according to norms for that organ. [26] Several researchers suggest that such individuated control provides an alternate conceptual base for homology that is biologically more reasonable than cladistic phylogeny. [27] Mutations also seem to be limited in their effects by being defined by such developmental/genetic coherencies. [28] Templeton and others argue for a new theory of species identity based on the possession of various genetically based cohesion mechanisms. [29] Thus, species too are defined by "individuated" genetic controls able to hold morphologies stable over millions of years. [30] Finally, the pattern for the emergence of new taxa suggests genetic constraints. The appearance of particular type forms is followed shortly by an adaptive radiation showing various more gradual (and often parallel) changes. [31]

Rieppel feels that some sort of morphogenetic "generative principles" dictate the possibilities of biological form. [32] To Goodwin also, such "structuralism" means that "the organismic domain as a whole has a 'form' and is therefore, intelligible (which does not mean predictable) and that the 'content'—the diversity of living forms, or at least their essential features—can be accounted for in terms of a relatively small number of generative rules or laws. [33] Such structural rules constrain GPS. They are a "programmed" restriction of living things to parts of GPS that contain permitted morphologies. Again, "Living organisms are devices which use the contingent 'noise' of history as a 'motor' to explore the set of structures, perhaps infinitely large, which are possible for them." [34] (Note that Goodwin's metaphor for exploration is a materially constrained "living device" rather than the "environmental breeder" of Darwin and Dawkins. Also, *both* mutation and environment are part of the contingent "noise" of history.) However, structuralism does not explain how such "living devices" have arrived at the (possibility enriched but certainly constrained) areas in GPS in which they exist.

The neglect of such structuralist insights suggests a high degree of "teleophobia" in evolutionary biology. Investigators seem to feel they must defend themselves against an accusation of teleological thinking as if it were a charge of moral turpitude.[35] Von Brucke (as quoted by systems theorist M. Mesarovic) described teleology "as a lady without whom no biologist can live—but he is ashamed to be seen with her in public." Mesarovic continued, "For an important class of situations, one can develop an effective specification of the system only if one is using a goal-seeking (i.e., teleological) description." [36] Such a reductionistic fervor has long separated the insights of physiological functional analysis from phylogenetic morphological analysis.[37] The neglected issue is not the search within the constraints, but the search *for* the constraints.

The Implication of Biotic Coherencies

How does the presence of coherent individuated blueprints in the genome affect the neo-Darwinian hope? (The hope to explain the major features of evolution as the undesigned products of environmentally based gradual selection of micromutations.) Will selection still suffice as formal and final cause, as well as efficient cause? If structuralism is correct—if the biosphere is indeed characterized by self-referencing programs on the genome—it seems unlikely. Blueprints programmed into the DNA define change in the genes that they control.[38] A major change in morphology would thus require a change in the constraining blueprint. Further, the initial forming of genetic coherencies must be explained.

Coherencies require genetic definitions. The best metaphor is probably human language. As in English, genetic "languages" are used to encode their own dictionaries (e.g., the structure of the aminoacyl synthetases is encoded using the very amino-acid code that they define). Since the meaning of genes is defined in this way, a lineage can not use small-effect genes to simply "walk away" from the part of GPS containing its current morphology. The increasing pleiotropic "developmental" stress will limit the walk, and draw the lineage back toward its original morphology.[39] Thus, *effective* change requires change in the programmed constraints.

It is true of course that a change in the control genes themselves would have larger effects than a change in the genes they control. In fact, a model of the genome as a hierarchy of controlling blueprints (individuations) could be reflected in the biosphere as a hierarchy in the scope of morphological transitions. However, since such large-effect genes take their meaning (definition/blueprint) from the coadapted array of genes that they control, a large-effect change will create a disproportionate increase in developmental tension/stress.[40] The longer the "leap" in morphology, the greater the tension and the likelihood that the genetic complex will dissolve into incoherency.

One can, of course, insist that such "punctuated" change has occurred, and thus that such a macromutant occasionally survives and flourishes.[41] But, how likely are unguided major morphological changes? A major morphological change *would* require a change in control genes, but it would also require that the change be understandable in terms of the genes controlled. Judging from the infrequency of such major transitions, they are like rare and narrow "wormholes" in GPS. A lineage would have to be exactly positioned to traverse such a path. But what is the probability of such positioning, and indeed, how rare are the holes? The more change is described by such leaps, the less reasonable the acceptance of unguided change becomes. But, to really know that, we would need a map of GPS. As David Jablonski put it, "The most dramatic kinds of evolutionary novelty, major innovations, are among the least understood components of the evolutionary process."[42] We are again playing on the field of dreams.

The origin of individuation is an even more difficult question.[43] If centipedes become insects, the first three body segments become a new entity—the thorax. Such individuation involves two new things. First, there is now a set of rules on the genome specifically governing the thorax, rules that give those segments new "definition." Second, that set of rules involves a great deal more information than that necessary to produce iterative (essentially fractal!) structures such as centipede segments. Thus, the GPS trajectory connecting these two genomes is far more complex than the phenotypic trajectory. Wagner concludes that we have no way "to assess the plausibility of the internalization mechanism. . . . The relevant type of data is not thus far available."[44]

There is a fundamental problem with the concept of natural selection as a simple directional tug across the adaptive landscape of GPS. It may be relatively easy to show how a path across *phenotypic* space could be progressively adaptive,[45] but explaining the necessary changes in the underlying genome is a different matter. The two seem identical only because neo-Darwinism assumes the presence of sufficient variability. For the "structuralist," however, one must demonstrate how the new genomic variation could be generated by the old. "A 'generative structuralism' is required in order to solve the problem of the origin of structures."[46]

Can selection accumulate the information for new genetic complexes? From where? There is no morphological information in the environment to accumulate. It must be generated by the genome itself. One can not breed horses for wings, no matter how clearly one visualizes Pegasus. But if so, variants represent *changes* in information, not *accumulations*. In Biomorph Land, visually complex forms contain the same amount of information as simple ones, and movement along a trajectory represents only change in information, not its accumulation. But even gene duplication does not free the "new" gene from its old definitions, nor give it new meaning. One can not select for control genes that do not yet exist. Self-referencing logic loops must come into existence as entire entities, not one component at a time. Once they are formed, *then* they can be modified, not before.

As for the probability that the world would turn out the same way if it was run a second time[47]—"Play it again, Sam!"—that obviously depends on the nature of GPS as well. If there are untold multitudes of low-probability outcomes, *and* there is no guidance, *then* it would not replay. As Gould would have it, we humans are "the embodiment of contingency: *Homo sapiens* is an entity, not a tendency."[48] We would not be back next time. But, that depends on Gould's projection of a necessary (richly branched) structure for GPS— necessary if we are to appear as a freaky accident, a product of *unguided* contingencies. Gould *assumes* lack of guidance, but if we are instead contingent products of a *guided* history, GPS might be otherwise empty.

Thus, we are again back on the "field of dreams." Shall we explain the appearance of new morphologies—and new individuations—as outside guidance given to lineages? Or shall we project back onto GPS the highly complex probability structure needed for their unguided realization? If the latter, what reason shall we give for so endowing GPS? The essentially religious nature of this choice is illustrated by Gould when he says of his conviction, "I have always regarded it as exhilarating, and a source of both freedom and consequent moral responsibility."[49]

Seeing Purpose without Proof

A biotic hierarchy of local teleologies might suggest that a vision of purpose is just that hierarchy projected across the universe, cloud faces sketched on chaos. But this will not do. In the absence of mental templates we perceive nothing at all—neither chaos nor design. Without local teleologies, we would not have formed such templates. Some perceive purpose in the cosmos, and others perceive its absence—which perception is valid? Local teleology can be a valid arrow pointing beyond itself to deeper meaning.

It may be that the God to which such teleologies point is not one we wish to acknowledge. Stephen Gould has based two arguments on such discomfort. First, he points out that imperfect adaptation (such as the panda's thumb) would be unworthy of the Divine Engineer.[50] Of course, that assumes that such an engineer would not work through directed historical processes. Second, Gould suggests that perfect adaptation achieved through neo-Darwinian mechanisms (directed selection?) requires relentless slaughter, and is thus morally repugnant.[51] He thus assumes that mutational search would be directionless—which is hardly reasonable if he is also assuming that *selection* is directed. In *both* arguments, Gould assumes that the divine intentions (final causes) are just what Paley and Curvier thought they were—individual environmental adaptation.

Darwin had the same problem with the shape of the biological world and the problem of evil. Warfield commented that "Mr. Darwin's difficulty arises on the one side from his inability to conceive of God as immanent in the universe and his consequent misapprehension of the nature of divine providence, and on the other from a very crude notion of final cause which posits a single extrinsic end as the sole purpose of the Creator. . . . No one would hold to a teleology of the raw sort which he here has in mind—a teleology which finds the end for which a thing exists in the misuse or abuse of it by an outside selecting agent." [52] In other words, we have no reason to follow Darwin and Gould in accepting Paley's limited vision of divine purpose.

But, does this make God evil? The question of God's providential governance always raises that question.[53] Philosopher Alvin Plantinga points out that if we assume that God is omniscient, omnipotent, and morally perfect, and that he created the world, we must *prove* that some possible world could have contained a better balance of broadly moral good to broadly moral evil to render his existence improbable. But, to do that, we would have to be omniscient ourselves. Thus, we simply cannot know enough to accuse God of evil.[54]

What then shall we believe? Materialism has tacitly rejected the presence of local teleology, a view clearly inadequate for biology. It has acted as a powerful constraint on theoretical work, inhibiting the formation of valid biological understanding (even perception) of local individuation/coherences. Likewise, this worldview has tacitly assumed a shape for genetic phase space. It is difficult to see any reason for the metaphysical "dogma" that nature must be viewed as undirected, and thus biotic systems *must* arise autonomously. How utterly circular a reason to reject statements about ultimate purpose! Is it likely to be a valid key to larger realities?

It has been said that to admit the possibility of the "God Hypothesis" is to make science impossible, for that hypothesis can never be falsified.[55] But, neither can the hypothesis that GPS is of such Byzantine complexity that known mechanisms, without guidance, are sufficient to produce biological morphologies. No matter what difficulty arises, the occult structure of genetic phase space can be modified to meet it. Is that a more reasonable faith than a belief that a wise intelligence stands behind GPS? Are we more reasonable if we locate our God in eternity, or if we build him in genetic phase space? I leave the reader to judge.

Endnotes

Introduction

[1] L. Eiseley, *The Firmament of Time* (New York: Atheneum, 1985), p. 5.

[2] K. C. Cole, "On Imagining the Unseeable," *Discover* (December 1982): 70.

[3] T. Kuhn, *The Structure of Scientific Revolutions*, 2nd edit. (Chicago: University of Chicago Press, 1970).

[4] A. Peacocke, *Intimations of Reality* (Notre Dame: University of Notre Dame Press, 1984), p. 16.

[5] McMullin, "The Relativist Critique of Science" in *The Sciences and Theology in the Twentieth Century*, edit. A. Peacocke (Notre Dame: University of Notre Dame Press, 1981), pp. 301-02.

[6] McMullin, "The Relativist Critique of Science," p. 26.

[7] T. Ferris, *Coming of Age in the Milky Way* (New York: William Morrow, 1988), p. 383.

[8] S. Gould, *Wonderful Life—The Burgess Shale and the Nature of History* (New York: W. W. Norton & Co., 1989).

[9] P. Davies, *The Cosmic Blueprint* (New York: Simon & Schuster, 1988), p. 140.

[10] D. Kenyon and G. Steinman, *Biochemical Predestination* (New York: McGraw Hill, 1969).

[11] C. Thaxton, W. Bradley, and R. Olsen, *The Mystery of Life's Origin: Reassessing Current Theories* (New York: Philosophical Library, 1984).

[12] Ibid., p. vii.

[13] L. Young, *The Unfinished Universe* (New York: Simon & Schuster, 1986), p. 57.

[14] Ibid., p. 76.

[15] Ibid., p. 87.

[16] Ibid., p. 89.

[17] L. Eiseley, *The Immense Journey* (New York: Vantage Books, 1957), p. 64.

[18] Ibid., p. 77.

[19] R. Lewin, *In the Age of Mankind* (Washington, DC: Smithsonian Books, 1988).

[20] K. Weaver, "The Search for Our Ancestors," *National Geographic*, 168 (1985): 578.

[21] C. B. Stringer, "The Emergence of Modern Humans," *Scientific American* (December 1990): 102-3.

[22] Ibid., p. 99.

[23] D. Wilcox, personal communications.

[24] Genesis 1:26, 27 in Holy Bible New International Version (Grand Rapids: Zondervan, 1978).

[25] C. G. Smith, *Ancestral Voices* (Englewood Cliffs, NJ: Prentice-Hall, 1985).

[26] J. Goodall, "The Behavior of Free-Living Chimpanzees in the Gombe Stream Reserve," *Animal Behavior Monographs* 1 (1968): 161–311.

[27] S. Gould, *Wonderful Life*, p. 319.

Chapter 1: Dare a Scientist Believe in Design?

[1] B. M. Olivera, *et al.*, "Diversity of *Conus* Neuropeptides," *Science* 249 (20 July 1990): 257-63.

[2] Marica Barinaga, "Science Digests the Secrets of Voracious Killer Snails," *Science* 249 (20 July 1990): 250-51.

[3] James L. Carew, "'Purposeful Evolution'" (letter), *Science* 249 (24 August 1990): 843.

[4] William Paley, *Natural Theology; or, Evidences of the Existence and Attributes of the Deity Collected from the Appearances of Nature* (Edinburgh, 1816), chapter 5, section 5, p. 61.

[5] Johannes Kepler, *Harmonies of the World*, p. 1085 in *Great Books of the Western World*, vol. 16 (Chicago, 1952).

[6] J. J. Rousseau, *Profession of Faith of a Savoyard Vicar* (1765), quoted in Alan Lightman and Owen Gingerich, "When Do Anomalies Begin?" *Science* 225 (February 7, 1992): 690-95.

[7] Ernst Mayr, "The Ideological Resistance to Darwin's Theory of Natural Selection," *Proceedings of the American Philosophical Society* 135 (1991): 123-39, on. p. 131.

[8] George Gaylord Simpson, *The Meaning of Evolution* (New York: Mentor Edition, 1951), p. 143.

[9] Fred Hoyle, "The Universe: Past and Present Reflections," pp. 8-12 in *Engineering and Science* (November 1981), esp. p. 12.

[10] Paley, *Natural Theology*, chapter 22.

[11] Walt Whitman, "Song of Myself," stanza 31, in *Leaves of Grass* (1891-92 edition).

[12] Lecomte du Noüy, *Human Destiny* (New York, 1947), p. 35.

[13] Ibid., p. 38.

[14] Mayr, "Ideological Resistance," p. 131.

[15] Simpson, *Meaning of Evolution*, p. 144.

[16] Stephen Hawking, *A Brief History of Time* (New York, 1988) p. 125.

[17] Slightly abridged and modified from my translation in *Great Ideas Today 1983* (Chicago, 1983), pp. 321-22.

[18] *First Things* no. 6 (October 1990): 23.

[19] Charles B. Thaxton, Walter L. Bradley, and Roger L. Olsen, *The Mystery of Life's Origin: Reassessing Current Theories* (New York, 1984).

[20] Phillip E. Johnson, *Darwin on Trial* (Washington, DC, 1991).

[21] Johannes Kepler, *Harmonice mundi*, IV, 7, p. 1619.

[22] Milton K. Munitz, *Cosmic Understanding: Philosophy and Science of the Universe* (Princeton, 1986).

[23] End of book 5, chapter 9 of *Harmonice mundi, Johannes Kepler Gesammelte Werke*, 6:362; my translation is based on the ones by Charles Glenn Wallis in *Great Books of the Western World* , 16, and by Eric J. Aiton, forthcoming, American Philosophical Society.

Chapter 2: God's Purpose in and Beyond Time

[1] A. Einstein, *Relativity: The Special and General Theory*, trans. R. W. Lawson (University Paperback, 1960), p. 150.

Chapter 3: The Unreasonable Effectiveness of Science

[1] Jacques Monod, *Chance and Necessity*, trans. A. Wainhouse (London: Collins, 1972), p. 167.

[2] Steven Weinberg, *The First Three Minutes* (London: Andre Deutsch, 1977), p. 149.

[3] For a fuller account see *The Mind of God* by Paul Davies (New York: Simon & Schuster, 1992).

[4] Paul Davies, *The Cosmic Blueprint* (New York: Simon & Schuster, 1988).

[5] See Davies, *The Mind of God*, chapter 7.

[6] L. J. Henderson, *The Fitness of the Environment*, reprint (Gloucester, MA: Peter Smith, 1970), p. 312.

[7] In *Religion and the Scientists*, ed. Mervyn Stockwood (London: SCM Press, 1959).

[8] Fred Hoyle, *The Intelligent Universe* (London: Michael Joseph, 1983).

[9] For a recent review see *Cosmic Coincidences* by John Gribbin and Martin Rees (New York: Bantam, 1989).

[10] Thomas Aquinas, *Summa Theologiae*, pt. 1, ques. 2, art. 3.

[11] Robert Boyle, *Works* (London, 1744), vol. 4, p. 522.

[12] Carl Sagan, *Contact* (London: Century, 1986).

[13] Richard Dawkins, *The Blind Watchmaker* (London: Longman, 1986).

[14] John Barrow, *Theories of Everything* (Oxford: Oxford University Press, 1991), p. 172.

[15] Ronald E. Mickens, *Mathematics and Science* (Singapore: World Scientific, 1990).

Chapter 5: Cosmology: Evidence for God or Partner for Theology

[1] Pope John Paul II, "Message," in *Physics, Philosophy, and Theology: A Common Quest for Understanding*, ed. by Robert John Russell, William R. Stoeger, and George V. Coyne (Vatican Observatory: Vatican City State and Notre Dame: University of Notre Dame, 1988). Reprinted with responses in *John Paul II on Science and Religion: Reflections on the New View from Rome*, same editors and publisher, 1990.

[2] For a very helpful survey of the field of science and religion and a typology that has become the "standard of the industry," see the writings of Ian G. Barbour. In particular see his "Ways of Relating Science and Theology" in Russell, *Physics, Philosophy, and Theology*, pp. 21-48. If we were to use his typology, what I am reject-

ing is Biblical Literalism and the Independence models, as well as design arguments (which do not figure prominently in his typology).

³ The Vatican Observatory and the Center for Theology and the Natural Sciences are cosponsoring a decade of international research conferences focusing on a variety of scientific and theological topics within the framework of "God's Action in the World." Several participants are working on the philosophical and theological elements at least implicitly present in scientific research. CTNS will also be involved, during the next three years, in a major research effort sponsored by the National Institutes of Health to analyze the theological and ethical issues raised by and, to some extent, implicit in the Human Genome Project. See endnote 42 below.

⁴ For an introduction to physical cosmology see Timothy Ferris, *Coming of Age in the Milky Way* (New York: William Morrow and Company, 1988); John Horgan, "Universal Truths: Trends in Cosmology," *Scientific American*, vol. 263 (October 1990); Joseph Silk, *The Big Bang: The Creation and Evolution of the Universe* (San Francisco: W. H. Freeman, 1980); James S. Trefil, *The Moment of Creation: Big Bang Physics from Before the First Millisecond to the Present Universe* (New York: Charles Scribner's Sons, 1983); and Steven Weinberg, *The First Three Minutes: A Modern View of the Origin of the Universe* (New York: Basic Books, 1977).

⁵ It turns out that the mass of the universe determines whether the universe is open or closed. The problem now is how to measure the actual mass of the universe. The amount of mass we can observe indicates that the universe is barely open (or "flat"). If there is significantly more matter in the universe than has so far been observed but as some indirect arguments suggest, the universe may be closed. This is referred to as the "missing mass" problem. See Trefil, *Moment of Creation*.

⁶ A very similar scenario is predicted for the future of a closed universe. As the universe passes the point of maximum expansion and begins to collapse into itself, its temperature will rise indefinitely. Ultimately the universe will end in a singularity much like the one from which it began. For the open and flat universes, the future will be one of endless cold and unending time, in which the universal temperature approaches nearer and nearer to absolute zero. Thus if the Big Bang scenarios are correct the future of the universe is either to "freeze or fry."

⁷ Here I simply assume that science as *method* presupposes that each state of affairs (event) is the result (effect) of a previous state of affairs (cause). The laws that relate cause and effect may or may not be deterministic in the Laplacian sense, as quantum physics has shown us. Still it is hard to see how science could stipulate the existence of an event for which there could *in principle* be no knowable cause. Hence if general relativity and its product, the standard Big Bang models, suggest that such an event actually occurred in nature and that it is not just a faulty prediction of the theory or a consequence of its own anomalous presuppositions, it leaves us with a difficult philosophical *and* scientific problem. Clearly it is for reasons like this that alternative theories to general relativity and the Big Bang models are being studied.

⁸ In the steady state model the universe is infinitely old and infinite in size. Moreover, it has always been expanding exponentially and it will continue to expand forever.

⁹ A very *rough* analogy for time here would be a circle: it has a finite circumference but no end.

¹⁰ For background reading, see Langdon Gilkey, *Maker of Heaven and Earth: The Christian Doctrine of Creation in the Light of Modern Knowledge* (Lanham: University Press of America, 1959; 1985); Philip J. Hefner, "The Creation," in *Christian Dogmatics*, eds. Carl E. Braaten and Robert W. Jenson (Philadelphia: Fortress Press, 1984). For a very recent comprehensive survey of the relationship between the theology of creation and the history of science, see Christopher Kaiser, *Creation and the History of Science* (London: Marshall Pickering, 1991).

¹¹ See Gilkey, *Maker of Heaven*, p. 310ff.

¹² *Summa Theologica*, part I, question 46, article 2.

¹³ According to Pope Pius XII, in an allocution to the Pontifical Academy of Sciences in Rome in 1951, contemporary cosmology discloses "the mark of the Eternal One" and, if developed further, "can provide a sure foundation for arguments which of themselves are outside the natural sciences." (Portions of the text are translated in the *Bulletin of the Atomic Scientists* 8 (1952): 143-46, 165. Representative of the views of some scientists was the comment made by Robert Jastrow that "science will never be able to raise the curtain on the mystery of creation." Yet Jastrow suggests that science leads us to that mystery that theologians have known "for centuries." See his *God and the Astronomers* (New York: W. W. Norton & Co., 1978), p. 115-16. A more nuanced view has been espoused by the authors of *Teaching Science in a Climate of Controversy* and a more theologically reflective argument was put forward by Lutheran theologian Ted Peters ("On Creating the Cosmos," in *Physics, Philosophy, and Theology: A Common Quest for Understanding*, ed. by Russell, Stoeger, and Coyne, pp. 273-96).

¹⁴ For a thorough introduction to the philosophical issues in cosmology see "Contemporary Cosmology and Its Implications for the Science-Religion Dialogue" by William Stoeger in Russell, et al., *Physics, Philosophy, and Theology*, pp. 219-47; see also Benjamin Gal-Or, *Cosmology, Physics, and Philosophy* (New York: Springer-Verlag, 1981).

¹⁵ Put another way, how can we study something scientifically if it is absolutely unique?

¹⁶ George Ellis has pointed in particular to the unobservability of the early universe and of its final state.

¹⁷ Additional questions should also be noted. For example (10) the passage of time and the difference between past and future are components of ordinary human experience. Yet most scholars argue that the "arrow of time" is not found in the fundamental laws of physics. How then are we to relate time in nature and time in human experience?

(11) The terms *finite* and *infinite* have a long and complex history in philosophy, mathematics, and the empirical sciences. Since they frequently occur in cosmological models, in particular in our discussion about the "finite past" suggested by "$t = 0$," their meaning deserves careful analysis before any theological conclusions can be drawn.

(12) A commonly held philosophical position among scientists is critical realism. But in what sense do concepts in cosmology, such as "the universe," "$t = 0$," "curvature," etc., refer in the same way that concepts in the other sciences do?

(13) Is our universe unique, or could all logically possible universes be real, as in so-called many-worlds theories? Why is the actual universe orderly and intelligible, given that one can imagine either an intelligible universe that is highly disorderly and an orderly universe that is unintelligible in detail? These and other questions are related to the controversial anthropic principle, which we will discuss below.

[18] See, for example, Michael J. Buckley, *At the Origins of Modern Atheism* (New Haven: Yale University Press, 1987).

[19] As Nancey Murphy pointed out to me, in *Revelation and Reason* Brunner shows increasing interest in the interaction between science (especially the human sciences) and theology. In his recent writings and lectures, Gilkey too has become increasingly interested in the interaction and will be a participant in the Vatican/ CTNS conferences as well as in the CTNS Human Genome conferences.

[20] The following arguments are in a sense the "other side" of the arguments I gave against strongly identifying theology and science in the preceding section.

[21] Bultmann's attempt to demythologize the New Testament Kerygma of myth is a standard example of a theologian uncritically accepting a worldview (the causally-closed mechanical universe) based on science and philosophy (the Cartesian/ Newtonian developments of the seventeenth century).

[22] The doctrine of creation in particular was an important intellectual element in the rise of experimental science. Because God's act is free the world as God's creation is contingent. Because it is created by divine rationality, the world is orderly. Hence one must experiment with the world to learn about it (deduction alone will not suffice). Because the world is not divine, one is morally free to experiment with the world. In this and other ways historically the doctrine of creation laid the theological and philosophical grounds for the rise of experimental science in the sixteenth century.

For an excellent discussion of these and related historical issues, the reader is again referred to Kaiser, *History of Science*. Other sources include Eugene Klaaren, *Religious Origins of Modern Science* (Grand Rapids: William B. Eerdmans, 1977); David C. Lindberg and Ronald L. Numbers, eds., *God and Nature: Historical Essays on the Encounter between Christianity and Science* (Berkeley: University of California Press, 1986). See also Nicholas Wolterstorff, *Reason within the Bounds of Religion* (Grand Rapids: William B. Eerdmans, 1976).

[23] To place this shift in perspective, we must first remember that until the Enlightenment nature, as well as human history, was a part of the theological problematic and a possible source of knowledge about God (at least as Creator).

This is certainly evident in Scripture. A sweeping theme of the Hebrew Scriptures is that the God who redeems Israel is the Creator of the universe. Theologies of creation are found in both the older Yahwistic stories of Eden (Gen. 2:4b-25) and the lofty Priestly version involving the entire biblical cosmology (Gen. 1:1-2:4a). Following the Flood—a catastrophe of cosmic proportions in the Priestly narrative (Gen. 7:11)—a new covenant is made that includes all life, not just humanity (Gen. 9:9-17). This covenant is reflected in the prophets (cf. Hos. 2:16-23) and taken up into the vision of "a new heaven and a new earth" (Isa. 66:17-25). Indeed the creation of the universe by the God of Israel is a theme running throughout the Hebrew testament, as Proverbs 8 so movingly portrays.

In the New Testament, Christ is seen as the new creation, the Word of God by which all things were made (John 1:1-3) and through whom the old has passed away (2 Cor. 5:17). Jesus teaches in parables drawn from nature, and his power as Messiah is evidenced in healings and nature miracles. The Resurrection of Christ is significant not only for humans but for all creation groaning in travail (Rom. 8:18-25). Finally, the Parousia will bring about a "new heaven and new earth" as promised to the prophets (2 Pet. 3:13; Rev. 21:1-4).

Patristic, medieval and even Reformation theologians by and large continued to speak about the creative power of God in both historical and natural terms until the rise of liberal Protestant theology in the nineteenth century. Since then mainline Protestant theologians have prescinded from articulating their theologies in terms of a cosmological perspective. Instead they by and large believe that the fundamental realm for religious discourse lies in value judgments and human subjectivity rather than in metaphysical interpretations of "objective facts" gained through the sciences.

[24] See Barbour, *Ways of Relating Science and Theology*, for a general discussion of these approaches.

[25] One of the central theological problems in assessing and appropriating science has been methodological: what constitutes epistemic progress in science? And can an answer to this question be appropriated fruitfully in the context of religion? i.e., what would really count as "progress in religion"?

Often a Popperian form of answer regarding science is given, that science is characterized by falsificationism: one must stipulate *in advance* what kinds of evidence can count *against* an hypothesis. Of course there is a wide spectrum of views on just what falsification means. I would emphasize the complexity of the process by which various domains of evidence are admitted, certain specific instances of data are acknowledged to count against the hypothesis, and the ways in which a core theory is protected from direct falsification by auxiliary (and possibly *ad hoc*) hypotheses. Nevertheless, during a significant portion of the history of the philosophy of science in this century, falsification via data was taken to demarcate scientific method from all other epistemological methods, and in this sense any field that adopts a falsificationist method can be considered to be "scientific."

On the other hand, beginning in the 1960s, "revisionist" philosophers of science such as Stephen Toulmin, Thomas Kuhn, Gerald Holton, Paul Feyerabend, and Imre Lakatos have expanded their understanding of science to include the influence of metaphysical and sociocultural elements in the competition between frequently incommensurate scientific paradigms. Imre Lakatos has given a particularly persuasive interpretation of scientific methodology in terms of a core hypothesis, a positive heuristic, a belt of auxiliary hypotheses that protect the core from direct falsification by anomalous data, and criteria of ad hoc-ness by which competing theories may be rationally judged. In a sense Lakatos incorporates the best of Popperian falsificationism with the most undeniable elements of the revisionist paradigmatic critique.

In my opinion what is therefore central to obtaining epistemic "progress in religion" will be insights gained from contemporary philosophy of science drawn from Lakatos, Kuhn, Popper, and others. This will begin with the acknowledgment by theologians that at least some of their theories (doctrines) are hypothetical, revisable, and ultimately refutable by evidence—and, most demandingly, the type of evidence that could falsify theological theory must be stipulated *in advance* (i.e., "predictions," where this term is properly understood in the theological context, must be made). Initial moves to acknowledge the hypothetical character of theology and the importance of falsification are being taken by some theologians, including Wolfhart Pannenberg, *Theology and the Philosophy of Science* (Philadelphia: Westminster Press, 1976).

Beyond this initial move we must draw on revisionist as well as Popperian insights. In this genre, a much more informed analysis of scientific methodology and its potential value to theology has recently been published by Nancey Murphy, *Theology in an Age of Scientific Reasoning* (Ithaca: Cornell University Press, 1990). Murphy draws on the arguments of Lakatos and other recent philosophers of science, and shows how this kind of method can be used fruitfully by theologians.

I would conclude that, though we can go further in appropriating scientific method for theology, we must not ignore the criterion of falsifiability: that, though one hopes that a theory is true, the theory must be formulated such that it can *in principle* be shown to be false. Clearly Lakatos and others incorporate this criterion; my concern is to keep theologians honest by not going too quickly beyond it to the full Lakatosian methodology. Too many theologians have failed to take seriously the first steps in meeting the rigors of contemporary epistemology. Thus being willing to be wrong must count as an unavoidable first step—though only a first step; confirmation as a tantalizing goal lies beyond.

This approach may also be an important clue to the meaning of what might somewhat ambiguously be called a "theology of humility." John M. Templeton, *The Humble Approach: Scientists Discover God* (New York: Seabury Press, 1981); John M. Templeton and Robert L. Herrmann, *The God Who Would Be Known: Revelations of the Divine in Contemporary Science* (New York: Harper and Row, 1989); John M. Templeton, "Theology of Humility" (private circulation). Such a theology is not so much to be characterized by the humble piety of the theologian (or scientist) advancing it—though it is hard to see how decent theology (or science) can be produced by someone lacking genuine religious convictions (or the values of a scientist). Nor does it involve a repristination of the design argument, for no matter how helpful science might be to a piety that is already based elsewhere, the path to God cannot be created out of science itself. Thus there can be no direct "evidence for design" or "evidence for God," since theories are never proven by data (only falsified by data) nor derived logically from data (only discovered through insight in the context of data). That is, theological conclusions should never be derived from scientific data, but only confirmed by science after the fact. (This holds equally for "New Age" religions and other science-based myths that seek to draw their support from science as for new arguments for design that seek to support the Bible using science!)

But, lying beyond the rigors of falsification, there awaits for those who have been willing to "go the distance" a form of "confirmation of God" or "confirmation of design" in the sense of the more complicated methodology described by Murphy, where a core theory's ability to explain increasing amounts of data without *ad hoc* auxiliary hypotheses count as *epistemic progress*. In this sense recent philosophy of science can help us toward a more scientifically informed theological methodology, one that I would identify closely with a true "theology of humility."

Still the basic, first-level challenge for theologians is to find ways in which evidence, appropriately defined for theology, can be brought to bear on theological doctrines like creation and redemption. It will require that the theologian be willing to stipulate in advance what will count, not for but *against*, one's most cherished views. It will mean being so convinced of what is true that one is willing to expose that belief to the test of being false. It will mean that theologians do not primarily defend their theories so much as put them, and themselves, to the test. In short it will mean faith seeking understanding by risking doubt. It will entail a true test of humility and it will promise the potential to have theological claims find confirmation in the data of science.

[26] Einstein's case illustrates the complexity of the role played by these presuppositions, for they sometimes prove fruitful while at other times they prove misleading. Shortly after formulating general relativity it became apparent that the theory would not admit a static model of the universe. However Einstein believed that nature was eternal and changeless, leading him then to alter his basic equations in general relativity by the addition of the so-called cosmological constant. Shortly thereafter, Hubble's discovery of the expansion of the universe showed the alteration to be wrong and the equations were returned to their original form.

In a similar vein several decades later, Fred Hoyle's commitments to atheism led him to attack Big Bang cosmology for its apparent support of Christian theism. Together with Bondi and Gold he constructed the steady state model as an alternative to Big Bang cosmology. Although the discovery of the universal microwave background eventually led to the demise of Hoyle's model as the discovery of the expansion of the universe led to the rejection of the cosmological constant, I would not conclude that it was mistaken of Einstein or Hoyle to have been guided by their convictions about nature (nor, obviously, in Hoyle's case that "atheism was proven wrong"). Rather it suggests to me that it is possible, at least in some cases, to put into testable form (i.e., to render falsifiable) one's presuppositions about nature, and thus to find a path between deeply held convictions and public experimentation. In general I believe that theological and philosophical assumptions can continue to play a fruitful role in ongoing scientific research where they will be exposed to public, empirical testing, although it will take an intense effort by dual-trained scholars to transform these assumptions into explicit scientific theories.

[27] I also expect the converse could happen if scientists will search for the philosophical and theological assumptions underlying their theoretical research and bring them to light more intentionally and less as an afterthought. This movement would be part of what I mean by an "interaction" between theology and science—not just the theological reformulation in light of science, as is the usual move in the field.

[28] Ernan McMullin, "How Should Cosmology Relate to Theology?" in *The Sciences and Theology in the Twentieth Century*, ed. by A. R. Peacocke (Notre Dame: University of Notre Dame Press, 1981).

[29] Ted Peters, ed., *Cosmos as Creation* (Nashville: Abingdon Press, 1989).

[30] *Religion in an Age of Science*, volume 1, The Gifford Lectures 1989-91 (San Francisco: Harper and Row, 1990).

[31] Willem Bernard Drees, *Beyond the Big Bang: Quantum Cosmologies and God* (La Salle: Open Court, 1990).

[32] See, for example, Robert John Russell, "Cosmology, Creation, and Contingency," in Peters, *Cosmos as Creation*, pp. 177-209.

[33] The careful reader will note that this understanding of consonance is based on an epistemological assumption, namely, that a *metaphorical* relation involving both a simile and a dissimile exists between specific theories in theology and science. This view is due in part to the work of Ian Barbour and Sallie McFague, who in turn draw on Paul Ricoeur. A metaphorical relation between theories in the two fields implies a tension between "is" and "is not," i.e., between similarities (read "consonance") and dissimilarities (read "dissonance"). Both are to be expected, although the precise form they take will vary from case to case. It should be noted that this argument is controversial; indeed, Janet Soskice has been critical of using metaphors as analogies between fields. In this paper I hope to discover the variation in the metaphor *as the theories in the related fields change.*

[34] For the technical meaning of *ad hoc* see Murphy, *Theology in an Age of Scientific Reasoning*, and her use of this term as taken from Lakatos.

[35] See endnote 1.

[36] I must admit—and emphasize—that I am relatively alone among scholars in theology and science in stressing the importance and value of dissonance.

[37] It should be repeated that scientists are divided on this issue. The universe may, in fact, be closed, i.e., finite in past, future, and size. Such a universe would obviously be more in consonance with Christian theology. However, the current evidence favoring the open scenario must be taken very seriously, and the more complex ways indicated above of relating such results to theology must be born in mind.

[38] Clearly these doctrines have complicated histories and are quite variously formulated. A very careful analysis needs to be undertaken to determine in precisely which ways the spatial infinity and future eternity of the universe depicted by an open Big Bang model challenges them.

[39] Recall the basis in *metaphor* for all language that I have referred to previously.

[40] This is in a sense a "win-win" strategy, until a theory becomes overwhelmed by strictly *ad hoc* moves.

[41] J. B. Hartle and S. W. Hawking, "Wave Function of the Universe," *Phys. Rev. D* (15 December 1983), pp. 2960-75. See also L. Z. Fang and R. Ruffini, eds., *Quantum Cosmology*, vol. 3, *Advanced Series in Astrophysics and Cosmology* (Singapore: World Scientific, 1987).

[42] Clearly there are tremendously subtle philosophical issues involved here. Some of these will be the subject of papers at the Vatican/CTNS conference in September 1991.

[43] Stephen W. Hawking, *A Brief History of Time: From the Big Bang to Black Holes* (Toronto: Bantam Book, 1988). In the introduction to Hawking's book Carl Sagan concludes that, since the universe has no beginning, there's nothing left for God to do. Obviously the "God" Sagan intends is more the god of deism than of Christianity. See my review in *America* (2 February 1991), pp. 95-97.

[44] Actually the status of the initial singularity in both classical cosmology and quantum gravity raises profound philosophical questions about the meaning and status of singularities in scientific and theological models—questions deserving of our *ongoing* attention.
Chris Isham has given a very insightful interpretation of the significance of

the Hawking/Hartle proposal for *creatio ex nihilo* in relation to Augustine's understanding of creation "of time." See "Creation of the Universe as a Quantum Process" in Russell, et al., *Physics, Philosophy, and Theology*, pp. 375-408. See also Drees, *Beyond the Big Bang,* for a helpful analysis of this issue.

These and other problems will be explored in the series of international research conferences mentioned in endnote 3. These conferences are being planned jointly by the Vatican Observatory and the Center for Theology and the Natural Sciences. The first conference, scheduled for September 1991, will focus on "The Quantum Creation of the Universe and the Origin of the Laws of Nature." The overall theme of the decade of conferences is "God's Action in the World."

[45] For a thorough discussion, see John Leslie, *Universes* (London: Routledge, 1989). Leslie developed these arguments in a variety of papers cited in *Universes*, including an article in Russell, et al., *Physics, Philosophy, and Theology*. See also John D. Barrow and Frank J. Tipler, *The Anthropic Cosmological Principle* (Oxford: Clarendon Press, 1986). See also Arthur Peacock, *Creation and the World of Science* (Oxford: Clarendon Press, 1979) and his more recent writings. See also John Polkinghorne, *Science and Creation* (Boston: Shambhala, 1988) and *Science and Providence* (Boston: Shambhala, 1989). See also Barbour, "Ways of Relating Science," Drees, *Beyond the Big Bang,* and McMullin in Peacocke, *Creation.*

[46] For a more traditional approach to natural theology see Stanley L. Jaki, *The Road of Science and the Ways to God* (Chicago: University of Chicago Press, 1978). Regarding ways that might be found within dogmatics proper for what was traditionally a prolegomenon to dogmatics (i.e., natural theology) see the revealing comments by Thomas F. Torrance about the methodology of Karl Barth in the preface to Torrance's *Space, Time, and Resurrection* (Grand Rapids: William B. Eerdmans, 1976). Torrance has also given a very helpful analysis of contingency as a theological principle relating the doctrine of creation to the methodology of science. See Thomas Torrance, *Divine and Contingent Order* (Oxford: Oxford University Press, 1981).

[47] For this and the following definitions of contingency, see Robert John Russell, "Contingency in Physics and Cosmology: A Critique of the Theology of Wolfhart Pannenberg," in *Zygon: Journal of Religion and Science*, vol. 23 (March 1988): 23-43. This article was written in response to Wolfhart Pannenberg, "The Doctrine of Creation and Modern Science," in *Zygon: Journal of Religion and Science*, vol. 23 (March 1988): 3-21. This discussion was picked up and rethematized by Ian Barbour in his recent Gifford Lectures, *Theology in an Age of Science,* pp. 142ff.

[48] Cosmology and fundamental physics may be able to answer some of these questions scientifically. But what is important here is that questions in the scientific arena are infused with philosophical questions about contingency, and that such questions have engaged theologians over the centuries as they wrestled with the central conviction that God is the transcendent creator of the universe. Since these are now *also* questions pondered by cosmologists, the way in which theologians interpret divine creation should take into account the ways cosmologists currently deal scientifically and philosophically with the contingency of the universe. (This does not imply that one starts with the scientific discussion and uses it as a basis for theological conclusions!)

[49] See Ernan McMullin, *Newton on Matter and Activity* (Notre Dame: University of Notre Dame Press, 1978); Ernan McMullin, ed., *The Concept of Matter in*

Modern Philosophy (Notre Dame: University of Notre Dame Press, 1963, 1978); Max Jammer, *Concepts of Mass in Classical and Modern Physics* (New York: Harper & Row, 1961). See also the article by Pannenberg in Peacocke, *Creation*, question 1.

[50] The presence of limit questions in science would be related to what David Tracy calls limit questions in general.

[51] One might then go on to relate global existential and global ontological contingency by why the only actual universe, among all possible universes, exists as the one in which life will evolve.

[52] For example, according to some forms of inflationary cosmology the actual universe is in effect divided into vast domains between which there can be little if any further communication. Just one of these domains could easily include our own "universe." As for the fine-tuning approach, what needs to be explained, i.e., the confluence of "the right" global features of this universe, may in principle be explainable in terms of the increasingly popular "Theories of Everything." Obviously these two arguments (domains and TOE's) are closely related.

[53] Robert John Russell, "Cosmology, Creation, and Contingency," in Peters, *Cosmos as Creation*, pp. 177-209.

[54] Of course since Hume we have known that design arguments are highly problematic on a *strictly philosophical* basis, since general conclusions can never be drawn logically or proven formally from a finite set of data (see Hume's famous problem of induction). See *An Enquiry concerning Human Understanding*, ed. L. A. Selby-Bigge (Oxford: Clarendon Press, 1902). Other problems, notably the problem of evil, were used by Hume in his attack on theism. For an important contemporary critique of the status of theology since Hume and its inability to meet Hume's challenge, see Jeffrey Stout, *Flight from Authority* (Notre Dame: University of Notre Dame Press, 1981).

[55] See Buckley, *Origins of Modern Theism*.

[56] This sort of approach surfaces in the writings of Ian Barbour, Teilhard de Chardin, Paul Davies, Arthur Peacocke, John Polkinghorne, Frank Tipler, and many others, with varying theological implications taken. What I would resist is the tendency in some writers to take this insight and make it into a design argument—that a home implies a home builder with a blueprint in mind beforehand and tools external to the material out of which the home is built. If, on the other hand, the metaphor were more organic, it might allow the builder to be immanent in the evolution of creation.

The problem here is that the universe doesn't look so much like an organism as it does a mechanism—admittedly a chaotic one. Perhaps, again, quantum field theory and general relativity can soften even this critique to allow for more connectivity at the global level than we have so far seen for the universe.

[57] A similar analysis should be carried out for other cosmological models, including inflation and quantum gravity, so that the shifting forms of this argument can be tracked as we did with the "t = 0" case.

[58] As it evolved, the four interactions eventually separated, producing the universe as we know it today.

[59] Wolfhart Pannenberg, "The Doctrine of Creation and Modern Science," in *Zygon: Journal of Religion and Science*, vol 23 (March 1988): 3-21.

[60] One could easily add here the laws of nature that contain these constants, but that would take us beyond the limits of the present paper.

[61] This argument bears strongly on the problem of theodicy.

[62] McMullin in Peacocke, *Creation*, p. 52.

Chapter 6: Science and God the Creator

[1] Paul Davies, *God and the New Physics* (New York: Simon & Schuster, 1983), preface, viii–ix.

[2] Ibid., p. 229.

[3] Robert Jastrow, *God and the Astronomers* (New York: Warner Books, 1984), pp. 124-25. (Lecture originally given to the American Association for the Advancement of Science, Washington, February 14, 1978).

[4] Q.v., Arthur Peacocke, *Intimations of Reality: Critical Realism in Science and Religion* (Notre Dame, Ind.: University of Notre Dame Press, 1984) and references therein; "Science and Theology Today: A Critical Realist Perspective," *Religion and Intellectual Life* 5 (1988): 45-58. A helpful account of and apologia for, its significance for systematic theology has been given by W. van Huysteen in *Theology and the Justification of Faith* (Grand Rapids, Mich.: Eerdmans, 1989), chap. 9. See also M. Banner, n. 23, below.

[5] J. Leplin, introduction in *Scientific Realism*, ed. J. Leplin (University of California Press, 1984), p. 2.

[6] Ernan McMullin, "The Case for Scientific Realism," in Leplin, *Scientific Realism*, p. 26.

[7] Ibid., p. 30.

[8] Ian Barbour, *Issues in Science and Religion* (New York: Harper and Row, 1971, paperback edition), p. 158.

[9] Janet Martin Soskice, *Metaphor and Religious Language* (Oxford: Clarendon Press, 1984), chap. 7; Sallie McFague, *Models of God* (London: SCM Press, 1987).

[10] Q.v., B. G. Mitchell, *The Justification of Religious Belief* (London: Macmillan, 1973; D. Pailin, *God and the Processes of Reality* (London: Routledge, 1989); M. Banner, *The Justification of Science and the Rationality of Religious Belief* (Oxford: Clarendon Press, 1990).

[11] For these laws are mathematical ones constituting a system if there is a TOE. Hence, like all such mathematical structures, a TOE would: (1) be based on axioms that could have been otherwise and cannot be proved to be consistent from within the system; and (2) not be complete. For the mathematician Kurt Godel proved that "from within the system it was impossible to prove the truth of all true statements contained in that system. This inherent, unavoidable lack of completeness must reflect itself in whatever mathematical system models our universe. As creatures belonging to the physical world, we will be included as part of that model. It follows that we shall never be able to justify the choice of axioms in the model—and consequently the physical laws to which those axioms correspond. Nor shall we be able to account for all the true statements that can be made about the universe" (Russell Stannard, physicist, see reference following).

[12.] Russell Stannard, "No Faith in the Grand Theory," the *Times*, 13 November 1989.

[13] E.g., Richard Swinburne, *The Existence of God* (Oxford: Clarendon Press, 1979), p. 8.

[14] P. W. Atkins, *The Creation* (Oxford and San Francisco: W. H. Freeman, 1981).

[15] H. Montefiore, *The Probability of God* (London: SCM Press, 1985); John Polkinghorne, *Science and Creation* (London: SPCK, 1988).

[16] Q.v., for example, the discussion of J. Leslie, "How to Draw Conclusions from a Fine-tuned Universe," in *Physics, Philosophy, and Theology: A Common Quest for Understanding* (Vatican City State: Vatican Observatory publication, 1988, distributed by University of Notre Dame Press), pp. 297-311; and his recently published *Universes* (London: Routledge, 1989).

[17] A. N. Whitehead, *Science and the Modern World* (New York: Mentor Books edn., 1949), p. 56.

[18] John Durant, 1988 Enschede lecture on "Is There a Role for Theology in an Age of Secular Science?" Second European Conference on Science and Religion.

[19] The use of the male pronoun here is not meant to exclude feminine aspects of God.

[20] Heisenberg systems are unpredictable in principle—and it now seems likely that this is also the case with nonlinear dynamic systems. (The unpredictability of these latter is beginning to make intelligible how the free will we experience might be grounded in neuronal networks.)

[21] Paul S. Fiddes, *The Creative Suffering of God* (Oxford: Clarendon Press, 1988) p. 3.

[22] Ibid., p. 45 .

[23] Stephen W. Hawking, *A Brief History of Time* (London: Bantam Press, 1988) pp. 134-36.

[24] Ibid., p. 135.

[25] Ibid., p. 136.

[26] Ibid., p. 174.

[27] Originally propounded, A. R. Peacocke, *Creation and the World of Science* (Oxford: Clarendon Press, 1979) pp. 105-6; developed in *Intimations of Reality* (n. 4, above), p. 72; and expounded more fully in *Theology for a Scientific Age* (Oxford: Blackwells, 1990), chap. 9.3.

Chapter 7: A Potent Universe

[1] J. C. Polkinghorne, *Science and Creation* (SPCK/New Science Library, 1988), chap. 2.

[2] J. D. Barrow and F. J. Tipler, *The Anthropic Cosmological Principle* (Oxford University Press, 1986); J. Leslie, *Universes* (Routledge, 1989).

[3] J. C. Polkinghorne, *One World* (SPCK/Princeton University Press, 1986), chap. 2; *Rochester Roundabout* (Longman/Freeman, 1989), chap. 21.

[4] See reference 2.

[5] See, e.g., J. C. Polkinghorne, *Quantum World* (Longman/Princeton University Press, 1984), chap. 4.

[6] It would satisfy current wisdom by corresponding to a renormalizable quantum field theory.

[7] See, e.g., Leslie, *Universes*, chap. 2.

[8] See, e.g., S. Weinberg, *The First Three Minutes* (Andre Deutsch, 1977).

[9] Leslie, *Universes*, chap. 1.
[10] J. C. Polkinghorne, *Reason and Reality* (SPCK, 1991), chap. 7.
[11] Ibid., chap. 6.
[12] Leslie, *Universes*, chap. 1.
[13] See, e.g., R. Swinburne, *The Existence of God* (Oxford University Press, 1979).

Chapter 8: The Evolution of Purpose

REFERENCES

Amsterdam, B. 1972. "Mirror Self-Image Reactions Before the Age of Two." *Devel. Psychobiol.* 5: 297-305.

Akert, K., Peper, K., and Sandri, C. 1975. "Structural Organization of Motor End Plate and Central Synapses." In *Cholinergic Mechanisms*, ed. P. G. Waser, pp. 43-57, New York: Raven Press.

Dobzhansky, T. 1967. *The Biology of Ultimate Concern*. New York: New American Library.

Eccles, J. C. 1979. *The Human Mystery*. Berlin, Heidelberg, New York: Springer Internat.

Eccles, J. C. 1989, *Evolution of the Brain: Creation of the Self*. New York, London: Routledge.

Eccles, J. C. 1990. "A Unitary Hypothesis of Mind-Brain Interaction in the Cerebral Cortex." *Proc. Roy. Soc. Lond.* B 240:433-51.

Gallup, G. G. 1977. "Self-recognition in Primates." *Amer. Psychol.* 32:329-38.

Granit, R. 1977. *The Purposive Brain*. Cambridge, MA, and London, England: MIT Press.

Jerison, H. J. 1990. "Fossil Evidence on the Evolution of the Neocortex." In *Cerebral Cortex*, vol. 8A, ed. E. G. Jones and A. Peters, pp. 285-309. New York: Plenum Press.

Kelly, R. B., Deutsch, J. W., Carlson, S. S., and Wagner, J. A. 1979. "Biochemistry of Neurotransmitter Release. *Annu Rev. Neurosci.* 2:399-446.

Monod. J. 1971. *Chance and Necessity*. New York: Knopf.

Popper, K. R., and Eccles, J. C. 1977. *The Self and Its Brain*. Berlin, Heidelberg, London, New York: Springer Internat.

Roland, P. E., Larsen, B., Lassen, N. A., and Skinhoj, E. 1980. "Supplementary Motor Area and Other Cortical Areas in Organization of Voluntary Movements in Man." *J. Neurophysiol.* 43:118-36.

Sherrington, C. S. 1940. *Man on His Nature*. Cambridge: Cambridge University Press.

Thorpe, W. H. 1974. *Animal Nature and Human Nature*. London: Methuen Co.

Thorpe, W. H. 1978. *Purpose in a World of Chance: A Biologist's View*. Oxford: Oxford University Press.

Ulinski, P. S. 1990. "The Cerebral Cortex of Reptiles." In *Cerebral Cortex*, vol. 8A, ed. E. G. Jones and A. Peters. New York, London: Plenum Press.

Chapter 9: A Physiologist Looks at Purpose and Meaning in Life

† In collaboration with T. M. Beverley, J. Butera, C. E. Chaffey, and F. M. Osmond.
[1] D. Lack, *Evolutionary Theory and Christian Belief* (Methuen, 1961), p. 64,

quoted in M. A. Jeeves, *The Scientific Enterprise and Christian Faith* (Tyndale Press, 1969), p. 103.

[2] J. D. Bernal, quoted in C. A. Coulson, *Science and Christian Belief* (Collins Fontana Books, 1964), p. 26.

[3] Voltaire, "Les Cabales," quoted in E. Gilson, *From Aristotle to Darwin and Back Again* (University of Notre Dame Press, 1984), p. 106.

[4] D. M. MacKay, *The Clock Work Image* (London: Inter Varsity Press, 1977), p. 95.

[5] H. Butterfield, *Christianity and History* (Collins Fontana Books, 1960), p. 43.

[6] Psalm 23, New International Version.

[7] Epistle to the Ephesians, especially chapter 1.

[8] Ephesians 2:10.

[9] Matthew 6:10.

[10] Matthew 28:18-20.

[11] H. F. R. Catherwood, *The Christian in Industrial Society* (Tyndale Press, 1964) pp. xiv and 8.

[12] J. W. Bready *Lord Shaftesbury and Social-Industrial Progress* (London: George Allen and Unwin Ltd., 1933), Preface and pp. 27-35.

[13] Ibid., p. 13 and foreword.

[14] S. Neill, *Christian Faith To-Day* (Penguin Books, 1955), pp. 198-99.

[15] Acts 9:3-8.

[16] 1 Kings 19:11-18.

[17] E. L. Mascall, *Christian Theology and Natural Science* (Archon Books, 1965), p. 1.

[18] R. L. Herrmann, executive director, American Scientific Application, P.O. Box 668, Ipswich, MA 01938, USA. Phone: 508-356-5656, FAX: 508-356-4375, from whom information about all the named organizations may be obtained.

[19] *Webster's Universal Dictionary*, Unabridged International Edition (Harver, 1970).

[20] C. S. Lewis, *The Problem of Pain* (Collins Fontana Books, 1940).

[21] V. E. Frankl, *Man's Search for Meaning* (Washington Square Press, 1984), pp. 121–22.

[22] V. E. Frankl, *The Will to Meaning* (New American Library, 1970), pp. 68-69.

[23] Matthew 13:45-46.

[24] Frankl, *Man's Search for Meaning*, p. 87.

[25] Ibid., p. 97.

[26] Ibid., p. 111.

[27] Coulson, *Science and Christian Belief*, p. 136.

[28] N. L. Giesler, *Philosophy of Religion* (Zondervan, 1974), p. 77.

[29] Ibid., pp. 80-81.

[30] Exodus, chaps. 6-15.

[31] 2 Chronicles 36:15-23.

[32] W. G. Plaut, "A Common Quest for Redemption," *Globe and Mail* (Toronto), Facts and Arguments section, 29 March 1991.

[33] C. Dawson, *The Crisis of Western Education* (Doubleday, 1965), pp. 160-62.

[34] Ibid., pp. 13-15; 104-5.

[35] Butterfield, *Christianity and History*, pp. 47 and 148.

[36] R. Hooykaas, *Religion and the Rise of Modern Science* (Eerdmans, 1972), pp. 161-62.

[37] Coulson, *Science and Christian Belief*, pp. 22-24.

[38] J. M. Templeton and R. L. Herrmann, *The God Who Would Be Known* (Harper and Row, 1989), p. 7.

[39] Genesis 8:22.

[40] S. L. Jaki, *The Road of Science and the Ways to God* (University of Chicago Press, 1978), p. vii.

[41] S. L. Jaki, *Science and Creation* (Scottish Academic Press, 1986), p. viii.

[42] J. N. Hawthorne, *Questions of Science and Faith* (Inter Varsity Press, 1972), pp. 27-33.

[43] C. S. Lewis, *Miracles* (Collins Fontana Books, 1974) pp. 18-19.

[44] D. R. G. Owen, *Scientism, Man, and Religion* (Westminster Press, 1952), pp. 18-21.

[45] M. A. Jeeves, *The Scientific Enterprise and Christian Faith* (London: Tyndale Press, 1969), p. 37.

[46] C. S. Evans, *Preserving the Person* (Downer's Grove, Ill.: Inter Varsity Press, 1977), chap. 7.

[47] MacKay, *The Clock Work Image*, p. 95.

[48] Plato, *Timaios*, 30E.

[49] R. Hooykaas, *Religion and the Rise of Modern Science*, pp. 3-13.

[50] Genesis 1:28; Matthew 6:9-13.

[51] W. Durant, *The Life of Greece* , vol 2 of *The Story of Civilization* (New York: Simon and Schuster, 1966), pp. 531-34.

[52] C. E. Hummel, "The Natural Sciences," in *Christ and the Modern Mind*, edited by R. W. Smith (Inter Varsity Press, 1973), pp. 230-31.

[53] Aristotle, *Metaphysics*, book 12, chap. 10.

[54] Aristotle, *Physics*, 2.3.194b 20.

[55] P. Edwards, editor, *Encyclopedia of Philosophy*, vol. 2 (Crowell, Collier and MacMillan Inc., 1967), pp. 56-57.

[56] J. Owens, "Teleology of Nature in Aristotle," *Monist* 52 (1968):159-73.

[57] H. Butterfield, *The Origins of Modern Science* (Clarke Irwin, 1977), p. 7.

[58] Gilson, *From Aristotle to Darwin*, pp. 4-9.

[59.] Hooykaas, *Religion and the Rise of Modern Science*, p. 31.

[60] E. L. Mascall, *Christian Theology and Natural Science* (Archon Books, 1965), p. 100.

[61] F. Copleston, *History of Philosophy II* (London, 1964), p. 302.

[62] A. P. Fishman and D. W. Richards, "The Output of the Heart," in *Circulation of the Blood, Men, and Ideas*, A. P. Fishman and D. W. Richards editors (American Physiological Society, 1982) p. 77.

[63] W. Harvey, *Exercitato anatomica de motu cordis et sanguinis in animalibus*, with an English translation by C. D. Leake (Springfield, IL: Thomas, 1928).

[64] F. Bacon, quoted in C. A. Coulson, *Science and Christian Belief*, p. 63.

[65] R. S. Westfall, *The Construction of Modern Science: Mechanisms and Mechanics* (New York: Cambridge University Press, 1977), pp. 30-31.

[66] Hooykaas, *Religion and the Rise of Modern Science*, pp. 17-19.

[67] In C. A. Coulson, *Science and Christian Belief* (Collins Fontana Books, 1964), pp. 63-64.

[68] Hooykaas, *Religion and the Rise of Modern Science*, p. 39.

[69] Ibid., p. 40.

[70] M. Polanyi, *Science, Faith, and Society* (University of Chicago Press, 1970), p. 65.

[71] In Coulson, *Science and Christian Belief*, p. 103.

[72] Ibid., pp. 64-65.

[73] S. Drake, "Wiegand Foundation Lectures on Encounters of Science and Faith," University of Toronto, November 1983. Reported by T. Lougheed in *The Newspaper*, University of Toronto, 30 November 1983, p. 2.

[74] In Polyani, *Science, Faith, and Society*, pp. 71-72.

[75] M. Midgley in *The Religion of Evolution in Darwinism and Divinity*, edited by J. Durant (Blackwell, 1985), p. 154.

[76] J. D. Bernal in Coulson *Science and Christian Belief*, p. 26.

[77] G. G. Simpson, *The Meaning of Evolution* (Yale University Press, 1949), p. 344.

[78] S. W. Hawking, *A Brief History of Time* (Bantam Books, 1988), p. 123.

[79] R. Dawkins, *The Selfish Gene* (Oxford University Press, 1976), preface.

[80] E. O. Wilson, *Sociobiology, the New Synthesis, Part Three: The Social Species* (Belknap Press of Harvard University Press, 1975), pp. 560-61.

[81] J. Monod, *Chance and Necessity* (London: Collins, 1972), pp. 110, 136, 137, 167.

[82] E. Gilson, *From Aristotle to Darwin*, pp. 10-11.

[83] Coulson, *Science and Christian Belief*, pp. 72-73.

[84] D. M. MacKay, *Science, Chance, and Providence* (Oxford, 1978), pp. 31-34.

[85] D. M. MacKay, American Scientific Affiliation, Annual Meeting, 1976, Wheaton, Illinois. Three taped lectures (1) "Basic vs Piecemeal Integration"; (2) "Economy vs 'Nothing Buttery'"; (3) "The Deterministic Bogey."

[86] William of Ockham, cited in W. Durant, *The Reformation*, vol 4 in *The Story of Civilization*. (New York: Simon & Schuster, 1957), pp. 246-51.

[87] D. M. MacKay, *Science and Christian Faith Today* (Falcon, 1973).

[88] T. A. Goudge, *The Ascent of Life* (University of Toronto Press, 1961), pp. 127-28.

[89] Butterfield, *Christianity and History*, pp. 157-58.

[90.] John 3:19; Ephesians 2:15.

Chapter 10: How Blind the Watchmaker?

[1] O. Rieppel, "Structuralism, Functionalism, and the Four Aristotelian Causes," *Journal of the History of Biology* 23, 2 (1990): 291-320.

[2] G. G. Simpson, *The Meaning of Evolution* (New Haven, Conn.: Yale University Press, 1967).

[3] B. B. Warfield, "A Review of *Darwinianism Today*, by Vernon L. Kellogg," *Princeton Theological Review* (1908): 640-50.

[4] N. Emerton, "The Argument from Design in Early Modern Theology," *Science and Christian Belief* 1, no. 2 (1989): 129-47.

[5] Ibid.

[6] M. J. S. Rudwick, *The Meaning of Fossils*, 2nd edition (New York: Neale Watson Academic Publications, 1976).

[7] N. C. Gillespie, "Divine Design and the Industrial Revolution," *Isis* 81 (1990): 214-29.

[8] A. Desmond, *The Politics of Evolution* (Chicago: University of Chicago Press, 1989).

[9] N. A. Rupke, *The Great Chain of History* (Oxford: Clarendon Press, 1983).

[10] Desmond, *Politics of Evolution*.

[11] J. H. Brooke, "Natural Theology and the Plurality of Worlds: Observations from the Brewster-Whewell Debate," *Ann. Sci.* 34 (1977): 221-86.

[12] A. Desmond, *Archetypes and Ancestors* (Chicago: University of Chicago Press, 1982).

[13] R. Owen, *On the Nature of Limbs* (London: Van Voorst Publishers, 1849).

[14] Rieppel, "Structuralism."

[15] J. R. Moore, "1859 and All That: Remaking the Story of Evolution-and-Religion," *Charles Darwin, 1809-1882: Centennial Commemorative*(Wellington, New Zealand: Nova Pacifica 1982), 167-94.

[16] E. D. Cope, *The Origin of the Fittest* (New York: D. Appleton and Company, 1887).

[17] S. J. Gould, "Darwinism and the Expansion of Evolutionary Theory," *Science* 216 (1982): 380-86.

[18] G. Webster and B. C. Goodwin, "The Origin of Species: A Structuralist Approach," *Constructional Biology*, ed. H. Wheeler and J. Danielli (London: Academic Press, 1982).

[19] N. Eldredge, *Unfinished Synthesis* (Oxford: Oxford University Press, 1985). Also see E. S. Vrba and S. J. Gould. "The Hierarchical Expansion of Sorting and Selection: Sorting and Selection Cannot Be Equated," *Paleobiology* 12, no. 2 (1986): 217-28.

[20] C. Darwin, *The Variation of Animals and Plants under Domestication* (New York: D. Appleton and Co., 1896).

[21] R. Dawkins, *The Blind Watchmaker* (New York: W. W. Norton and Co., 1986).

[22] D. R. Brooks, J. Collier, B. A. Maurer, J. D. H. Smith, and E. O. Wiley, "Entropy and Information in Evolving Biological Systems," *Biology and Philosophy* 4 (1989): 407-32.

[23] Ibid.

[24] G. P. Wagner, "The Biological Homology Concept," *Annual Review of Ecology and Systematics* 20 (1989): 51-69.

[25] Rieppel, "Structuralism."

[26] "Anatomy emerges at the level of the organ but not at the level of the parts." The organ is thus ontologically prior to the parts—it defines them and gives them a local "purpose" or limited "final cause," Wagner, "Biological Homology."

Emergence is a characteristic of a group of cells committed to form an organ and error-checked according to norms for that organ. P. J. Bryant and P. Simpson, "Intrinsic and Extrinsic Control of Growth in Developing Organs," *Quarterly Review of Biology* 59 (1984): 387-415.

Wagner refers to control by such sets of developmental constraints as *individuation* or entity formation. Thus, an adequate understanding of embryonic tissues involves their *purpose* to the forming organ, and implies the existence of a genomic organ "blueprint" (formal cause). Wagner, "Biological Homology."

Waddington termed such control of developmental trajectories *Homeorhysis* in C. H. Waddington, "Fields and Gradients," *Major Problems in Developmental Biology*, ed. M. Locke (London: Academic Press, 1966), pp. 105-24.

[27] The problems addressed include:

(1) The phylogenetic reappearance of "lost" structures (avian clavicles)—R. T. Bakker, *The Dinosaur Heresies* (New York: William Morrow and Company, 1986)

(2) Alternate inducers of the same organs—B. K. Hall, "Epigenetic Control in Development and Evolution," *Development and Evolution*, ed. N. Holder, C. C. Wylie, and B. C. Goodwin (Cambridge: Cambridge University Press, 1983) pp. 353-79

(3) Alternate paths of development in related species—R. A. Raff and J. C. Kaufmann, *Embryos, Genes, and Evolution: The Developmental-Genetic Basis of Evolutionary Change* (New York: Macmillan, 1983).

(4) The same control genes used by different developmental pathways ("genetic piracy")—V. L. Roth, "The Biological Basis of Homology," *Ontogeny and Systematics*, ed. C. J. Humphries (New York: Columbia University Press, 1988), pp. 1-26.

(5) L. Van Valen, "Homology and Causes," *Journal of Morphology* 173 (1982): 305-12

(6) Iterative homology (parallels in repeated organs) and the growth of "homologous" organs from different embryonic primordia or germ layers—Wagner, "Biological Homology."

Thus, "Structures from two individuals or from the same individual are homologous if they share a set of developmental constraints, caused by locally acting self-regulatory mechanisms of organ differentiation. These structures are thus developmentally individualized parts of the phenotype"—Wagner, "Biological Homology."

[28] Random mutation can act as a search process—B. Borstnik, D. Pumpernik, and G. L. Hofacker, "Point Mutations as an Optimal Search Process in Biological Evolution," *Journal of Theoretical Biology* 125 (1987): 249-68.

Mutational rates increase in stressed populations, indicating that they play an adaptive role for some coherent level—P. A. Parsons, "Evolutionary Rates under Environmental Stress," *Evolutionary Biology* 21 (1987): 311-47.

Mutation rates per *character* are three- or fourfold higher than the rate per *locus*—N. H. Barton, and M. Turelli, "Evolutionary Quantitative Genetics: How Little Do We Know?" *Annual Review of Genetics* 23 (1989): 337-70, 778.

Evaluation of new mutants must be based on the function of the original sequence—A. A. Pakula and R. T. Saner, "Genetic Analysis of Protein Stability and Function," *Annual Review of Genetics* 23 (1989): 289-310.

Mutated genes must be understood within their higher level constraints—H. Wilkins, "Prinzipien der Manifestation Polygener Systeme," *Z. Zool. Syst. Evolutions Forschung* 18 (1980): 103-11.

Belyaev demonstrated very high existing levels of masked genetic variability in fox populations—D. K. Belyaev, "Destabilizing Selection as a Factor in Domestication," *The Journal of Heredity* 70 (1979): 301-8.

Thus such mutational patterns make sense only if a gene's action is highly constrained by its purpose to a more comprehensive biotic entity (its role within a higher set of rules of blueprint).

[29] H. E. H. Paterson, "The Recognition Concept of Species," *Species and Speciation*, ed. E. S. Vrba (Pretoria: Transvaal Museum Monograph, 1985), pp. 21-29.

Templeton points out problems with the usual species definitions of reproductive coherence or isolation. For instance, parthenogenic species may remain morphologically coherent despite a total lack of interbreeding. Or, in syngameons, interbreeding species may remain morphologically separated despite millions of years of gene flow. He suggests that species identity is due to their possession of various genetically based cohesion mechanisms—thus species too are characterized by individuated genetic controls. A. R. Templeton, "The Meaning of Species and Speciations: A Genetic Perspective," *Speciation and Its Consequences*, ed. D. Otte and J. A. Endler (Sunderland, MA: Sinauer, 1989), pp. 3-27.

Vrba's work with the alcelaphine tribe of African antelope suggests that the whole tribe might be viewed as an entity controlled by such a common coherency—E. S. Vrba, "Evolutionary Pattern and Process in the Sister-Groups Alcelaphini-Aepycerotini (Mammalia: *Bovidae*)," *Living Fossils*, ed. N. Eldredge and S. M. Stanley (New York: Springer-Verlag, 1984), pp. 62-79.

[30] Stanley points to millions of years of stasis for typical species—S. M. Stanley, "Rates of Evolution," *Paleobiology* 11, no. 1 (1985): 13-26.

Michaux shows that even the changes that are seen in fossil morphologies are within the morphological limits of the modern representatives of those species—B. Michaux, "Morphological Variation of Species through Time," *Biological Journal of the Linnean Society* 38 (1989): 239-55.

[31] *Diacodexis*, the stem Artiodactyl, appeared at the base of the Eocene with the basic adaptive complex of the artiodactyl limb in place, but without clear ancestry—K. D. Rose, "Skeleton of *Diacodexis*, Oldest Known Artiodactyl," *Science* 216 (1982): 621-23.

Also see K. D. Rose, "Climbing Adaptions in the Early Eocene Mammal *Chriacus* and the Origin of the Artiodactyla," *Science* 236 (1987): 314-16.

By the end of the Eocene, fifteen families of Artiodactyla had emerged. As time passed, these families showed a number of parallel changes in such structures as legs, teeth, horns, etc. This is the typical pattern shown by major emergences. Ichtheostega appears related to the contemporary osteolepiform lobe-fins, but has the individuated limb bones of the tetrapod complex instead of the iterative fin bones of its contemporaries. R. L. Carroll, *Vertebrate Paleontology and Evolution* (New York: W. H. Freeman and Company, 1988).

The same pattern holds for the explosive appearance of seventy-plus new phyla in the Cambrian—D. Erwin, J. W. Valentine, and J. J. Sepkoski, Jr., "A Comparative Study of Diversification Events: The Early Paleozoic versus the Mesozoic," *Evolution* 41, no. 6 (1987): 1177-86.

It holds for the speciation pattern of Miocene grazing horses—B. J. MacFadden and R. C. Hulbert, "Explosive Speciation at the Base of the Adaptive Radiation of Miocene Grazing Horses," *Nature* 336 (1988): 466-68.

Thus, in each case, the appearance of new taxa seems related to the sudden appearance of packages of individuated structural information.

[32] Rieppel, "Structuralism." Also see Webster and Goodwin, "A Structuralist Approach."

[33] Webster and Goodwin, "A Structuralist Approach."

[34] Ibid.

[35] For example, in W. A. Mitchell, and T. J. Valone, "The Optimization Research Program: Studying Adapations by Their Function, *Quarterly Review of Biology* 65, no. 1 (1990): 43-52.

[36] M. D. Mesarovic, "Systems Theory and Biology—View of a Theoretician," *System Theory and Biology: Proceeding, Systems Symposium Three*, Case Western Reserve University (New York: Springer-Verlag, 1968), pp. 59-87.

[37] G. V. Lauder, "Functional Morphology and Systematics: Studying Functional Patterns in a Historical Context," *Annual Review of Ecology and Systematics* 21 (1990): 317-40.

[38] Pakula and Saner, "Protein Stability and Function." See also Wilkins, "Prinzipien."

[39] Barton and Turelli, "Evolutionary Quantitative Genetics."

[40] Ibid.

[41] W. Arthur, *Mechanism of Morphological Evolution* (New York: John Wiley & Sons, 1989).

[42] Erwin et al., "Early Paleozoic versus the Mesozoic."

[43] Wagner, "Biological Homology."

[44] Ibid.

[45] J. G. Kingslover and M. A. Koehl, "Aerodynamics, Thermoregulation, and the Evolution of Insect Wings: Differential Scaling and Evolutionary Change," *Evolution* 39 (1985): 488-504.

[46] Rieppel, "Stucturalism."

[47] S. J. Gould, *Wonderful Life* (New York: W. W. Norton and Co., 1989).

[48] Ibid.

[49] Ibid.

[50] S. J. Gould, *The Panda's Thumb* (New York: W. W. Norton and Co., 1980).

[51] S. J. Gould, "Darwin and Paley Meet the Invisible Hand," *Natural History* 11 (1990): 8-16.

[52] B. B. Warfield, "Charles Darwin's Religious Life," *Princeton Theological Review* (1888): 569-601.

[53] J. R. Topham, "Teleology and the Concept of Natural Law: An Historical Perspective," *Science and Christian Belief* 1, no. 2 (1989): 149-60.

[54] A. Plantinga, *God, Freedom, and Evil* (Grand Rapids: W. B. Eerdmans, 1977).

[55] B. Wallace, *Chromosomes, Giant molecules, and Evolution* (New York: Norton, 1966).

BIBLIOGRAPHY

Bakker, R.T. *The Dinosaur Heresies*. New York: William Morrow and Company, 1986.

Barton, N. H., and M. Turelli. "Evolutionary Quantitative Genetics: How Little Do We Know?" *Annual Review of Genetics* 23 (1989): 337-70, 778.

Belyaev, D. K. "Destabilizing Selection as a Factor in Domestication." *Journal of Heredity* 70 (1979): 301-08.

Borstnik, B., D. Pumpernik, and G. L. Hofacker. "Point Mutations as an Optimal Search Process in Biological Evolution." *Journal of Theoretical Biology* 125 (1987): 249-68.

Brooke, J. H. "Natural Theology and the Plurality of Worlds: Observations from the Brewster-Whewell Debate." *Ann. Sci.* 34 (1977): 221-86.

Brooks, D. R., J. Collier, B. A. Maurer, J. D. H. Smith, and E. O. Wiley. "Entropy and Information in Evolving Biological Systems." *Biology and Philosophy* 4 (1989): 407-32.

Bryant, P. J., and Simpson, P. "Intrinsic and Extrinsic Control of Growth in Developing Organs." *Quarterly Review of Biology* 59 (1984): 387-415.

Carroll, R. L. *Vertebrate Paleontology and Evolution.* New York: W. H. Freeman and Company, 1988.

Cope, E. D. *The Origin of the Fittest.* New York: D. Appleton and Company, 1887.

Darwin, C. *The Variation of Animals and Plants under Domestication.* New York: D. Appleton and Co., 1896.

Dawkins, R. *The Blind Watchmaker.* New York: W. W. Norton and Co., 1986.

Desmond, A. *Archetypes and Ancestors.* Chicago: University of Chicago Press, 1982.

———.*The Politics of Evolution.* Chicago: University of Chicago Press, 1989.

Eldredge, N. *Unfinished Synthesis.* Oxford: Oxford University Press, 1985.

Emerton, N. "The Argument from Design in Early Modern Theology." *Science and Christian Belief* 1, no. 2 (1989): 129-47.

Erwin, D., J. W. Valentine, and J. J. Sepkoski, Jr. "A Comparative Study of Diversification Events: The Early Paleozoic versus the Mesozoic." *Evolution* 41, no. 6 (1987): 1177-86.

Gillespie, N. C. "Divine Design and the Industrial Revolution." *Isis* 81 (1990): 214-29.

Gould, S. J. "Darwin and Paley Meet the Invisible Hand." *Natural History* 11 (1990): 8-16.

———. "Darwinism and the Expansion of Evolutionary Theory." *Science* 216 (1982): 380-86.

———. *The Panda's Thumb.* New York: W. W. Norton and Co., 1980.

———. *Wonderful Life.* New York: W. W. Norton and Co., 1989.

Hall, B. K. "Epigenetic Control in Development and Evolution." In *Development and Evolution* ed. by N. Holder, C. C. Wylie, and B. C. Goodwin, 353-79 Cambridge: Cambridge University Press, 1983.

Kingslover, J. G., and M. A. Koehl. "Aerodynamics, Thermoregulation, and the Evolution of Insect Wings: Differential Scaling and Evolutionary Change." *Evolution* 39 (1985): 488-504.

Lauder, G. V. "Functional Morphology and Systematics: Studying Functional Patterns in a Historical Context." *Annual Review of Ecology and Systematics* 21 (1990): 317-40.

MacFadden, B. J., and R. C. Hulbert. "Explosive Speciation at the Base of the Adaptive Radiation of Miocene Grazing Horses." *Nature* 336 (1988): 466-68.

Mesarovic, M. D. "Systems Theory and Biology—View of a Theoretician." In

System Theory and Biology: Proceeding, Systems Symposium Three, 59-87. Case Western Reserve University. New York: Springer-Verlag, 1968.

Michaux, B. "Morphological Variation of Species through Time." *Biological Journal of the Linnean Society* 38 (1989): 239-55.

Mitchell, W. A., and T. J. Valone. "The Optimization Research Program: Studying Adaptations by Their Function." *Quarterly Review of Biology* 65, no. 1 (1990): 43-52.

Moore, J. R. "1859 and All That: Remarking the Story of Evolution-and-Religion." In *Charles Darwin, 1809-1882: Centennial Commemorative,* 167-94. Wellington, NZ: Nova Pacifica, 1982.

Owen, R. *On the Nature of Limbs.* London: Van Voorst Publishers, 1849.

Pakula, A. A., and R. T. Saner. "Genetic Analysis of Protein Stability and Function." *Annual Review of Genetics* 23 (1989): 289-310.

Parsons, P. A. "Evolutionary Rates under Environmental Stress." *Evolutionary Biology* 21 (1987): 311-47.

Paterson, H. E. H. "The Recognition Concept of Species." In *Species and Speciation,* ed. E. S. Vrba, 21-29. Pretoria: Transvaal Museum Monograph, 1985.

Plantinga, A. *God, Freedom, and Evil.* Grand Rapids: W. B. Eerdmans, 1977.

Raff, R. A., and J. C. Kaufmann. *Embryos, Genes, and Evolution: The Developmental-Genetic Basis of Evolutionary Change.* New York: Macmillian, 1983.

Rieppel, O. "Structuralism, Functionalism, and the Four Aristotelian Causes." *Journal of the History of Biology* 23, no. 2 (1990): 291-320.

Rose, K. D. "Skeleton of *Diacodexis,* Oldest Known Artiodactyl." *Science* 216 (1982): 621-23.

———. "Climbing Adaptations in the Early Eocene Mammal *Chriacus* and the Origin of the Artiodactyla." *Science* 236 (1987): 314-16.

Roth, V. L. "The Biological Basis of Homology." In *Ontogeny and Systematics,* ed. C. J. Humphries, 1-26. New York: Columbia University Press, 1988.

Rudwick, M. J. S. *The Meaning of Fossils.* 2nd edition. New York: Neale Watson Academic Publications, 1976.

Rupke, N. A. *The Great Chain of History.* Oxford: Clarendon Press, 1983.

Simpson, G. G. *The Meaning of Evolution.* New Haven, CT: Yale University Press, 1967.

Stanley, S. M. "Rates of Evolution." *Paleobiology* 11, no. 1 (1985): 13-26.

Templeton, A. R. "The Meaning of Species and Speciations: A Genetic Perspective." In *Speciation and Its Consequences,* ed. D. Otte and J. A. Endler, 3-27. Sunderland, MA: Sinauer, 1989.

Topham, J. R. "Teleology and the Concept of Natural Law: An Historical Perspective." *Science and Christian Belief* 1, no. 2 (1989): 149-60.

Van Valen, L. "Homology and Causes." *Journal of Morphology* 173 (1982): 305-12.

Vrba, E. S. "Evolutionary Pattern and Process in the Sister-Groups Alcelaphini-Aepycerotini (Mammalia: Bovidae)." In *Living Fossils,* ed. N. Eldredge and S. M. Stanley, 62-79. New York: Springer-Verlag, 1984.

Vrba, E. S., and S. J. Gould. "The Hierarchical Expansion of Sorting and Selection: Sorting and Selection Cannot Be Equated." *Paleobiology* 12, no. 2 (1986): 217-28.

Waddington, C. H. "Fields and Gradients." In *Major Problems in Developmental*

Biology, ed. M. Locke, 105-24. London: Academic Press, 1966.

Wagner, G. P. "The Biological Homology Concept." *Annual Review of Ecology and Systematics* 20 (1989): 51-69.

Wallace, B. *Chromosomes, Giant Molecules, and Evolution*. New York: Norton, 1966.

Warfield, B. B. "Charles Darwin's Religious Life." *Princeton Theological Review* (1888): 569-601.

———. "A Review of *Darwinianism Today*, by Vernon L. Kellogg." *Princeton Theological Review* (1908): 640-50.

Webster, G., and B. C. Goodwin. "The Origin of Species: A Structuralist Approach." In *Constructional Biology*, ed. H. Wheeler and J. Danielli. London: Academic Press, 1982.

Wilkins, H. "Prinzipien der Manifestation Polygener Systeme." *Z. Zool. Syst. Evolutions Forschung* 18 (1980): 103-11.

Contributors

SIR JOHN TEMPLETON is widely known and highly respected in the financial and business community. Since 1954, he has become one of the most successful managers of mutual funds in the world. But, exceeding even his practical interest in economics is the significance he places on the role he believes religion plays in life. He thinks that religion is important whatever anyone does, and that a relationship to God is the most important thing there is. To act upon what he believes, an integral part of the Templeton philosophy, he has taken great personal responsibility in communicating this message worldwide. One method is awarding the Templeton Prize for Progress in Religion to men and women who have made an original and innovative contribution to religion. The Templeton Prize rewards persons in a field where there is no Nobel Prize, and by making it the world's largest annual cash prize emphasizes the value its founder places upon spiritual knowledge.

Also, John Templeton, since boyhood, has been extremely interested in science. In *The God Who Would Be Known*, with Robert Herrmann, he demonstrates that science and faith should never have been considered antagonists, and helps lead the way to a reconciliation, a "new journey of faith."

He has a degree in economics from Yale University and studied at Oxford as a Rhodes scholar. He has written several other books, including *The Templeton Plan* and *The Humble Approach*. He established the Templeton Foundation and the Templeton Prize and is the originator of Templeton College, Oxford. He has served on the Princeton Seminary Board of Trustees for many years and is an elder in the United Presbyterian Church.

PAUL DAVIES has been professor of mathematical physics at the University of Adelside, South Australia, since 1990. He received his Ph.D. from University College, London, where he lectured for eight years before going on to be professor of theoretical physics at the University of Newcastle-upon-Tyne. His research has ranged across much of fundamental physics and cosmology, and he is known internationally for his books: *Other Worlds, The Runaway Universe, The Edge of Infinity, God and the New Physics, Superforce,* and *The Cosmic Blueprint.*

SIR JOHN ECCLES is a fellow of the Royal Society and winner of the 1963 Nobel Prize for physiology and medicine. He has devoted his scientific life to the study of mammalian brain, and has written over five hundred articles and several books of international acclaim, including *Understanding the Brain* (1973), *The Self and Its Brain* (with K. R. Popper, 1977), *The Human Mystery* (1979), *The Human Psyche* (1980), and *The Wonder of Being Human* (with D. Robinson, 1984). He is professor emeritus of the State University of New York at Buffalo, and has been associated with the Max Planck Institute for Biophysical Chemistry in Gottingen, Germany. He currently resides in Switzerland.

DR. OWEN GINGERICH is professor of astronomy and the history of science at Harvard University, and a senior astronomer at the Smithsonian Astrophysical Observatory. Since February, 1992, he has also chaired Harvard's History of Science Department. Professor Gingerich's research interests have ranged from the recomputation of an ancient Babylonian mathematical table to the interpretation of stellar spectra. He is a leading authority on the seventeenth-century German astronomer Johannes Kepler and on Nicholas Copenicus, the sixteenth-century cosmologist who proposed the heliocentric system. His class for nonscientists, "The Astronomical Perspective," has won the Harvard-Radcliffe Phi Beta Kappa Prize for excellence in teaching.

WALTER R. HEARN is presently adjunct professor of science at the New College for Advanced Studies, Berkeley. He is a graduate of Rice University and received his doctorate in biochemistry from the University of Illinois at Urbana. He was for many years a member of the faculty of the Department of Biochemistry and Biophysics of Iowa State University and subsequently a visiting professor at the University of California at Berkeley. He has been a freelance writer and editor since 1972, during which time he has edited the *Newsletter of the American Scientific Affiliation* and contributed chapters to several books, including Richard Bube, ed., *Encounter between Christianity and Science* (1968), Hatfield, ed., *The Scientist and Ethical Decision* (1973), and Sider, ed., *Living More Simply* (1980). He is currently author of a widely circulated book *Teaching Science in a Climate of Controversy.*

DANIEL H. OSMOND is professor of physiology and medicine at the

University of Toronto. He is a graduate of the University of British Columbia and received his Ph.D. from the University of Toronto. He has been involved in extensive research of the renin-angiotensin system for the control of blood pressure and is an elected fellow of the Council for High Blood Pressure Research of the American Heart Association. Dr. Osmond is also an elected fellow and past president of the Canadian Scientific and Christian Affiliation. He has published a number of papers dealing with ethical problems in the conduct of research, and is listed in *Who's Who in Theology and Science*.

The **REVEREND DR. ARTHUR PEACOCKE** followed an academic scientific career in the Universities of Birmingham and Oxford in the field of the physical chemistry of biological macromolecules. His principal interest for the last twenty years has been in the relation of science and theology and associated questions. (His most recent book: *Theology for a Scientific Age*, Blackwell: Oxford, 1990.) Peacocke was ordained as a priest in the Church of England in 1971 and was for twelve years dean of Clare College, Cambridge. He later directed the Ian Ramsey Centre, Oxford, and is currently the warden of the Society of Ordained Scientists, as well as an honorary chaplain at Christ Church Cathedral, Oxford. He gave the Gifford Lectures at St. Andrew's University for 1992-93.

DR. JOHN POLKINGHORNE was elected the chair of mathematical physics at Cambridge University in 1968. A fellow of the Royal Society, he was engaged in research in elementary particle physics for over twenty-five years. In 1979 he resigned to train for the Anglican ministry and has since written a very important series of books on science and religion, including the recent trilogy, *One World, Science and Creation* and *Science and Providence* (London: SPCK). He is now president of Queens' College, Cambridge.

ROBERT JOHN RUSSELL was born and raised in Southern California. In 1968 he completed his undergraduate training at Stanford University with a major in physics and minors in music and religion. He then began concurrent studies in physics and theology, receiving an M.A. in theology from the Pacific School of Religion, Berkeley, in 1972. His Ph.D. in experimental solid-state physics was received from the University of California, Santa Cruz, on the same day that he was ordained in the United Church of Christ (Congregational). He is founder and director of the Center for Theology and the Natural Sciences, and professor of theology and science in residence at the Graduate Theological Union. Other recent activities include his work as coeditor of the book *Physics, Philosophy, and Theology: A Common Quest for*

Understanding (Vatican Observatory Press, 1988), and as book review editor for Zygon (1985-88).

RUSSELL STANNARD is professor of physics and head of department at the Open University, Milton Keynes, United Kingdom. London-born, he was educated at University College London, receiving his Ph.D. in cosmic-ray physics in 1956. In 1983 he began studies of the relationship between science, religion, psychology, and philosophy. More recently he has explored better ways to teach physics to young children and to incorporate modern thinking into school religious education lessons. His recent books in science and religion include *Grounds for Reasonable Belief* (Scottish Academic Press, 1989) and a children's book, *Holes and Uncle Albert*, (Faber & Faber, 1991). He is also a trustee of the John Templeton Foundation.

DAVID WILCOX is professor and chair of the Department of Biology of Eastern College, St. Davids, PA. He graduated from Geneva College and received his Ph.D. in population genetics from Pennsylvania State University. He is a fellow and member of the Executive Council of the American Scientific Affiliation and a frequent lecturer on evolutionary biology and the biblical view of creation. His most recent work includes a Pascal Centre Symposium paper entitled "Of Messages and Molecules—What Is the Essence of Life?" and a book in preparation: *The Creation: Spoken in Eternity, Unfolded in Time*.